Get Ready! for Social Studies
WORLD HISTORY

Books in the *Get Ready! for Social Studies* Series:

Essays, Book Reports, and Research Papers
Geography
Government and Citizenship
U.S. History
World History

Nancy White and Francine Weinberg, series editors, have been involved in educating elementary and secondary students for more than thirty years. They have had experience in the classroom as well as on dozens of books and electronic projects. They welcome this partnership with parents and other adults to promote knowledge, skills, and critical thinking.

Get Ready! for Social Studies
WORLD HISTORY

Steven Otfinoski

Series Editors
Nancy White
Francine Weinberg

McGraw-Hill
New York   Chicago   San Francisco
Lisbon   London   Madrid   Mexico City
Milan   New Delhi   San Juan   Seoul
Singapore   Sydney   Toronto

Contents

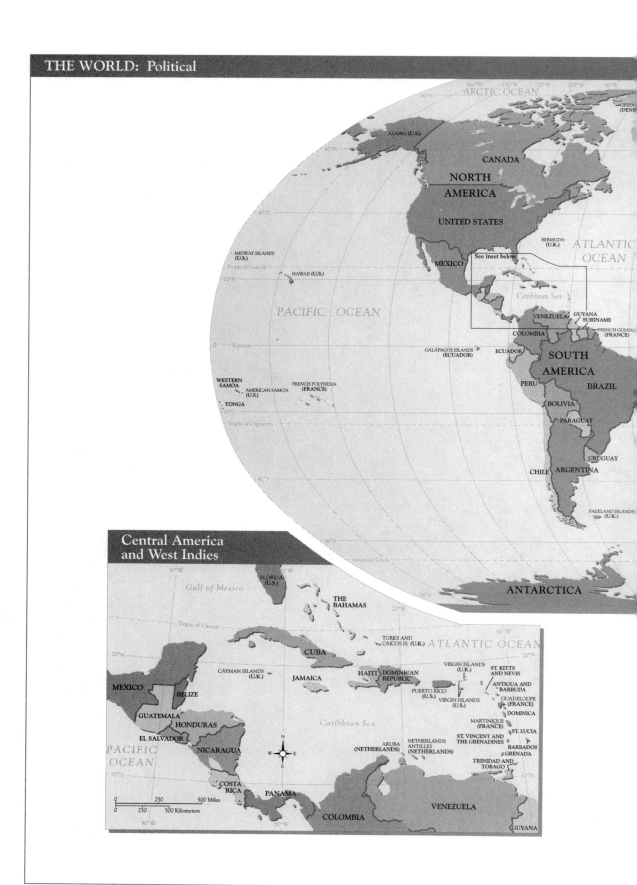

Central America and West Indies

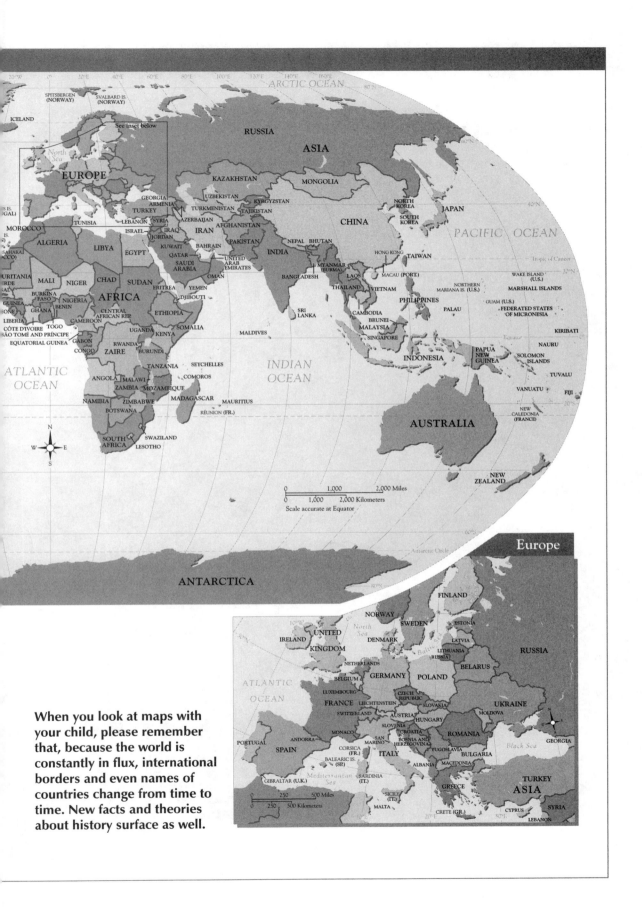

When you look at maps with your child, please remember that, because the world is constantly in flux, international borders and even names of countries change from time to time. New facts and theories about history surface as well.

Introduction

In recent years, the media have told us that many students need to know more about history, geography, and government and to improve their writing skills. While schools are attempting to raise standards, learning need not be limited to the classroom. Parents and other concerned adults can help students too. *Get Ready! for Social Studies* provides you with the information and resources you need to help students with homework, projects, and tests and to create a general excitement about learning.

You may choose to use this book in several different ways, depending on your child's strengths and preferences. You might read passages aloud; you might read it to yourself and then paraphrase it for your child; or you might ask your child to read the material along with you or on his or her own. To help you use this book successfully, brief boldface paragraphs, addressed to you, the adult, appear from time to time.

Here is a preview of the features you will find in each chapter.

Word Power

To help students expand their vocabulary, the "Word Power" feature in each chapter defines underlined words with which students may be unfamiliar. These are words that students may use in a variety of contexts in their writing and speaking. In addition, proper nouns and more technical terms appear in boldface type within the chapter, along with their definitions. For example, the word underline decade is defined as "period of ten years" on a "Word Power" list. The word **cartography** would appear in boldface type within the chapter and be defined there as "the science of mapmaking."

What Your Child Needs to Know

This section provides key facts and concepts in a conversational, informal style to make the content accessible and engaging for all readers.

Implications

This section goes beyond the facts and concepts. Here, we provide the answers to students' centuries-old questions, "Why does this matter?" and "Why is this important for me to know?"

Fact Checker

A puzzle, game, or other short-answer activity checks children's grasp of facts—people, places, things, dates, and other details.

The Big Questions

These questions encourage students to think reflectively and critically in order to form a broader understanding of the material.

Skills Practice

Activities provide the opportunity for children to learn and to apply reading, writing, and thinking skills basic to social studies and other subjects as well. These skills include learning from historical documents, map reading, identifying cause and effect, comparing and contrasting, and writing analytically and creatively.

Top of the Class

In this section, creative suggestions help students stand out in class. By taking some of these suggestions, students can show their teachers that they have been putting in the extra effort that means the difference between average and excellent performance.

The book you are now holding in your hand is a powerful tool. It will help you boost your child's performance in school, increase his or her self-confidence, and open the door to a successful future as a well-educated adult.

Nancy White and Francine Weinberg

Prologue

When we speak of world history in this book, we mean the history of *human* life on Earth. Of course, the world existed before humans, but we refer to that time as part of **prehistory.** Before looking into human history, let's take a brief look at the time that led up to the appearance of modern human beings on our planet.

Scientists have found evidence that creatures called **hominids** (human*like* creatures), appeared on Earth before modern human beings. In the grasslands of East Africa, scientists have found fossilized footprints of a humanlike creature dating back more than 3 million years. They call this creature *Australopithecus* ("southern ape"). But *Australopithecus* was not an ape. The footprints show that it walked on two legs and stood upright. For this reason, scientists consider *Australopithecus* to be the earliest ancestor of today's humans.

By about 2 million years ago, a larger hominid appeared on Earth. Scientists call this human ancestor *Homo habilis* ("handy man") because it was the first to make and use tools. *Homo habilis* made a kind of crude cutting tool by using one rock to sharpen another. For this reason, the period of prehistory that began at this time is sometimes called the **Stone Age.**

The next step toward modern humans appeared about 1.5 million years ago. *Homo erectus* ("upright man") was somewhat smaller than modern humans. This hominid, which also originated in Africa, was the first to move into what is now Europe and Asia. *Homo erectus* was also the first creature to control and use fire.

Much later—about three hundred thousand years ago—the human ancestor we call Neanderthal man (*Homo sapiens neanderthalensis,* which means "wise man found in the Neander valley") appeared. Bones of this early human have been found in Germany. Neanderthals lived in caves. The Neanderthals were the first to bury their dead and care for the sick and elderly.

Our closest known human ancestor appeared at least forty thousand years ago. The scientific name for this creature is *Homo sapiens sapiens* ("wise, wise man"), the same name used for modern humans. It is also called Cro-Magnon man. The Cro-Magnons and Neanderthals existed at the same time, but the Neanderthals died out about twenty-eight thousand years ago. Some people once believed that the Cro-Magnons killed off the Neanderthals, but that theory has been rejected. The Cro-Magnons created more advanced tools for hunting. They also made jewelry and created art, notably their beautiful paintings on the walls of caves in France, Spain, and the Sahara.

The Cro-Magnons were the only hominids to survive the last ice age. During that time, some of them crossed a bridge of land that once connected Asia with North America. Within a few thousand years, both North and South America were populated by the first modern human beings. They learned how to use metals to make tools and other objects. They began to live in organized villages and towns. This is where Chapter 1 picks up the story, in the year 5000 B.C.

CHAPTER 1
The First Civilizations
5000 B.C.–1200 B.C.

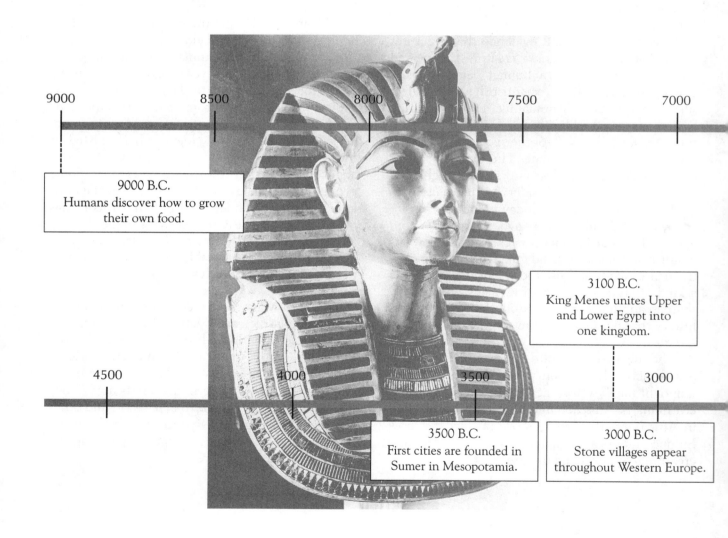

9000   8500   8000   7500   7000

9000 B.C.
Humans discover how to grow their own food.

3100 B.C.
King Menes unites Upper and Lower Egypt into one kingdom.

4500   4000   3500   3000

3500 B.C.
First cities are founded in Sumer in Mesopotamia.

3000 B.C.
Stone villages appear throughout Western Europe.

This timeline provides an overview of the period of the first civilizations. The narrative in the following pages offers more details and discusses the significance of the events.

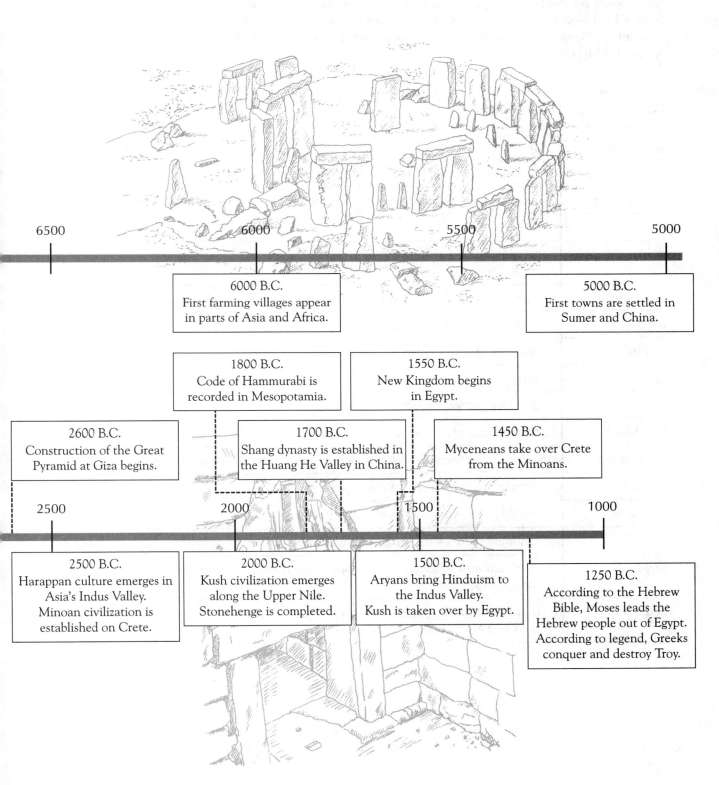

6500   6000   5500   5000

6000 B.C.
First farming villages appear
in parts of Asia and Africa.

5000 B.C.
First towns are settled in
Sumer and China.

1800 B.C.
Code of Hammurabi is
recorded in Mesopotamia.

1550 B.C.
New Kingdom begins
in Egypt.

2600 B.C.
Construction of the Great
Pyramid at Giza begins.

1700 B.C.
Shang dynasty is established in
the Huang He Valley in China.

1450 B.C.
Myceneans take over Crete
from the Minoans.

2500   2000   1500   1000

2500 B.C.
Harappan culture emerges in
Asia's Indus Valley.
Minoan civilization is
established on Crete.

2000 B.C.
Kush civilization emerges
along the Upper Nile.
Stonehenge is completed.

1500 B.C.
Aryans bring Hinduism to
the Indus Valley.
Kush is taken over by Egypt.

1250 B.C.
According to the Hebrew
Bible, Moses leads the
Hebrew people out of Egypt.
According to legend, Greeks
conquer and destroy Troy.

Word Power

Word	Definition
agriculture	farming
ancestor	family member from the distant past
archaeologists	persons who study the past by digging up old objects
artisans	craftspeople
delta	triangular area of land made from mud deposited by a river as it enters the sea
domesticate	tame an animal so it can live with humans or be used by them
dynasty	series of rulers from one family
empire	number of states ruled by one state or leader
epic	long
fertile	good for growing crops and plants
flourished	thrived and grew; made advances; prospered or did well
mummified	dried and preserved and wrapped in cloth so as to last a long time
nomadic	wandering from place to place
ousted	forcibly removed from position of power
reeds	tall grass plants with long, slender stems
surplus	extra amount; enough food or other goods so that some can be stored for later use
taxes	in addition to the price of an item, money or goods that must be paid to a government

What Your Child Needs to Know

You may choose to use the following text in several different ways, depending on your child's strengths and preferences. You might read the passage aloud; you might read it to yourself and then paraphrase it for your child; or you might ask your child to read the material along with you or on his or her own.

WHAT IS A CIVILIZATION?

Historians usually define *civilization* as an organized society in which people live in cities, specialize in different tasks, use a written language, and have a religion and a government. People have lived on Earth for hundreds of thousands of years, yet civilization, according to this definition, arose only within the last six thousand years. Why? For most of human history, people lived <u>nomadic</u> lives. They hunted animals, fished in rivers and streams, and gathered wild plants. They had no permanent homes. The term for people who live in this way is **hunter-gatherers.**

Around 9000 B.C., humans discovered how to grow their own food. This was the beginning of <u>agriculture</u>. Later they learned to <u>domesticate</u> animals such as goats, sheep, and cattle. These animals produced milk and meat, as well as wool to make clothing. The ability to provide food for themselves allowed people to stay in one place. Soon villages developed. Over time, the villages grew. Some became large cities.

Once people had a <u>surplus</u> of food to store away, not everyone had to farm. Some people could do other jobs. Some became traders of goods. Others were craftspeople who made pottery, wood carvings, or jewelry. Still others were free to become artists, builders, musicians, and writers.

Specialization leads to trade. For example, a person who makes pottery but does not grow food might get food from a farmer in return for clay pots in which to store grain. Because people who trade need a way to keep track of their goods, trade leads to a system of writing. Trade also leads to contact between different peoples and therefore to the need for peace and order—a need filled by both a religion with a strong priesthood and a government with a strong leader.

MESOPOTAMIA

The world's first civilizations arose in a <u>fertile</u> valley between two rivers in the area that is present-day Iraq. The rivers, the **Tigris** (TYE gruhs) and the **Euphrates** (yoo FRAY teez), formed what is sometimes called the **Fertile Crescent** and sometimes called the **Cradle of Civilization.** We call the area Mesopotamia (*meh* suh puh TAY mee uh), which means "land between the rivers" in Greek. The two rivers provided fertile soil for growing crops, water for farming, and transportation routes for trade—easier and faster than land routes.

Sumer

The civilization born about 3500 B.C. in Mesopotamia is known as Sumer (SOO muhr). Much of what we know about Sumer comes from the findings of <u>archaeologists</u>, who unearthed the ancient Sumerian city of **Ur** in 1927. From what they found, we know that the Sumerians developed powerful city-states. A **city-state** is a city that, with its surrounding areas, is also a state unto itself. It has its own government and is not controlled by any larger state.

Some Sumerians lived outside of the cities, farming and raising pigs, oxen, and sheep. A complex network of canals led water from the rivers to the farmers' crops. Those who lived in the cities were merchants, tradespeople, or <u>artisans</u>. The upper class in Sumerian society was made up of nobles, wealthy landowners, government officials, priests, and kings. Merchants, farmers, artisans, tradespeople, and soldiers made up the middle class, while the lowest class was made up of slaves. Sumerian civilization gave birth to both the wheel and the earliest known written language.

The Sumerians had a system of writing that took the form of wedge-shaped characters called **cuneiform** (kyoo NEE uh *fawrm*). They scratched cuneiform characters onto clay tablets with the sharp ends of <u>reeds</u>. On these tablets, the Sumerians wrote legal documents, religious texts, and literary works. We know this because thousands of cuneiform tablets have been dug up by archaeologists.

The Sumerians were also great builders. They constructed towering, pyramid-shaped temples called **ziggurats** (ZI guh *rats*). They believed the many gods of their religion lived on top of the ziggurats.

The Sumerians were probably the first people to make glass, brew beer, and create pottery on a potter's wheel. Our system of time based on a sixty-minute hour is derived from the Sumerian system of mathematics. So is the method of dividing a circle into 360 degrees. The Sumerians had an army and weapons, and they traded with other peoples.

The Sumerians were not united under a central government. Therefore, city-states often quarreled and fought with one another. It is probably for this reason that they were easily conquered by the **Akkads** (AH *kahds*), people from an area north of Sumer, led by their king, **Sargon.** From around 2330 B.C. to around 2275 B.C., Sargon united all Mesopotamia and built the world's first <u>empire</u>. He was a strong leader, but he was also noted for his cruelty. After only about fifty years, the city-states rebelled against the empire.

Babylon

At the time that Sargon's empire fell, people from the area that is now Syria started moving into southern Mesopotamia. Their main city was called Babylon (BAH buh luhn). In about 1800 B.C., Babylon began to seize power and soon controlled most of Mesopotamia.

Hammurabi, one of Babylon's most important kings, created one of civilization's first set of laws. We know it as **Hammurabi's Code.** Some of the laws seem cruel, but others are fair and good. For example, one law said the strong and rich could not take advantage of the weak and poor.

The Babylonians traded with neighboring peoples including the **Phoenicians** (fi NEE shuns), who occupied the area where Syria and Lebanon (LE buh nuhn) are today. The Phoenicians were the greatest seafarers of the ancient world. Their name comes from the Greek word for purple be-

cause they had discovered a process for dying fabric purple. They also invented glassblowing and were skilled craftspeople.

Around 1595 B.C., Babylon fell to the **Hittites,** a people who had settled in Turkey. The warlike Hittites were the first to use iron for tools and weapons. For the next hundred years, Babylon would be under the power of foreign rulers, and then it would be controlled by the Assyrians for another five hundred years.

EGYPT

When the Sumerian civilization was reaching its height, a new civilization was emerging in the valley of another river. The **Nile,** the world's longest river, threads its way from central Africa north to the Mediterranean Sea. The land around it is lush and fertile. Near the mouth of the Nile, where it empties into the Mediterranean Sea, the river fans out into several branches and forms a <u>delta</u>. Here the kingdom of Lower Egypt developed. Farther south emerged the kingdom of Upper Egypt, so called because it was farther *up*stream on the Nile. To the south, east, and west lay deserts. The Mediterranean Sea was on the north. Because of their geographical location, the Egyptians were not seriously threatened by invasion. Their civilization <u>flourished</u> for two thousand years.

The Old Kingdom

In 3100 B.C., King **Menes** (MEE nez) of Upper Egypt conquered Lower Egypt. He united the two kingdoms, established **Memphis** as his capital city, and founded ancient Egypt's first <u>dynasty</u>. Under this dynasty, Egyptian culture flourished. The Egyptians developed **hieroglyphics,** a kind of writing using pictures and symbols. They wrote on **papyrus,** a kind of paper made from the stems of reeds. **Scribes,** or people who knew how to write, were very important in Egyptian society.

The Egyptians believed that the most important god in their religion—the sun god, Ra—was the <u>ancestor</u> of their **pharaohs,** or rulers. They also believed in a life after death. For this reason, they often <u>mummified</u> dead bodies to get them ready for their lives in the "next world."

Golden death mask of King Tutankhamen of Egypt

Dead pharaohs and their families were entombed in great pyramids made of huge stone blocks. The largest is the Great Pyramid at Giza, built under the pharaoh **Khufu** about 2600 B.C. More than one hundred thousand people labored for twenty years to create this monument, which still stands today. Many of the workers were slaves, and many were forced to work against their wills.

The Middle Kingdom

Most people in Egypt who were not slaves were farmers. Others were artisans, merchants, scribes, or soldiers. To meet the huge expense of building the pyramids, farmers had to give a large part of their crops in <u>taxes</u> to the pharaoh each year. Other people had to contribute goods or services. About 2000 B.C., the people of Upper Egypt rebelled. They set up a new pharaoh in the city of **Thebes** (THEEBZ). This began the period called the Middle Kingdom. During this four-hundred-year era, Egypt reached out to the rest of the world.

Trade increased with neighboring peoples and with western Asia. The Egyptian army conquered kingdoms in **Nubia** (NOO bee uh), to the south, enslaved many of its people, and took gold from the mines in the area. But the Egyptians themselves were attacked in 1650 B.C. by the **Hyksos** (HIK *sahs*), who came from western Asia. The Hyksos took over Lower Egypt and ruled for one hundred years.

The New Kingdom

Eventually, the armies of Upper Egypt drove the Hyksos out and began the New Kingdom—the third and greatest period of ancient Egypt's power. The pharaoh **Ahmose** (AH mohs) made Egypt's army one of the strongest in the world. By 1400 B.C., Egypt had established an empire by reconquering Nubia, seizing the kingdom of Kush (KUHSH), farther south, and gaining control of the lands that are now Syria, Lebanon, and Israel. (The kingdom of Kush is discussed later in this chapter.)

The **Hebrews** had lived among the Egyptians for many years. They had originally come from the Mesopotamian city of Ur. According to the Hebrew Bible, **Abraham,** their founder, unlike most ancient peoples, believed in only one god. He took his family to **Canaan** (KAY nuhn), where they worked as shepherds. (Canaan was later known as Palestine.) Much later, the Hebrews immigrated to Egypt. The Egyptians let the Hebrews live peacefully for many years but eventually enslaved them. The Bible goes on to tell that a leader named **Moses** led his people out of Egypt into the desert—and to freedom. This would have happened about 1250 B.C., during the reign of the pharaoh **Ramses II.** The Hebrews eventually returned to Canaan, where they founded their own kingdom.

From about this time, Egypt's power began to decline. Rulers became weaker, priests became more powerful, and the army began to lose control over the region. Finally, Egypt fell to a series of foreign invaders.

INDIA

Around the year 2500 B.C., a civilization arose along the **Indus River** in what is now Pakistan.

Although the people who lived there flourished for eight hundred years, little is known about them. We do not even know what they called themselves. They were named the **Harappan** civilization after their main city, **Harappa** (huh RAH puh). Their other major cities were called **Mohenjo Daro** (moh *hen* joh DAR *oh*) and **Lothal.** What we do know about the Harappans comes from archaeological findings. Remains of canal systems that carried water for crop irrigation and sewer systems in their cities show that the Harappans were excellent engineers. Archaeologists have so far been unsuccessful in understanding their writing.

By 1700 B.C., the Harappans disappeared. Earthquakes and floods may have destroyed their cities. Invaders may have driven them out. They may have used up the land and moved away. About two hundred years later, a new people arrived in the Indus Valley. They were **Aryans** (AHR ee uhns) from central Asia. They brought with them their language, **Sanskrit,** and new ideas that, later on, would form the **Hindu** religion. The Aryans are the ancestors of today's Indian people.

CHINA

Around 4000 B.C., farming communities began to develop along the lower part of the the **Huang** (HWONG) **River** valley in northern China. Villages grew into towns, towns into cities, cities into small kingdoms. By around 1700 B.C., one of these kingdoms controlled the entire region. This kingdom centered on the city of **Shang,** and the civilization that grew there is known as the **Shang dynasty.** Much of what the Shang people achieved is lost. Their buildings of earth and wood crumbled and disappeared long ago. Fortunately, some of their writing has survived. Shang priests scratched questions about the future on animal bones. When the bones were thrown into a fire so that they cracked from the heat, the priests studied the pattern of cracks, believing that they represented answers from the gods of their religion. The Shang people worshiped their ancestors as gods.

The Shang made beautiful craft works and weapons from bronze. They were the first people to raise silkworms and weave cloth with silk. Their written language contained more than three thousand characters and is the basis for modern Chi-

nese. Unlike most peoples of the period, they used money rather than simply trading goods. The Shang ruled for about six hundred years. The last Shang king, both cruel and a drunkard, was <u>ousted</u> around 1100 B.C. by the **Zhou** (JOH) people, a group of wandering herders who had settled in western China.

AFRICA

By the time of ancient Egypt's Middle Kingdom, the vast Sahara desert covered most of northern Africa, as it does today. But it had not always been so. For thousands of years, the Sahara was grassland that was used by early farmers for cattle grazing. Sometime before 2000 B.C., there was a change in climate. The land became drier and drier. Farmers moved out of the region. Some of them went east to Egypt. Others headed south to the kingdom of **Kush.**

Kush developed along the banks of the Nile River in what is present-day Sudan. Its civilization was based on trade. People from different parts of Africa and western Asia came to Kush to trade goods for gold, ebony, ivory, and things made of iron. Egyptian trade made Kush rich, but about 1500 B.C., the Egyptians conquered Kush; Kush became part of Egypt's empire.

EARLY GREECE

The first Greek civilization developed on the island of **Crete** (KREET) in the Aegean (uh JEE uhn) Sea around 2500 B.C. Unlike the fertile river valleys, Crete, like most of Greece, is dry and rocky. The people here turned to the sea, rather than to the land, for their living. They became skilled sailors and traders. They are known as the Minoans.

The Minoans

The Minoans (muh NOH uhns) were named after their legendary king **Minos** (MYE nuhs). Minos and the kings that followed him built lavish palaces with beautiful artwork covering their walls. The greatest of these was the Palace of Minos in the city of Knossos (NAH suhs).

Minoan culture flourished for about five hundred years. About 1450 B.C., an earthquake struck a nearby island, causing a massive tidal wave. The wave probably swept over and destroyed most Minoan towns and cities. Soon after, the Mycenean (*mye* suh NEE uhn) people from the Greek mainland invaded Crete.

The Myceneans

The Myceneans ruled Crete and the rest of Greece for four hundred years. Around 1250 B.C., legends tell that their general, **Agamemnon** (*ah* guh MEM *nuhn*) led an army to fight and defeat the people of Troy, a city-state on the eastern Mediterranean. The beginning of the Trojan War is the subject of a famous <u>epic</u> poem called *The Iliad* by **Homer,** a blind poet of ancient Greece. Another epic poem by Homer, *The Odyssey*, tells of the wonderings of Odysseus (oh DIH see uhs), one of the Greeks who, according to legend, fought in the Trojan War.

Not long after, the Myceneans were themselves conquered by wandering invaders called the **Sea Peoples.** Then Greece entered a dark age that lasted three hundred years. People abandoned their towns and lived in tribes controlled by warlords. The Dorians, people who came from the Balkan Mountains to the east, occupied much of Greece. Dorian culture was less developed than the Mycenean or Minoan culture had been. Written language was lost or forgotten during Dorian times; storytellers passed Greek culture orally from one generation to the next. Around 800 B.C., Greek civilization rose again—this time to new

Lion Gate at Mycenae

WESTERN EUROPE

In western Europe during these early times, people lived in small villages and grew crops. There were no cities, no unifying governments, and no literature or arts. Little was known about these early Europeans until A.D. 1850. That year, a storm on the Orkney Islands off the Scottish coast blew away tons of sand to reveal a buried village nearly five thousand years old. The village was **Skara Brae,** and it contained a number of stone houses. Everything in Skara Brae, including utensils, was made of stone or the bones of animals. The island had no trees for wood.

Some of these early European peoples did incredible things with the stone available to them. They used **megaliths**—gigantic standing stones—to build huge circular monuments. Megalithic monuments have been found in Spain, France, England, and Sweden. The most famous megalith in Europe is **Stonehenge** in England. Stonehenge was built over a thousand-year period from 3000 to 2000 B.C. Another well-known megalith is the one at Carnac, France. Scientists believe the people who built megaliths set the huge stones in circles to mark the rising and setting positions of the sun and moon at different times of the year. These standing stones may also have been part of religious ceremonies and possibly animal and human sacrifice.

THE AMERICAS

In North America during the time period discussed in this chapter, people were mainly living as

Stonehenge

hunter-gatherers. People of Central and South America were taking first steps toward civilization. In what is now Mexico, people were farming by 3000 B.C. and cultivating corn by 2000 B.C. In South America, in the Andes Mountains in what is now Peru, temples were built by 2600 B.C., about the same time as the pyramids in Egypt. By 2000 B.C., people were living in villages. They grew cotton and corn and had an irrigation system for bringing water to their crops. They also made jewelry. By 1800 B.C., a huge pyramid had been built near present-day Lima.

The great Olmec civilization of Central America advanced during the time period covered by Chapter 2 in this book.

! Implications

To answer the question, "Why does all this matter?" or "What does it mean?," share the following insights with your child.

For most people on Earth today, living in permanent cities or towns, conducting trade, communicating through writing, obeying laws, and recognizing the control of a central government are accepted parts of everyday life. These aspects of society were in an early stage of development at the time of the first civilizations. While much has been lost from each civilization discussed in this chapter, it is important to remember that each civilization had contact with and influenced others. That influence is not lost. The most basic building blocks of our own societies today trace their foundations to people who lived five thousand years ago.

Another thing passed down to us from earliest times is war. Reading about the very earliest civilizations, one can't help noticing how many times this chapter mentions that a civilization eventually fell to attack or invasion. It seems that, after thousands of years of civilization, we have made little progress toward respecting human rights and getting along peacefully with neighboring peoples.

Fact Checker

To check that your child knows or can find the basic facts in this chapter, here is a matching game using facts about the first civilizations.

The top row names early civilizations. The bottom row names things or ideas in our own culture. Match the items on the top with the civilization that they come from. More than one item may be matched with the same civilization.

Sumerians   Babylonians   Shang   Egyptians

the wheel   a system of laws   paper   silk   glass   a written language   the potter's wheel

Answers appear in the back, preceding the index.

 The Big Questions

The following questions encourage your child to think critically rather than simply recall facts. If necessary, review the specific information from the preceding pages that will help your child make the appropriate inferences to come up with reasonable answers.

1. Explain why the beginning of agriculture was the first step toward civilization.
2. What characteristics of the geography of the Fertile Crescent made it ideal as one of the first places for civilization to begin?
3. Historians think that the Harappan civilization disappeared because of earthquakes and floods, destruction by foreign invaders, or overuse of the land. Compare these possibilities with the threats to modern civilization.

Suggested Answers

1. *When people began planting crops, they could stay in one place rather than leading nomadic lives as hunter-gatherers. This enabled villages, towns, and cities to grow. Having more than just enough food meant that not everyone had to farm—some could do other jobs, and some could be craftspeople and artists. Because things besides food were being produced, people began trading with each other. With trade, record keeping, which requires a written language, became necessary. Another result of trade is to bring people of different cultures together. Because contact among different peoples often leads to conflict, the need for law and order arose. That need was fulfilled by religion and government.*
2. *The Fertile Crescent was an ideal place for civilization to begin because it offered three important things: fertile soil, water for irrigation of crops, and rivers for transporting goods for the purpose of trade.*
3. *The threats to civilization are much the same as they were when civilization first began. While modern technology makes us better equipped today to survive natural disasters, it also increases the threat of destruction due to war and also puts a greater strain on our supply of natural resources.*

Skills Practice

The following activities give your child practice in applying the skills basic to social studies. For some of the activities, your child may need to review the information in the preceding pages.

A. DISTINGUISHING FACT FROM OPINION

Review with your child the definitions of the words *fact* and *opinion*. Establish that statements of fact can be checked to find out whether they are true or false, while statements of opinion are neither true nor false—they represent the judgments people have made. Then ask your child to identify the following statements as facts or opinions. Encourage your child to explain each identification.

1. The Babylonian civilization was the greatest of all those discussed in this chapter.
2. The Egyptians believed that the sun god was the ancestor of their pharaohs.
3. The Aryans are the ancestors of today's Indian people.
4. Learning about early civilizations is very important.
5. By 2600 B.C., civilization in parts of South America was as advanced as it was in Egypt.

Answers

1. opinion; 2. fact; 3. fact; 4. opinion; 5. opinion

Evaluating Your Child's Skills: If your child has trouble, point out key words and phrases that are typical in statements of opinion: *greatest* and *very important*.

B. SUPPORTING OPINIONS WITH FACTS

Review with your child that a person's opinion cannot be true or false because it is a judgment that the person has made—not a statement of fact. However, to be convincing, a person should be able to back up his or her opinions with facts. If necessary, have your child return to the "What Your Child Needs to Know" section to find at least one fact to back up the following opinions.

1. The Babylonian civilization was the greatest of the early civilizations discussed in this chapter.
2. The Sumerian civilization was the greatest.
3. By 2600 B.C., civilization in parts of South America was as advanced as it was in Egypt.

Suggested Answers

1. *The Babylonians gave us one of the first written systems of laws—the Code of Hammurabi.*
2. *The Sumerians invented the wheel.*
3. *Around 2600 B.C., the same time that the pyramids were built in Egypt, temples were built in parts of South America.*

Evaluating Your Child's Skills: In order to complete this activity successfully, your child needs to be able to distinguish between fact and opinion. He or she also needs to recall information already learned. If your child has difficulties, help him or her look through the "What Your Child Needs to Know" section, looking for key words such as *Babylonians* to find the information needed.

Top of the Class

Children interested in delving more deeply into the topic of this chapter can choose one or more of the following activities. They may do the activities for their own satisfaction or share what they have done in class to show that they have been seriously considering the first civilizations.

A POINT TO PONDER

Suggest to your child that he or she raise the following issue in class.

Since the earliest civilizations, humans have made progress. We now have electricity, telephones, computers, airplanes, and space shuttles. But we also have guns and nuclear weapons. In fact, humans are still as warlike as ever. Why don't we make progress in finding a peaceful way to live?

ART PROJECTS

Encourage your child to do one of the following projects and share it with the class.

- Make a map of the area called Mesopotamia or the Fertile Crescent. Show the locations of the Sumerian and Babylonian civilizations.
- Draw or make a model of a ziggurat, a pyramid, or a megalith such as the one at Stonehenge in England.

CHAPTER 2

Civilization Expands
1200 B.C.–500 B.C.

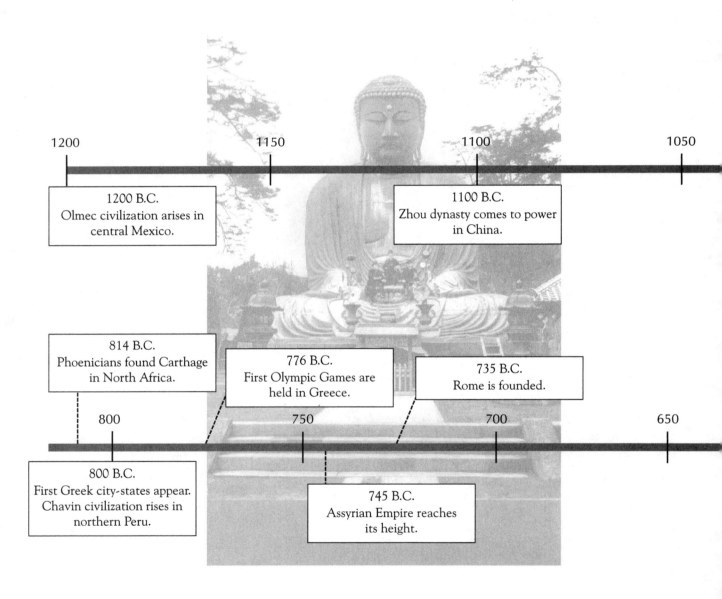

1200   1150   1100   1050

1200 B.C.
Olmec civilization arises in central Mexico.

1100 B.C.
Zhou dynasty comes to power in China.

814 B.C.
Phoenicians found Carthage in North Africa.

776 B.C.
First Olympic Games are held in Greece.

735 B.C.
Rome is founded.

800   750   700   650

800 B.C.
First Greek city-states appear. Chavin civilization rises in northern Peru.

745 B.C.
Assyrian Empire reaches its height.

This timeline provides an overview of the period of 1200 B.C. to 500 B.C. The narrative in the following pages offers more details and discusses the significance of the events.

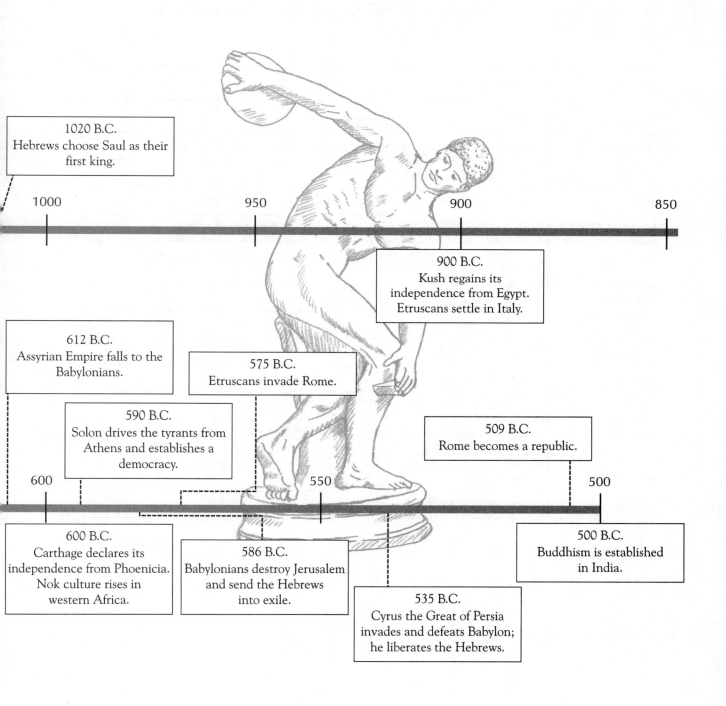

1020 B.C.
Hebrews choose Saul as their first king.

1000   950   900   850

900 B.C.
Kush regains its independence from Egypt.
Etruscans settle in Italy.

612 B.C.
Assyrian Empire falls to the Babylonians.

575 B.C.
Etruscans invade Rome.

590 B.C.
Solon drives the tyrants from Athens and establishes a democracy.

509 B.C.
Rome becomes a republic.

600   550   500

600 B.C.
Carthage declares its independence from Phoenicia.
Nok culture rises in western Africa.

586 B.C.
Babylonians destroy Jerusalem and send the Hebrews into exile.

500 B.C.
Buddhism is established in India.

535 B.C.
Cyrus the Great of Persia invades and defeats Babylon; he liberates the Hebrews.

Word Power

Word	Definition
colony	place that is under foreign rule
crossbow	weapon with a bow mounted across a piece of wood
enlightenment	wisdom
exile	send someone away and order him or her not to return
lacquered	coated with a shiny finish
monetary	having to do with money (as in "Our *monetary* system is based on the dollar.")
nurture	tend to the needs of
orally	spoken, not written
provinces	districts; regions
psalms	sacred songs or poems
rivals	people in competition with one another; enemies
smelted	melted down rock so that the metal in the rock can be separated out and removed.
subjugated	controlled
vulnerable	open (to attack)

What Your Child Needs to Know

You may choose to use the following text in several different ways, depending on your child's strengths and preferences. You might read the passage aloud; you might read it to yourself and then paraphrase it for your child; or you might ask your child to read the material along with you or on his or her own.

MESOPOTAMIA

The Cradle of Civilization that gave rise to the world's earliest civilizations continued to <u>nurture</u> rising civilizations during this period. Some of these civilizations were new and others already existed but reached new heights of power and influence during the years covered by this chapter.

The Hebrews

According to the Bible story, the Hebrew people spent forty years wandering in the Sinai (SYE *nye*) Desert after their flight from Egypt. Then they returned to Canaan and established the kingdom of Israel. In 1020 B.C., threatened by the Philistines, a neighboring people, they elected their first king, **Saul.** Saul was weak in many ways, but his successor, **King David,** was a great ruler. He was also a poet who supposedly wrote many of the <u>psalms</u> in the Bible. David also enlarged the kingdom of Israel and established Jerusalem as his capital city. His son **Solomon,** who followed him, built Jerusalem into a fine city with a magnificent temple. King Solomon was known for his great wisdom.

The Assyrians

Unlike the Hebrews, the Assyrians' first interest was warfare. These fierce warriors had been living in the Fertile Crescent at least since 1350 B.C. About 900 B.C., they began a plan of conquest. Their expert armies attacked towns and cities, either killing or enslaving the people they conquered. At its height, about 745 B.C., the Assyrian

Empire included Babylon, Arabia, and the lands that are now Syria, Egypt, and Israel.

The Assyrians were great builders of cities and palaces. Their last king created the world's first known library. It contained more than twenty-two thousand clay tablets written in Sumerian cuneiform. (See Chapter 1.)

The Assyrians' cruelty finally led their subjects to rebel, and internal disorder weakened their empire. In 612 B.C., the Babylonians, whom the Assyrians had <u>subjugated</u>, for more than five hundred years, rose against Assyria. Along with other subjugated peoples, the Babylonians brought down Assyrian power and destroyed **Nineveh** (NIH nuh vuh), the capital. The Assyrian Empire was no more.

The Babylonians

Soon after the downfall of Assyria, **King Nebuchadnezzar II** (*neh* byuh kuhd NEH zuhr) came to power in Babylon and made Babylon a great power once again. He took over parts of the Assyrian Empire and enlarged the city of Babylon. Perhaps his greatest achievement was the Hanging Gardens of Babylon. These gorgeous gardens draped over steps built high above the city. Later, the Greeks would name them one of the Seven Wonders of the World, along with the Egyptian pyramids. Nebuchadnezzar also built a giant ziggurat, which may be the famous Tower of Babel mentioned in the Hebrew Bible.

By this time, the Hebrew people were divided into two kingdoms, **Judah** (JOO duh) in the south and **Israel** in the north. In 586 B.C., Nebuchadnezzar captured Jerusalem in Judah and destroyed the city and its great temple. He forced most of the Hebrews of Judah to go into <u>exile</u> in Babylon.

Nebuchadnezzar's successors were less capable rulers than he. The Babylonian Empire was once again weakened by poor leadership and <u>vulnerable</u> to invasion.

The Persians

The Persians came out of central Asia and settled in the area of present-day Iran. Their king, **Cyrus** (SYE ruhs) **the Great,** came to the throne in 557 B.C. and set out to build his own empire. He invaded Babylon in 535 B.C. The Persians, unlike the Assyrians and Babylonians, treated the people they conquered with kindness and gave them some degree of freedom. They freed the captive Jews in Babylon and allowed them to return home to Canaan.

Cyrus's successor, **Darius II,** expanded the Persian Empire to include India and Greece. Darius divided his empire into twenty <u>provinces</u>. Each province was ruled by a governor. Darius made the city of **Persepolis** (pur SE puh luhs) his capital and built good roads to improve transportation throughout his empire. He also established a <u>monetary</u> system of gold and silver coins to encourage trade. He lived up to the title he gave himself, *Shahanshah,* which means, "king of kings."

AFRICA

Kush

By 900 B.C., Egypt had lost much of its power in the ancient world. Kush regained its independence from Egypt and established a new capital at **Napata.** In 770 B.C., the Kushites went to war against Egypt and defeated the once powerful Egyptian army. About a hundred years later, Kush began a long decline. The kingdom moved its cultural center south to the city of **Meroë** (MER oh ee), where iron deposits allowed them to continue to prosper for a time.

The Nok People

Meanwhile, across the continent in western Africa, a new civilization emerged about 600 B.C. Like the Kushites, the Nok people of what is now Nigeria mined iron ore and <u>smelted</u> it in furnaces lined with clay. They used the iron to make knives, ax blades, and arrowheads. The axes were used to clear land for farming. The Noks were highly artistic as well and created new styles of pottery with elaborate designs and figures.

The Rise of Carthage

The Phoenicians, who occupied the area on the eastern coast of the Mediterranean Sea, had outlived many of their more powerful neighbors. This was probably due to the fact that the Phoenicians made their living mostly by trading rather than by warfare. About 1000 B.C., Phoenician ships began exploring the coastline of the Mediterranean. In 814 B.C., they founded the <u>colony</u> of Carthage on the northern coast of Africa, in present-day Tunisia. Carthage rapidly became the largest trading center on the African coast outside of Egypt. It was an important trading link between the Mediterranean lands and the rest of Africa. By 600 B.C., Carthage was so powerful that it broke its ties with Phoenicia and became an independent city.

INDIA

The Aryans, the ancestors of today's Indian people, were strong warriors who spread out from the Indus Valley to occupy a large area of northern India. By 500 B.C., they had established sixteen separate kingdoms. The Aryans adopted much of the older Harappan culture, such as Hinduism, with its **caste system.** In this system, a person was born into one of four castes, or classes: priest, soldier, farmer or merchant, or servant. A person could not move from one class to another. However, Hinduism teaches that when the body dies, the soul is reborn. A person who has led a good life might be born into a higher caste. This concept of rebirth is called **reincarnation.**

The Aryans spoke the Sanskrit language, but they had no written language, so they passed their history and religious beliefs from one generation to the next <u>orally</u>. Much later, their words were written down in books called the *Vedas,* now considered the ancient bible of the Hindus.

In 560 B.C., a child named **Siddhartha Gautama** (sih DAHR tuh GOH tuh muh) was born to a wealthy Aryan family. Later, at the age of twenty-nine, he gave up his life of luxury to go out into the world and seek <u>enlightenment</u>. The religion **Buddhism,** based on his ideas, was established by 500 B.C. Siddhartha Gautama was called **Buddha,** which means "the enlightened one." Buddhism teaches that all people are equal. It also teaches respect for all living things. Like Hinduism, Buddhism teaches a belief in reincarnation. Soon Buddhism would spread to China, Japan, and other countries.

CHINA

The Zhou people, who had ousted the last king of the Shang dynasty, did not establish a unified king-

Great bronze statue of Buddha, Kamakura, Japan, photo c. 1900

dom. Instead, a number of large estates were ruled by wealthy nobles who owed loyalty to the king.

The Zhou introduced ironworking to China. Iron was used to make weapons, such as the <u>crossbow</u>, which gave Zhou soldiers an advantage in war. It was also used for practical household items and farm tools, such as plows. The Zhou also made beautiful <u>lacquered</u> artwork.

EUROPE

Greece

During Greece's dark age following the fall of the Myceneans, there was no written language in Greece, but language and literature were kept alive by storytellers. They passed Greek heritage down orally from one generation to the next. As noted in Chapter 1, one such storyteller may have been the blind poet Homer, who is said to have composed the famous poems that tell of the Trojan War (*The Iliad*) and of the adventures of the Greek hero Odysseus (*The Odyssey*). The stories were written down at the end of Homer's life, when writing was introduced in Greece.

By about 800 B.C., small city-states began to appear across Greece. Each city-state, or **polis** (POH luhs), had its own government, culture, and gods, to whom the people turned for protection. The highest point in the city was called the **acropolis** (uh KRA puh luhs). At the foot of the acropolis, the city's leaders met to discuss important issues. The **agora** (A guh ruh) was an open space used as a marketplace.

The most important city-states were **Sparta** in southern Greece and **Athens** to the north. The Spartans were warlike and aggressive. Spartan boys and girls were trained as soldiers from an early age. Sparta was the largest city-state and had many slaves who farmed the land and did other jobs.

Athens was a very different kind of place. Athens was the trading and cultural capital of Greece. Children were not trained in warfare but were taught philosophy and poetry. Athens and Sparta often quarreled with each other. These quarrels eventually led to war.

Although the Greek city-states had their differences, they all came together for the Olympic Games. This festival in honor of **Zeus** (ZOOS), king of the Greek gods, first took place in 776 B.C. at the city of Olympia near Mount Olympus, where the Greeks believed their gods and goddesses lived. The Olympic Games included contests in sports, music, and drama. The sports events included a footrace, a long jump, a discus throw, a javelin throw, and wrestling matches.

Powerful governors called **tyrants** ran many of the Greek city-states. These men had complete power over the people in their cities. Some cities were controlled by a group of tyrants. In 590 B.C., the people of Athens, led by a wealthy and influential citizen named **Solon** (SOH luhn), drove the tyrants from their city. After that, the people had more power. Citizens were allowed to help choose the people who would rule them. This was the beginning of **democracy,** which is based on two Greek words that mean "rule by the people."

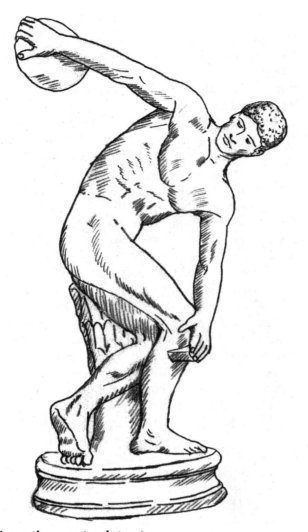

Discus thrower (sculpture)

The Etruscans

Italy lies west of Greece on the Mediterranean Sea. Around 900 B.C., the Etruscans (ih TRUHS kuhnz) settled in what is now Italy northwest of the **Tiber** (TYE buhr) **River.** They controlled nearly all of west and central Italy.

We know little about the Etruscans because the language they spoke has never been translated into a modern language. We do know they were much influenced by the neighboring Greeks. They prayed to Greek gods and goddesses and adapted the Greek alphabet for their writing. They also excelled at trading, navigating, and metalwork. Their main <u>rivals</u> were the people who lived in central Italy known as **Latins.**

Rome

In 735 B.C., a new city was established in what is now Italy on seven hills along the Tiber River. It was named Rome after its supposed founder **Romulus** (ROM yuh luhs). The legend goes that a cruel king had Romulus and his twin brother **Remus** (REE muhs) thrown into the Tiber as babies. The children did not drown but were washed ashore and cared for by a female wolf. Some shepherds found the two boys and raised them. Later, the two brothers founded a city along the Tiber but argued over what to name it. Romulus killed Remus in a fight, and so the city of Rome got his name. In reality, Rome's founding was probably far less dramatic. Rome most likely began as a group of small Latin villages scattered over the seven hills. They eventually grew and joined together into one large town.

The Etruscans invaded Rome about 575 B.C. The last Etruscan king, a cruel man, was finally driven out by the Romans in 509 B.C. The Etruscans were soon absorbed by the Romans and disappeared as a people. The Romans declared themselves the world's first **republic.** In a republic, citizens choose the people who govern them, much as they did in Athens. Every free man could vote in elections, although slaves and women could not vote.

Over the next five hundred years, Rome would build an empire of such size and scope as the world had never seen before.

THE AMERICAS

While civilization was on the rise in Europe, Africa, and Asia, across the Atlantic Ocean in what is now North America, life went on as it had for centuries. Two civilizations, very different from those of Europe, arose in **Mesoamerica,** the region that is now Mexico and Central America, and in South America in what is now Peru.

The Adena People

One of the first cultures to develop in North America was the Adena (uh DEE nuh). From about 1000 to 300 B.C., the Adena people lived on riverbanks in today's central and southern Ohio, Kentucky, Indiana, Virginia, and West Virginia. The Adena were hunter-gatherers who did some simple farming of corn, beans, and squash. Most of what people today know about the Adena is from their burial mounds. These rounded mounds of earth range from twenty feet (six meters) to more than three hundred feet (ninety meters) wide. Inside, archaeologists have found spear points, pipes for smoking, copper bracelets, and stone tablets.

The Olmec

The Olmec emerged about 1200 B.C. in what is today central Mexico. A cluster of villages on the Gulf of Mexico slowly developed into the first and most important Olmec city, **La Venta.** The Olmec were great builders and gifted artists. They created large pyramids of earth and stone for religious worship. They developed their own written language, calendar, and counting system. But they are best remembered today for the strange, enormous heads they carved out of stone. More than sixteen of these heads have been unearthed. It is thought that the heads represent early Olmec leaders. Little more is known of this early American civilization. Unfortunately, most of the Olmec written documents were destroyed. The Olmec disappeared about 700 B.C.

The Chavin Culture

Around 1000 B.C., the Chavin (tchah VEEN) civilization appeared in the high Andes Mountains of northern Peru in South America. Like the Olmec, the Chavin built great temples, made stone carvings, and built cities. They also were among the first American peoples to work with gold.

Centuries later, new civilizations would arise in both the regions first inhabited by the Olmec and the Chavin. These civilizations would be as advanced as any in the ancient world.

! Implications

To answer the question, "Why does all this matter?" or "What does it mean?," share the following insights with your child.

One good reason for learning about history is that knowledge about the past often helps us to see our own times more clearly. For example, while newspaper accounts of the current conflict between the Israelis and the Palestinians may seem confusing, it seems less so to one who knows the background of that conflict. As mentioned in this chapter, when the Hebrews came out of the Sinai Desert forty years after their escape from slavery, they returned to the land they had come from—Canaan. There they established the kingdom of *Israel.* If there is any truth to this biblical account, the competition between the Israelis and the Palestinians for land has been going on for three thousand years or so.

Another example of the past shedding light on modern times is evident in our own history. A person who understands that the democratic ideals born more than twenty-five hundred years ago in ancient Athens form the basis for our own government has a deeper appreciation for democracy than someone who thinks our system of government was born when the Declaration of Independence was signed less than 250 years ago.

Fact Checker

To check that your child knows or can find the basic facts in this chapter, here is a puzzle that uses names of peoples and places discussed.

PEOPLE AND PLACES

For each clue, fill in the name of a people or place you learned about in this chapter.

Across

2. The _____ people lived in northern Peru.
3. Buddhism and Hinduism started in _____.
6. _____ was the world's first republic.
7. A king of _____ created hanging gardens.
10. The _____ invaded Rome in 575 B.C.
12. David was a great king of the _____.
13. _____ defeated the Egyptian army.

Down

1. The _____ were seafarers and traders.
4. A king of the _____ built the first-known library.
5. Athens and Sparta were city-states in ancient _____ .
8. The _____ people made heads out of stone.
9. Cyrus the Great was king of the _____.
11. The _____ people mined iron in West Africa.

Answers appear in the back, preceding the index.

The Big Questions

The following questions encourage your child to think critically rather than simply recall facts. If necessary, review the specific information from the preceding pages that will help your child make the necessary inferences to come up with reasonable answers.

1. So far, the story of civilization seems to be one endless war story. One after another, civilizations rose. They developed skills, languages, and systems of government. They built cities. Then they fell, usually as a result of warfare. Note, however, that this chapter mentions that the Phoenicians survived longer than many of their neighbors because they "lived by trade rather than warfare." How does trade prevent war? What can we, today, learn about survival from the ancient Phoenicians?

2. Some of the things discussed in this chapter are still in our lives today: the democratic form of government, the psalms of David in the Bible, the epic poems of Homer, the Buddhist and Hindu religions, and the Olympic games. Consider the fact that these things have lasted for more than twenty-five hundred years. What does this tell us about ourselves and the people who lived so long ago? Although the world is, in many ways, very different from two thousand five hundred years ago, are we, today, more different from or similar to these early peoples?

Suggested Answers

1. *When two nations trade with each other, both of them profit. But nations that are at war with each other cannot trade. In order to trade, nations have to cooperate and communicate. The lesson we can learn from the Phoenicians is that cooperation rather than competition leads to survival.*

2. *We are not so different from human beings who lived a long time ago. While much has changed, the basic fears, hopes, and desires of human beings remain the same from earliest times up to the present.*

Skills Practice

The following activities give your child practice in applying the skills basic to social studies. For some of the activities, your child may need to review the information in the preceding pages.

A.   READING A TIMELINE

With your child, examine the timeline at the beginning of the chapter. Encourage your child to use the timeline to answer the following questions.

1. What was happening in Peru (in South America) when the Greek city-states first appeared?

2. For how many years did the Babylonian Exile last for the Hebrews?

3. About how long ago was democracy established as the form of government in Athens?

4. Which was established first—the Olmec civilization in Mexico or the Chavin civilization in Peru?

5. What important religion was established in 500 B.C.?

Answers

1. *The Chavin civilization arose.*
2. *51 years.*
3. *About twenty-six hundred years.*
4. *The Olmec.*
5. *Buddhism.*

Evaluating Your Child's Skills: In order to complete this activity successfully, your child needs to use several skills. Question 1 requires skimming the timeline to look for years for which more than one event is listed; Question 2 requires skimming for the word *Hebrews* and subtracting one date from the other; Question 3 requires skimming to locate the word *democracy* and knowing that adding rather than subtracting is the way to find the answer; Question 4 requires reasoning that, since "The Olmecs . . ." is the first item on the timeline, it must precede the Chavin; Question 5 requires locating the year 500 B.C.—understanding that B.C. dates go from higher to lower numbers. If your child has trouble, go over the particular skill he or she needs help with.

B.   FINDING SIMILARITIES

The civilizations discussed in this chapter are different in many ways, but the chapter notes certain important similarities. Help your child go into the text to find them in order to answer the following questions.

1. What do the *Vedas* of the Hindu religion and the poems of Homer have in common?
2. In what way were the Assyrians, Aryans, and Spartans similar?
3. In what way were the Zhou people of China similar to the Nok people of western Africa?
4. In what way were the governments of Greece and Rome alike?
5. In what way did the Olmecs resemble the Chavin people?

Answers

1. *They were both originally part of an oral tradition and written down later.*
2. *All three were warlike.*
3. *They both worked with iron.*
4. *They were both democratic.*
5. *Both made temples, carved stone, and built cities.*

Evaluating Your Child's Skills: In order to complete this activity successfully, your child needs to make connections among ideas that are basically dissimilar. You can help by looking up and reviewing with your child the main points made about the civilizations mentioned in each question.

 # Top of the Class

Children interested in delving more deeply into the topic of this chapter can choose one or more of the following activities. They may do the activities for their own satisfaction or share what they have done in class to show that they have been seriously considering the time period from 1200 B.C. to 500 B.C.

A POINT TO PONDER

Suggest to your child that he or she raise the following issue in class.

Studying about this period of time, we begin to hear about ideas and works that seem to last forever. Democracy, begun in ancient Greece, is still the form of government chosen by many countries in the modern world. Buddhism, Hinduism, and Judaism are still living religions. We still read King David's psalms and Homer's epic poems, *The Iliad* and *The Odyssey*. Are there any ideas or works generated in our period of history that will last as long? If so, what are they? If not, why not?

FURTHER RESEARCH

Suggest that your child do further research to find out more about the great contributions made by the civilizations under discussion in this chapter. He or she could present the findings as a written or oral report.

Use books in the library or a good encyclopedia to find out more about the Hindu and Buddhist religions or the Greek alphabet. In a copy of the Bible, read some of the psalms written by King David.

BOOKS TO READ

Suggest that your child read simplified versions of the famous poems of Homer—great literature composed during the time period discussed in this chapter. Your child may want to recommend these books to other students or respond to what he or she has read by offering an oral or written critique in class.

Strachan, Ian. *The Iliad.* Kingfisher, 1997.

Sutcliff, Rosemary. *The Wanderings of Odysseus: The Story of the Odyssey.* Delacorte, 1996.

CHAPTER 3
The Classical World
500 B.C.–A.D. 1

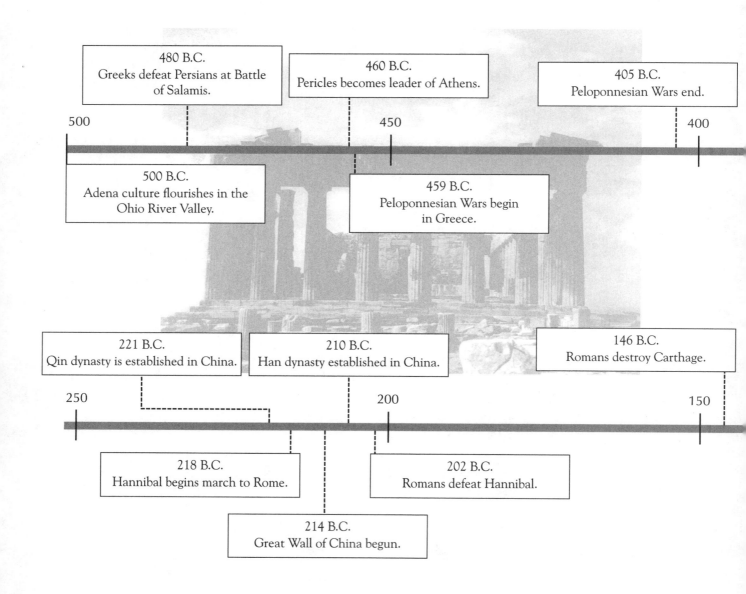

480 B.C.
Greeks defeat Persians at Battle of Salamis.

460 B.C.
Pericles becomes leader of Athens.

405 B.C.
Peloponnesian Wars end.

500

450

400

500 B.C.
Adena culture flourishes in the Ohio River Valley.

459 B.C.
Peloponnesian Wars begin in Greece.

221 B.C.
Qin dynasty is established in China.

210 B.C.
Han dynasty established in China.

146 B.C.
Romans destroy Carthage.

250

200

150

218 B.C.
Hannibal begins march to Rome.

202 B.C.
Romans defeat Hannibal.

214 B.C.
Great Wall of China begun.

This timeline provides an overview of the period from 500 B.C. to A.D. 1. Then a narrative describes this period in greater detail and discusses its significance.

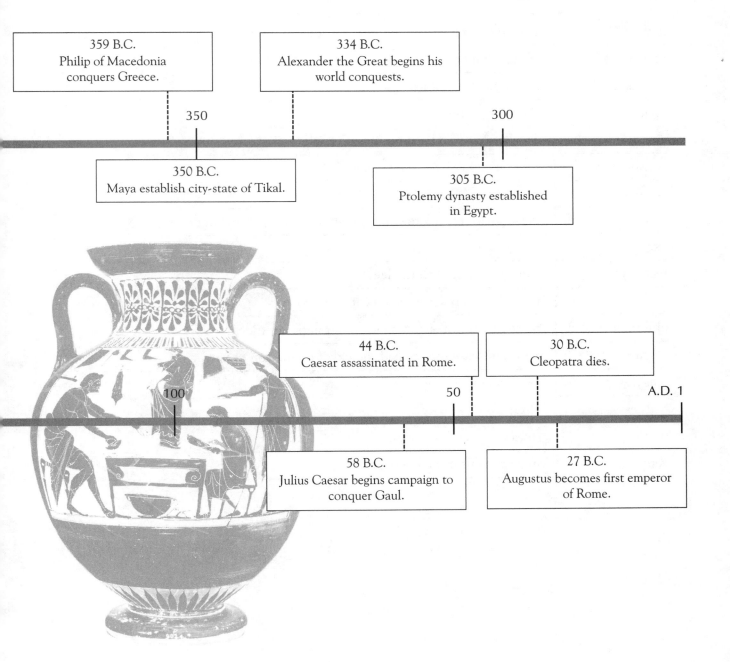

359 B.C.
Philip of Macedonia
conquers Greece.

334 B.C.
Alexander the Great begins his
world conquests.

350

300

350 B.C.
Maya establish city-state of Tikal.

305 B.C.
Ptolemy dynasty established
in Egypt.

100

50

A.D. 1

44 B.C.
Caesar assassinated in Rome.

30 B.C.
Cleopatra dies.

58 B.C.
Julius Caesar begins campaign to
conquer Gaul.

27 B.C.
Augustus becomes first emperor
of Rome.

Word Power

Word	*Definition*
ally	person or country that gives support to another
aqueducts	bridges built to carry water from one place to another over land
assassinated	murdered for political reasons
chaos	complete confusion
civil war	war between different groups of people in the same country
conspirators	partners in a secret, illegal plot
currency	money
dictator	person with complete control over a country; often, an unfair person
exquisite	very beautiful
meditate	calm one's mind; think deeply
outmaneuvered	moved in such a way as to beat an opponent
philosopher	person who writes or teaches about important ideas
plague	serious disease that spreads quickly from person to person
preside	be in charge
textiles	cloth
tragedies	stories that end unhappily
veto	stop; prevent from making a law

What Your Child Needs to Know

You may choose to use the text that follows in several different ways, depending on your child's strengths and preferences. You might read the passage aloud; you might read it to yourself and then paraphrase it for your child; or you might ask your child to read the material along with you or on his or her own.

Ruins of the Parthenon

GREECE

For more than half a century, the Persians had tried to conquer Greece and make it part of their empire. Faced with a common enemy, the Greek city-states banded together to fight the Persians.

In 490 B.C., the Athenians defeated the Persians at the Battle of Marathon. Ten years later, 380 swift Greek ships outmaneuvered a fleet of 1,200 Persian vessels at the Battle of Salamis (SA luh muhs). It was a great victory for the Greeks. The Persians withdrew and were never again a serious threat to Greece.

The Age of Pericles

In 461 B.C., **Pericles** (PER uh *kleez*) became leader of Athens, which he governed for the next thirty years, until 431 B.C. Pericles encouraged learning and the free exchange of ideas. He gave more rights to ordinary citizens than they had enjoyed before. He saw that citizens were paid to serve on juries or hold public office. This allowed common people to participate in government. Before that, public officials were not paid, so only the wealthy could afford to hold office.

Pericles also ordered great buildings and temples to be erected in Athens. The greatest of these was the **Parthenon** (PAR thuh *nahn*), a temple to Athena, goddess of wisdom. It was built in Athens at the top of the acropolis, where parts of it still stand today.

The Age of Pericles and the years following were a golden age for Greece. People flocked to spacious outdoor theaters to hear the great tragedies of the playwrights **Aeschylus** (ES kuh luhs), **Sophocles** (SAH fuh *kleez*), and **Euripides** (yoo RI puh *deez*) and the comedies of **Aristophanes** (ar uh STAH fuh *neez*)—plays that people still read and perform today. They listened to the ideas of the great philosopher **Socrates** (SAH kruh *teez*), who spoke with his students about the right way to live, about what makes a good government, and about what we mean when we use words such as *good* and *beautiful*. The Greeks read the works of the first historians, **Herodotus** (hih RAH duh tuhs) and **Thucydides** (thuh SIH duh *deez*). Greek architects designed great buildings supported by graceful columns. Greek sculptors created statues of gods and heroes that were remarkable for their realism, grace, and beauty. Many of these works are on exhibit today in museums around the world.

The Peloponnesian Wars

Sparta and other city-states grew jealous of the culture and wealth of Athens. Other city-states joined Sparta against Athens in the Peloponnesian (*peh* luh puh NEE shun) Wars in 459 B.C. The first of these wars ended in a Spartan victory. Fifteen years later, Athens attacked **Corinth,** Sparta's ally, and sparked a second war. This one lasted for nearly forty years. During this time, a terrible plague struck Athens and killed one-third of its population. Among the dead was Pericles.

In 404 B.C., the Spartan navy destroyed the entire Athenian fleet. With this defeat, the golden age of Athens came to an end, and Sparta became the leader of the Greek city-states.

Attic black-figured amphora showing shoemaker's shop, sixth century B.C.

Even so, Athens remained the cultural leader of Greece. The philosophers **Plato** (PLAY toh) and **Aristotle** (AR uh *stah* tul) wrote and taught during this time. Socrates, Plato's teacher, had discussed important ideas with his students, but he had never written any of these ideas down. Plato wrote down and elaborated on these discussions. His writings are called **Plato's Dialogues.** Aristotle offered theories as to how the universe worked. Because of his careful observation of the world around him and his logical methods of reasoning, he is said to have given birth to modern science.

Alexander the Great

To the north of Greece lay **Macedonia** (*ma soh DOH nee uh*), a nation of fierce warriors. Its king **Philip II** conquered Greece in 338 B.C. When Philip was <u>assassinated</u> in 336 B.C., his twenty-year-old son, Alexander, took over the Macedonian empire, including Greece. Alexander, even at this early age, was a courageous soldier and a bril-

liant military leader. The Greek philosopher Aristotle had been Alexander's tutor when he was a child. Through Aristotle, Alexander came to love Greek culture and learning.

In 334 B.C., Alexander set out on a campaign of conquest that would change the ancient world. He led his army into Turkey, then Syria and Egypt. In 333 B.C., he defeated Persian troops, went on to conquer Babylon, and then marched eastward into India.

Everywhere he went, Alexander spread Greek culture and ideas. He built temples and buildings in the Greek style, settled Greek people in each conquered land, and founded a great Greek city in Egypt he named after himself—**Alexandria.** He created the largest empire in the ancient world and came to be called Alexander the Great.

While in India, Alexander was called back to Persia to put down a rebellion. On the way, he came down with a fever and died suddenly in Babylon in 323 B.C. at the age of thirty-three. Alexander's empire quickly fell apart. By 146 B.C., both Macedonia and Greece were under the control of the growing Roman Empire.

AFRICA

Alexander's empire was split up among his generals. Egypt went to **Ptolemy** (TAH luh mee), who became king of Egypt in 305 B.C. Ptolemy made Alexandria his new capital. Alexandria remained a great city. The library of Alexandria was one of the finest in the world and an important center of learning. The **Pharos** (FAR *uhs*) **lighthouse,** completed in 280 B.C., was one of the world's first lighthouses. The Greeks named it one of the seven wonders of the ancient world.

The Ptolemy dynasty ruled Egypt for nearly three hundred years. The last Ptolemy ruler was the queen **Cleopatra** (*klee* uh PAH truh). She committed suicide in 30 B.C. when the Roman leader **Marc Antony,** with whom she was in love, was defeated by rival Roman leaders at the Battle of Actium. After that, Egypt became part of the Roman Empire.

ROME

The governing body of the young Roman republic was the **Senate.** The senators, who were elected for life, decided how all tax money would be spent and determined how Rome would interact with foreign peoples. Only **patricians,** wealthy landowners and other members of the ruling class, could be senators.

The **plebeians** (plih BEE uhnz), ordinary citizens of Rome, did not want to be ruled by the patricians. They wanted more of a say in how the republic was run. In 494 B.C., the plebeians won the right to elect representatives called **tribunes** who would protect their interests in the Senate. In addition, the Senate selected two **consuls,** or officers, each year to <u>preside</u> over the Senate. The consuls also served as army commanders and judges. The consuls were powerful, but they served for only one year and the tribunes could <u>veto</u> any one of their actions. By 287 B.C., the republic had become much more democratic than in its earlier days, and the plebeians had won complete equality.

By about 265 B.C., Rome was in control of all Italy. Now the Romans looked to extend their power to the rest of the Mediterranean world.

The Punic Wars

Rome had one serious rival in the Mediterranean. It was Carthage, on the northern coast of Africa. In 264 B.C., Roman soldiers invaded the island of Sicily, controlled by Carthage. This act began the Punic (PYOO nik) Wars between Rome and Carthage. *Punic* comes from the Latin word for Phoenicia, the country that had founded Carthage some five hundred years earlier. The first war ended in defeat for Carthage, which lost its power on the Mediterranean.

But Carthage was still a threat to Rome. In the 230s B.C., Carthage founded a colony in Spain, giving it a foothold of power in Europe. The commander of New Carthage in Spain was a brilliant, fearless general named **Hannibal.** In 218 B.C., Hannibal set off to achieve what many thought was impossible. He decided to march across Gaul (the ancient Roman name for France) and cross the Alps, Europe's highest mountain range, to attack Rome by land. Hannibal's army consisted of ninety thousand soldiers and forty elephants. He hoped to frighten the Romans with the elephants, but most of the animals died crossing the Alps.

For thirteen years, Hannibal attacked Italy, but won no decisive victory over the Romans. The Roman general **Scipio** (SIH pee *oh*) was as clever as Hannibal and avoided fighting him directly. Instead, Scipio marched south and attacked Carthage itself. Hannibal was forced to return to Carthage to defend the city. There he was finally defeated.

Carthage rose up against Rome one last time in 149 B.C. This third Punic War ended when the Romans destroyed Carthage three years later.

The Roman Empire

With Carthage in ruins, Rome ruled the entire Mediterranean area, including Macedonia and Greece. Now it was ready to seek new lands to conquer.

The **Celts** (KELTZ) were a warrior people who, by 500 B.C., were living in present-day Spain, France, Germany, and Great Britain. They were a tribal people with no central government. Their lives were governed largely by a class of priests and wise men called **Druids** (DROO idz). The Celts had no written language but kept their literature and history alive orally. They also made <u>exquisite</u> metalwork. The Romans set out to conquer the Celts and succeeded in controlling most of their lands by 44 B.C. The Celts accepted Roman rule and even fought on the Roman side against invading barbarians from the north.

The Romans, who by 44 B.C. controlled much of present-day Europe, built a great civilization. But they borrowed much of their culture from the Greeks. They copied the works of Greek artists and the architectural styles of Greek buildings. They even adopted the Greek gods, simply changing their names from Greek to Roman. For instance, Zeus, king of the Greek gods, became the Roman god Jupiter; Athena, the Greek goddess of wisdom, became Minerva.

The Romans excelled at building, engineering, and governing more than in the arts. They built cities, sturdy bridges, and thousands of miles of fine roads throughout their growing empire. Roman <u>aqueducts</u> carried fresh water from rivers into the cities. Some still stand today.

Julius Caesar

The struggle between the patricians and the plebeians in Rome, however, continued to be a problem. In 60 B.C., a group of three men attempted to establish order. The leading member of this trio was the popular politician Julius Caesar (JOOL yus

SEE zuhr). In 58 B.C., Caesar led a Roman army against Gaul and, by 50 B.C., conquered the entire country. He returned to Rome a hero to the plebeians but a threat to the patricians, who feared he would try to seize power. In 49 B.C., Caesar did just that and made himself <u>dictator</u>.

Caesar was not unpopular. He gave land to his soldiers and provided the poor with food. He granted rights of citizenship to many people within the Roman Empire who were not Romans. He created the modern calendar still in use today. The month of his birth was named July in his honor.

A group of <u>conspirators</u>, including some senators, thought Caesar had too much power. They plotted to kill him and restore the republic. On March 15, 44 B.C., they assassinated Caesar as he arrived at the Senate.

The Age of Augustus and the End of the Republic

The death of Caesar led to years of <u>chaos</u> and <u>civil war</u>. Finally, Caesar's grandnephew and adopted son, **Octavian** (ahk TAY vee uhn), emerged as the new ruler of Rome. In 27 B.C., he declared himself its first emperor. Octavian took the name **Augustus,** which in Latin means "honored one." The Roman republic was at an end.

Although a dictator, Augustus used his power wisely. He was generous to those people he conquered. He made the government more effective and increased trade with countries as far away as India and China. He also ordered the building of many great structures in Rome. Perhaps the greatest of these is the **Colosseum** (*kah* luh SEE uhm), a stadium that held about fifty thousand people (see page 42). Romans came to the Colosseum to see spectacular chariot races and **gladiator** fights, in which men battled wild animals and each other.

Under Augustus, the Roman Empire would experience a time of great peace and prosperity. This came to be called the *Pax Romana,* or "the Roman peace." It would last for two hundred years.

CHINA

The period from about 485 B.C. to 221 B.C. is known as the **Warring States period** in China. China was divided into several kingdoms and states dominated by warlords fighting to take each other's lands. In this troubled time, two great thinkers arose in China: Confucius and Lao-tzu.

Confucius (kuhn FYOO shuhs) believed that order was important in society. He gave people rules to live by and stressed the importance of polite behavior and respect for laws and traditions. Confucius traveled all over China spreading his teachings.

The other great thinker was **Lao-tzu** (LOU TZUH). He believed people should live simply and in harmony with nature. He founded the philosophy of **Taoism** (DOU *ih* zuhm), based on the word *Tao,* which means "the path" or "the way." Lao-tzu told his followers to <u>meditate</u> and be satisfied with what they had. This, he said, would lead to inner peace and happiness.

In 221 B.C., the leader of the kingdom known as **Qin** (CHIN) took control and united China for the first time. He called himself *Qin shi hunagdi,* which means "First Emperor of Qin." From this title the word *China* was derived. Qin, a bold, harsh ruler, established a strong army, organized the government, and set up a standard system of <u>currency</u>. Under his rule, trade with other countries increased, and China became wealthy.

Soon after Qin died in 210 B.C., the **Han dynasty** took over China. It continued Qin's policies. To protect China's northern border from invaders, the Han people repaired and joined together a system of walls. These walls eventually formed the **Great Wall of China,** which stretched for fourteen hundred miles. The Great Wall is one of the greatest building feats of history and much of it still stands today.

Han officials followed the teachings of Confucius. They worked together as a team for the greater good of the Chinese people and not for their own gain. The Han dynasty ruled for four hundred years.

THE AMERICAS

In Central America, the **Maya** (MYE yuh) people founded their first city-state, **Tikal** (tih KAHL), in present-day Guatemala about 350 B.C. This civilization would develop and reach its peak after the year A.D. 1.

As noted in Chapter 2, one of the first major civilizations to emerge in North America between

1000 and 300 B.C. was the Adena. They lived in settlements along the Ohio River Valley in what are now the states of Ohio, Indiana, Kentucky, Virginia, and West Virginia. The Adena people hunted and grew corn, beans, and sunflowers. They built large earthen mounds in which they buried their leaders. Later North American people would build similar mounds, many of which can still be seen today. The most extraordinary mound is the **Great Serpent Mound,** built by the Adena sometime between 1000 B.C. and A.D. 700 in present-day Ohio. This mound twists and turns across the countryside. Archaeologists believe the mound represented a serpent, an Adena symbol for the life force. Near the serpent's head is an egg, which it appears about to devour, perhaps symbolizing the cycle of birth and death for the Adena.

 # Implications

To answer the question, "Why does all this matter?" or "What does it mean?," share the following insights with your child.

The empires created by Alexander the Great and Augustus spread first Greek and then Roman influence far and wide. Peoples they ruled accepted not only the political authority of these empires, but adopted their social and cultural values as well. Many people in lands invaded by Alexander the Great welcomed Alexander's modern ideas. Gauls, Germans, and later Egyptians, too, considered themselves citizens of Rome.

Today, the United States has come to dominate the world in similar ways. Although the United States is not an empire—we do not send our military forces around the world to conquer other countries—our products, technology, movies, music, fashions, and ideas and values have spread around the world. For this reason, the twentieth century has been called the "American century."

While many people in other countries have accepted and welcomed aspects of American culture, others have come to resent and reject them. Some feel resentment toward Americans for controlling so much of the world's wealth and for trying to force our ideas and values upon the rest of the world. It will be interesting to see how, in the twenty-first century, other countries relate to America and Americans and how we deal with feelings of anti-Americanism from abroad.

 # Fact Checker

To check that your child knows or can find the basic facts in this chapter, here is a fill-in-the-blanks activity that uses information discussed.

Fill in the blanks with terms you have learned from this chapter. All the terms appear in boldface type within the chapter.

1. The leader of Athens during its golden age was _____.
2. The Greek philosopher who wrote down the ideas of Socrates was _____.
3. The ruler who spread Greek ideas throughout the ancient world was _____.
4. _____ was the Carthaginian general who fought the Romans.
5. _____ was the first emperor of Rome.
6. Two great philosophers of ancient China were _____ and _____.
7. The first emperor of China was named _____.
8. The people in North America who are famous for building great burial mounds were the _____.

Answers appear in the back, preceding the index.

? The Big Questions

> The following questions encourage your child to think critically rather than simply recall facts. If necessary, review the specific information from the preceding pages that will help your child make the necessary inferences to come up with reasonable answers.

1. In what ways can the culture of ancient Athens be said to still survive, even more than two thousand years after its defeat? Why do you think that the culture of a little city-state has survived for centuries, while powerful empires such as the Assyrian and Babylonian died and disappeared?

2. It is said that Caesar, although he made himself a dictator, did many good things for the people of Rome. It is also said that Augustus, the first emperor of Rome, used his power wisely for the good of the people. If a dictator can be good for the people, why do we, in the United States, think that a dictatorship is not a good form of government?

Suggested Answers

1. *The literature, the arts, and the ideas that originated in ancient Greece are still appreciated today. Perhaps those who create art and spread ideas are more powerful than those who amass power and build empires.*

2. *Since a dictator is not controlled by the people or by any other branch of the government, he or she may or may not act for the good of the people.*

Skills Practice

> The following activities give your child practice in applying the skills basic to social studies. For some of the activities, your child may need to review the information in the preceding pages.

A. BUILDING VOCABULARY

> The ability to recognize Greek and Latin roots is a tool for figuring out the meanings of unfamiliar words while reading.

Many words in the English language come from the language spoken by the ancient Greeks and from Latin, the language of ancient Rome. See if you can figure out the meanings of the following words by using the information given.

1. In Greek, the word *philos* means "loving," and the word *sophos* means "wise." Therefore, the word *philosophy* means "the _____ of wisdom."

2. In Greek, the word *biblion* means "book." You already know that the Greek word *philos* means "loving." Therefore, the word *bibliophile* means "one who loves _____."

3. You already know that the Greek word *sophos* means "wise." The Greek word *moros* means "foolish." Therefore, the real meaning of the word *sophomore* is "one who is both _____ and _____."

4. The Latin word *monos* means "alone," and the Latin word *arkhein* means "to rule." Therefore a *monarch* is one who rules _____.

5. In Latin, *sub* means "under," and *scribere* means "to write." Therefore, when you *subscribe* to something, you usually _____ your signature at the bottom of a sheet of paper.

Answers

1. love; 2. books; 3. wise, foolish; 4. alone; 5. write

> **Evaluating Your Child's Skills:** This activity will require some creative thinking on your child's part, since not all the Greek and Latin words translate into English exactly as they were originally used. If your child

needs an example to get started, explain that the word *education* is really a combination of two Latin words: *e*, which means "out" or "out of" and *ducere*, which means "to lead." Therefore, the real meaning of the word *education* is "leading out." Education involves *leading out* or *bringing out* ideas about a subject.

B. COMPARING AND CONTRASTING

Comparing-and-contrasting activities are very common in school.

Compare means "show how two things or ideas are similar." *Contrast* means "show how two things are different." Practice comparing and contrasting the following things or ideas.

1. Compare Alexander the Great and Julius Caesar.
2. Contrast Pericles and Julius Caesar.
3. Compare and contrast the cultures of Greece and Rome.

Answers

1. *Both Alexander and Julius Caesar expanded their empires by conquering other peoples.*
2. *Pericles gave his people more rights and freedoms, while Julius Caesar became a dictator.*
3. *Compare: The Romans copied styles of Greek art and architecture and even adopted the Greek religion. Contrast: While the Athenians excelled in the arts, the Romans excelled more at building, engineering, and governing.*

Evaluating Your Child's Skills: In order to complete this activity successfully, your child will need to single out the *main ideas* about the topics mentioned in each question. While Athens and Sparta, as described in Chapter 2, were located in different parts of Greece, *location* is not the most meaningful basis for contrast between them.

 # Top of the Class

Children interested in delving more deeply into the topic of this chapter can choose one or both of the following activities. They may do the activities for their own satisfaction or share what they have done in class to show that they have been seriously considering the period of world history from 500 B.C. to A.D. 1.

GREEK AND ROMAN ART AND ARCHITECTURE

With your child, look through an art history book to see how the Romans copied Greek styles of art and architecture.

In an art history book, which you can easily find in the library, look at photographs of Greek statues and buildings—for example, the Parthenon on the Acropolis in Athens. Then look at photos of the Colosseum and the Pantheon in Rome, as well as some of the sculptures. Can you see how the Romans used Greek styles of architecture and sculpture?

BOOKS TO READ AND RECOMMEND IN CLASS

Suggest that your child read one or more of the following nonfiction books and respond by giving an oral or written critique in class.

Green, Robert. *Alexander the Great.* Watts, 1996.
Green, Robert. *Cleopatra.* Watts, 1996.
Green, Robert. *Julius Caesar.* Watts, 1996.
Lazo, Caroline. *The Terra Cotta Army of the Emperor Quin.* Macmillan, 1993.

CHAPTER 4
Decline of the Ancient World
A.D. 1–A.D. 400

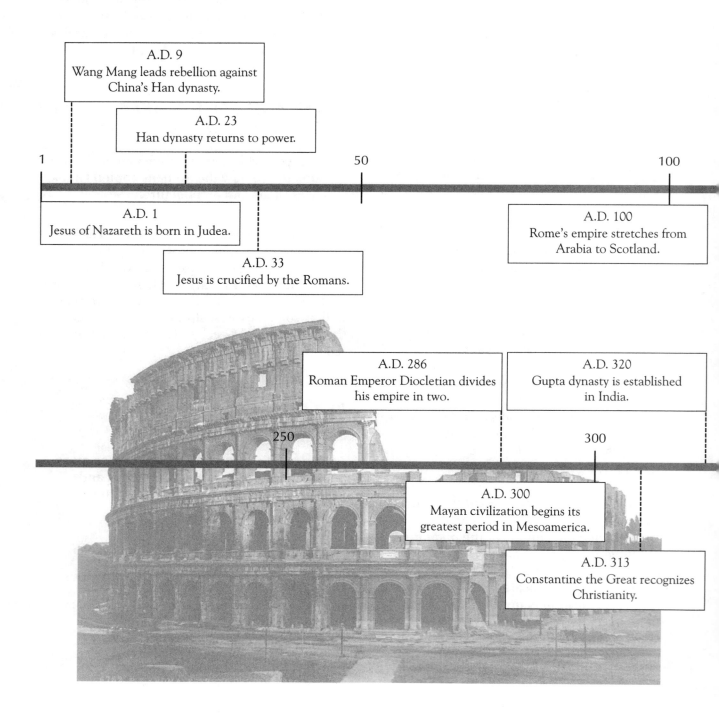

A.D. 9
Wang Mang leads rebellion against
China's Han dynasty.

A.D. 23
Han dynasty returns to power.

1

50

100

A.D. 1
Jesus of Nazareth is born in Judea.

A.D. 100
Rome's empire stretches from
Arabia to Scotland.

A.D. 33
Jesus is crucified by the Romans.

A.D. 286
Roman Emperor Diocletian divides
his empire in two.

A.D. 320
Gupta dynasty is established
in India.

250

300

A.D. 300
Mayan civilization begins its
greatest period in Mesoamerica.

A.D. 313
Constantine the Great recognizes
Christianity.

This timeline provides an overview of the period from A.D. 1 to A.D. 400. The narrative in the following pages offers more details and discusses the significance of the events.

A.D. 165
Plague kills thousands of Romans.

150

200

A.D. 167
Yamato dynasty is established
in Japan.

A.D. 225
Parthians are overthrown in Persia.

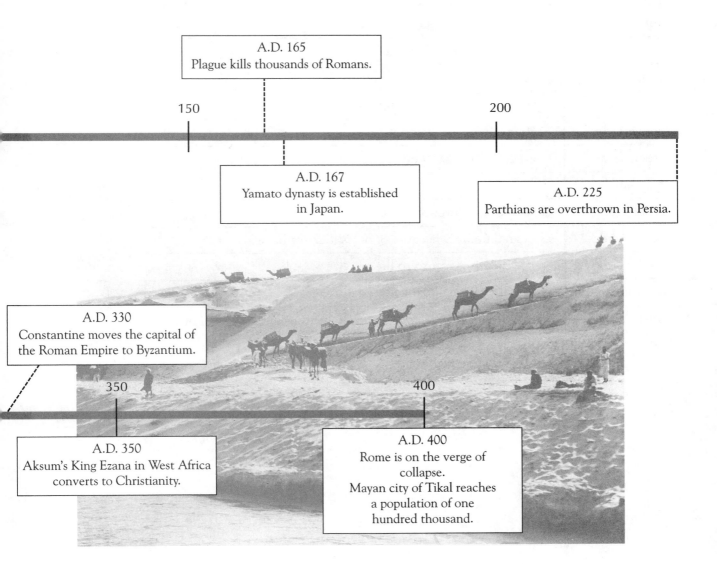

A.D. 330
Constantine moves the capital of
the Roman Empire to Byzantium.

350

400

A.D. 350
Aksum's King Ezana in West Africa
converts to Christianity.

A.D. 400
Rome is on the verge of
collapse.
Mayan city of Tikal reaches
a population of one
hundred thousand.

Word Power

The words on the following chart are underscored in the section called "What Your Child Needs to Know." Explain their meanings to your child as needed when they come up in reading or discussion. Keep the list handy for you and your child to use.

Word	*Definition*
apostles	followers of a person or cause
barbarians	uncivilized savages or outsiders
blasphemy	act of saying offensive things about God or a religion
caravans	groups of people traveling together
converted	changed one's religion
crucifixion	execution on a wooden cross
cultivated	grew
descendants	people born after others in a culture
persecuted	treated unfairly because of one's ideas or beliefs
resurrection	after death, a return to life
sophisticated	worldly, highly advanced
tolerance	willingness to respect and accept customs and beliefs of others

What Your Child Needs to Know

You may choose to use the following text in several different ways, depending on your child's strengths and preferences. You might read the passage aloud; you might read it to yourself and then paraphrase it for your child; or you might ask your child to read the material along with you or on his or her own.

BEGINNINGS OF CHRISTIANITY

Among the many peoples who lived under Roman rule were Jews, <u>descendants</u> of Hebrews and Israelites. The Romans conquered the Jews in 37 B.C. in the area we now refer to as the Middle East. Unlike the Romans and other peoples, the Jews believed in only one god. The Romans <u>persecuted</u> the Jews for their beliefs.

Jesus Christ

At this time, a Jew named Jesus of Nazareth (NA zuh ruhth) was born. Around the age of thirty, Jesus began preaching and teaching in the towns and villages of Judea (joo DEE uh), the Roman name for Judah, mentioned in Chapter 2. He taught that people should love God and their neighbor as much as they loved themselves. He urged people to live lives devoted to others and to forgive those who wronged them. He was reported to have performed miracles.

The Jews believed that a **Messiah** (muh SYE uh), a special leader, would one day be sent by God to guide them. The Jewish leaders accused Jesus of <u>blasphemy</u> when he claimed to be this Messiah. Romans thought Jesus was a political threat. They arrested him and tried him before the Roman governor **Pontius Pilate** (PAHN chus PYE luht), who sentenced Jesus to death by <u>crucifixion</u>.

The <u>apostles</u> (uh PAHS ulz) of Jesus claimed to have seen him alive after his death. Such a <u>resurrection</u> would mean that Jesus was divine—that he was God. The apostles traveled throughout the Roman Empire spreading Christianity, a religion based on Jesus' life and teachings and on the belief that Jesus and God are one. The Romans persecuted the Christians because they put their God and Jesus above the emperor. Nevertheless, Christianity continued to thrive and grow.

Peter and Paul

Two especially important early Christian leaders were Peter and Paul. Peter was one of Jesus' original apostles and became the first **pope,** or leader, of what later was named the **Roman Catholic Church.** Paul's letters, or **epistles,** to Christian churches are an important part of the Bible's **New Testament.** By A.D. 300, Christianity had spread to Greece, Egypt, France, Britain, and as far away as India.

THE ROMAN EMPIRE

During the *Pax Romana,* which gave the Roman Empire peace and security, strong emperors conquered other lands until the empire reached its greatest extent—including parts of Europe, Asia, and Africa. This period ended in A.D. 180. After that, Rome faced many problems.

The vast empire became harder and harder to govern. To maintain the enormous army necessary for this task, taxes increased until the people could no longer pay them. A plague struck Rome in A.D. 165 and wiped out thousands of people. This further weakened the state. <u>Barbarians</u> from the north began to boldly invade many parts of the empire. Worst of all, there was no strong leadership.

Most of the emperors after A.D. 180 were weak and corrupt. What could the Romans do to keep the Roman Empire, like so many empires before it, from falling apart?

A Divided Empire

In A.D. 286, the emperor **Diocletian** (*dye* uh KLEE shuhn) decided the Roman Empire was too big for one person to govern, and he divided it in two. The eastern empire included Greece, Egypt, Turkey, and Palestine (the larger area of which Israel and Judea were parts). The western empire included Rome, the rest of Italy, Gaul (France), Britain, and Germany. Diocletian ruled the eastern empire, and

Ruins of Colosseum in Rome, completed A.D. 80

Maximilian (*mak* suh MIL yuhn), general of Gaul, ruled the western empire.

This split, however, did not help. In A.D. 306, the Emperor **Constantine** (KAHN stuhn *teen*) **the Great** reunited the two parts of the empire and ruled them single-handedly. But like Diocletian, he favored the eastern lands.

In A.D. 330, Constantine moved his capital from Rome to the Greek colony of **Byzantium** (buh ZAN tee uhm) on the western coast of Turkey, facing the Mediterranean. He later renamed the city **Constantinople** (*kahn stan* tuhn OH puhl) in honor of himself. Today it is **Istanbul,** Turkey.

Constantine had made one other bold move that changed the course of world history. In A.D. 313, he had recognized Christianity as a religion and allowed Christians to worship openly. He took this approach for practical reasons as well as religious ones. The Christian faith had grown despite Roman persecution and had united peoples of different backgrounds. Constantine hoped Christianity would unify the empire and make it strong again. He himself converted to the new religion on his deathbed in A.D. 337. Christianity soon became the state religion of the Roman Empire.

The Decline of Rome

By the late 300s, the empire again had two rulers—one for the eastern empire and one for the western. Christianity did make the eastern empire stronger and more unified, but the western empire continued to decline. Barbarian tribes such as the **Goths, Franks,** and **Vandals** boldly attacked, and the western rulers were not strong enough to hold them back. By A.D. 400, the barbarians were at the gates of Rome. The eastern empire, now called the **Byzantine** (BIH zuhn *teen*) **Empire,** was secure, however, and would continue to flourish for another thousand years.

AFRICA

After the fall of Carthage in 146 B.C. (see Chapter 3), Rome dominated the northern coast of Africa from Morocco to Egypt. The introduction of the camel about 100 B.C. changed life in this desert region. Caravans using camels to carry goods and people crossed the Sahara Desert and brought goods from West Africa to parts of the Roman Empire. In West Africa, great trading towns sprang up

Camel caravan

to become the first African states in that region. In A.D. 193, a North African soldier, **Septimius Severus** (suh VIR uhs) became Roman emperor. He further developed North African cities and gave Roman citizenship to free men in Roman Africa and elsewhere.

The Kingdom of Aksum

The African kingdom that benefited most from increased trading with Rome was Aksum (AK *sum*) on the Red Sea coast in the area later known as Ethiopia. This kingdom exported ivory, perfume, and precious stones to Rome and Greece. Aksum was also famous for its fine cities and great **monoliths,** tall stone monuments erected for religious purposes. About A.D. 350, the Aksum king became one of the first African leaders to convert to Christianity.

ASIA

China

The Han dynasty of China (see Chapter 3) grew weaker, but the nobles grew stronger. Then in A.D. 9, a relative of the last emperor led a rebellion against the nobles. He reformed the government and gave more rights to the people. However, the nobles ousted him in A.D. 23, and the Han dynasty returned to power. It moved its capital eastward and became known as the **East Han.**

During the East Han period, China experienced great growth in the arts and technology (**technology** is the use of science to do practical things). Far ahead of the rest of the world, the Chinese invented paper, porcelain, and the first seismograph, to record earthquake activity. The East Han came to an end in A.D. 220 during a period of civil war and barbarian invasions.

India

By A.D. 100, northern India was ruled by the **Kushans,** Asian nomads from present-day Afghanistan. Their greatest king was **Kanishka,** a follower of Buddha (see Chapter 2). Kanishka promoted the arts and believed in <u>tolerance</u> toward all peoples. But the Kushan Empire fell apart, and a line of princes called **Gupta** (GOOP tuh) came to power about A.D. 320. **Chandragupta** (shuhn druh GOOP tuh) **II,** the third ruler in this dynasty, ruled for nearly forty years as **maharajah,** which means "emperor." Under him ruled a number of local **rajahs,** or kings.

During Chandragupta's reign, India experienced a golden age and became the greatest nation in Asia. Both Buddhism and Hinduism continued to develop. Great literature, music, and dance developed. Many fine palaces and temples went up. The Buddhist University had thirty thousand students from all over Asia. Indian doctors developed new medical procedures such as injections to prevent diseases. Indian mathematicians invented the **decimal system** that was based on multiples of ten and further developed the Arabic numerals that we still use today. Science and technology here exceeded levels reached in Europe during this period.

Japan

In about 300 B.C., a group of people immigrated to the island nation of Japan from Korea and Manchuria, a part of China. They made tools and weapons from bronze and iron, <u>cultivated</u> rice and barley, and introduced the **Shinto** religion, which at that time centered on the worship of one's ancestors and of spirits in nature.

The **Yamato** came to power in A.D. 167. Their first ruler was a priestess who united most of the Japanese tribes into one state for the first time. To this day, Japanese emperors trace their ancestry back to the Yamato dynasty.

Persia

In A.D. 225, the Parthians of Persia were overthrown by a local king who wanted to return Persia to its former glory. Persia conquered Armenia, Syria, Afghanistan, and the Indus Valley, which is in present-day Pakistan. The Persians even fought against Rome and captured and killed the Roman emperor.

THE AMERICAS

Mesoamerica

Of the civilizations that flourished in Mesoamerica during this period, none was greater than the Maya. Centered in what is today southern Mexico and Central America, the Maya reached their peak between A.D. 300 and A.D. 900. They built magnificent cities with stone temples, pyramids, palaces, and ball courts. The Maya, it is believed, did perform human sacrifice on some religious occasions.

The Maya cities were home to nobles, priests, and government officials. Farmers, who made up most of the population, lived in the countryside, where they grew corn, squash, beans, and cotton. They entered the cities only for trade, business, and religious festivals. By about A.D. 400, Tikal, the largest Mayan city, had one hundred thousand people, more than Rome itself at that time.

The Maya were keen observers of the stars and planets and used the tops of temples and pyramids as observatories. Based on their observations, they developed two accurate calendars. Each calendar was written on a geared wheel, and the two wheels meshed together. One of their calendars was very similar to our own, with 365 days in a year.

The Maya also developed a mathematical system based on multiples of twenty and were among the earliest people to deal with the concept of zero. Their written language was the most sophisticated in the Americas, with about eight hundred **glyphs,** or symbols.

The **Moche** (mo SHAY) developed a culture along the coast of Peru. They also built pyramids for religious ceremonies. The Moche created elegant pottery without the use of a potter's wheel and were also the first culture in South America to make clay objects from molds.

North America

At least two civilizations developed in North America during this time. In what is now southern Arizona, the **Hohokam** (100 B.C.–A.D. 700), who had probably come from Mesoamerica, found a way to grow crops successfully in a difficult climate. They set up a complex series of canals, some as long as ten miles, to irrigate their fields. They planted corn, beans, squash, and cotton. The Hohokam also developed advanced art techniques.

The **Hopewell** people flourished until A.D. 400 in what are now the southern Ohio and Mississippi river valleys. These people were named after **Captain Hopewell,** on whose land thirty of their large rectangular mounds were discovered in the 1800s. These mounds may have served as burial places for their leaders and as religious ceremonial centers.

![!] Implications

> **To answer the question, "Why does all this matter?" or "What does it mean?," share the following insights with your child.**

In this chapter, we see that the world is no longer dominated by the ancient Greeks, and that the Roman Empire expands greatly, only to be on the verge of partial collapse by A.D. 400.

Constantine's friendliness to Christianity, a religion that had been condemned by earlier emperors, was another signal that the times were changing. The significance of Constantine's move to Christianity comes right down to this day. Although Constantine's empire is gone, Christianity in its many forms remains one of the most popular and powerful religions in the world.

During the same four hundred years of Rome's ups and downs, we see peoples outside the boundaries of the Roman Empire achieving their own remarkable accomplishments. It's important to keep in mind that at the very time the western Roman Empire was about to fall, the Maya were at a peak culturally.

Fact Checker

To check that your child knows or can find the basic facts in this chapter, here is a fill-in activity that uses key names and terms discussed in the preceding pages. Your child may find the answers in the list that follows the activity or may try to do the items without looking at the box in the right column.
Note: Three items in the answer list do not fit in any blanks.

1. The first emperor to divide the Roman Empire in two was _____.
2. By A.D. 400, the most popular religion in the Roman Empire was _____.
3. One of the Germanic tribes that attacked Rome was the _____.
4. People with camels crossed the Sahara Desert in groups called _____.
5. *Maharajah* means _____.
6. Two religions that flourished in India during its golden age were Buddhism and _____.
7. The Mayan writing system was made up of about eight hundred _____.
8. The ancient Maya lived in present-day _____.
9. A culture developing between 100 B.C. and A.D. 700 in the Southwest of what is now the United States is called _____.
10. One of the products that Aksum in Africa exported to Rome and Greece was _____.

Arizona	glyphs	Mexico
caravans	Hinduism	Pontius Pilate
Christianity	Hohokam	tea
Diocletian	ivory	Vandals
emperor		

Answers appear in the back, preceding the Index.

 # The Big Questions

The following questions encourage your child to think critically rather than simply recall facts. If necessary, review the specific information from the preceding pages that will help your child make the appropriate inferences to come up with reasonable answers.

1. Why couldn't the Roman Empire last forever?
2. What does the word *barbarian* mean today, and how did it get that meaning?
3. Why did so many groups—the Sumerians, the Egyptians, the Olmec, the Maya, and the Moche—build pyramids?
4. Of all the discoveries and inventions mentioned in this chapter—paper, the seismograph, the decimal system, calendars, the concept of zero—which surprised or impressed you most? Why?

Answers

1. *The empire got too big to manage and so fell prey to other powers.*
2. *Today,* barbarian *often means "lacking in learning or culture" and suggests that the person it is applied to is inferior. In ancient days, the term was used, disparagingly, to refer to a person from outside the Mediterranean civilization of Greece and Rome. Over the years, this very specific Roman meaning generalized so that now we use the word* barbarian *in many contexts.*
3. *Accept any reasonable answer—for example, that lots of different people had the idea that height, being nearer to the heavens, or sheer bigness was desirable. It is unlikely that one of these ancient groups saw another group's pyramid and copied it.*
4. *The point of this question is to make your child think about how people two thousand years ago needed and created some of the same tools that we use every day.*

45

Skills Practice

The following activities give your child practice in applying the skills basic to social studies. For some of the activities, your child may need to review the information in the preceding pages.

A. RESEARCHING MYTHOLOGY

The names of the planets in our solar system are a reminder of ancient times. They are names of gods and goddesses and heroes.

Use textbooks or reference books to fill in the chart. For each god, goddess, or hero, tell his or her specialty. Then give an example of something the Greeks and Romans believed this god, goddess, or hero had done. The first row is filled in for you.

PLANETS AND MYTHOLOGY

Planet	Named for	Something about him or her
Mercury	in Roman mythology, a hero famous for his strength	slew two serpents when he was an infant
Venus		
Mars		
Jupiter		
Saturn		
Uranus		
Neptune		
Pluto		

Answers

Answers for column 3 may vary.

Venus: *In Roman mythology, the goddess of love, known for her great beauty; she fell in love with the mortal Adonis.*

Mars: *In Roman mythology, the god of war; he was the father of Romulus, the legendary founder of Rome.*

Jupiter: *In Roman mythology, the king of the gods, worshiped as god of the sky, rain, thunder, and lightning; he formed a triad with Juno and Minerva.*

Saturn: *In Roman mythology, an ancient god; he ruled over Italy during a prosperous time.*

Uranus: *In Greek mythology, the god of the heavens; he was the father of the Titans, who later produced the gods.*

Neptune: *In Roman mythology, the god of the sea; he was a son of Saturn and a brother of Jupiter.*

Pluto: *In Roman mythology, the god of the dead; his brothers were Jupiter and Neptune.*

Evaluating Your Child's Skills: **In order to succeed with this task, your child needs to find information and, where possible, paraphrase it for the chart. If your child has difficulty with this activity, do a few rows with him or her.**

B.   FINDING THE MAIN IDEA AND SUPPORTING DETAILS

Remind your child that, when reading, he or she should always look for the main idea of a passage and its supporting details.

The main idea is what a paragraph or section of text is mostly about. Each main idea carries with it details that support it. The following paragraph is from a social studies textbook. The questions following it are about its main idea and its supporting details.

Maya farmers grew a plentiful supply of food for a large population. They used their knowledge of the environment to get the most out of their land. In hilly areas farmers built terraces to make level surfaces for planting. In swampy areas they built raised islands by piling up soil above the water. Farmers also moved their fields from place to place to help keep the soil from wearing out.

—from United States: Adventures in Time and Place, *McGraw-Hill, 2001*

1. What part of Mayan life is this paragraph mostly about?
2. Find three examples that support, or prove, the answer to Question 1?

Answers

1. *The paragraph is about the knowledge that Maya farmers had (the first two sentences create this main idea).*

2. *One example is farmers building terraces to level the land; another example is farmers building islands to farm on; the third example is farmers moving, or rotating, their fields. (These answers are in sentences 3 to 5.)*

Evaluating Your Child's Skills: **In order to succeed with this task, your child needs to distinguish generalizations (main idea) from specifics (supporting details). If your child has difficulty, remind him or her that the main idea of a paragraph very often appears in the first sentence or two and that the rest of the paragraph often consists of examples in support of the beginning sentences.**

 # Top of the Class

Here is an activity that children can do on their own or share in class to show that they have been seriously considering the period from A.D. 1 to 400.

REVIEWING A WEB SITE

Send your child to the Internet to evaluate the medium, as described here.

Spend some time at www.mayadiscovery.com, and then write a review of the Web site. Consider the audience for your review to be children of your age. In the review, describe the site by telling the following:

- What categories of information it offers
- How easy or hard it is to find your way around the site
- How interactive the site is (that is, are there things the site lets you do?)
- Whether the site is educational, entertaining, or both
- The quality of the links that the site provides
- The cost of the site: which parts of the site are free, and which parts do you have to pay for?

At the end of your review, tell whether or not you recommend this Web site to your friends and classmates, to younger children, or to adults. You may hand the review in to your teacher.

CHAPTER 5
Religious Empires
A.D. 400–1000

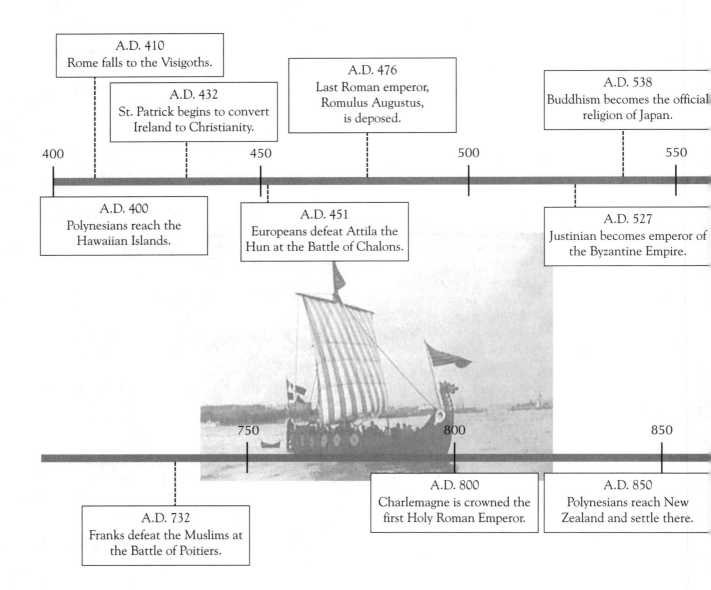

A.D. 410
Rome falls to the Visigoths.

A.D. 432
St. Patrick begins to convert
Ireland to Christianity.

A.D. 476
Last Roman emperor,
Romulus Augustus,
is deposed.

A.D. 538
Buddhism becomes the official
religion of Japan.

400   450   500   550

A.D. 400
Polynesians reach the
Hawaiian Islands.

A.D. 451
Europeans defeat Attila the
Hun at the Battle of Chalons.

A.D. 527
Justinian becomes emperor of
the Byzantine Empire.

750   800   850

A.D. 732
Franks defeat the Muslims at
the Battle of Poitiers.

A.D. 800
Charlemagne is crowned the
first Holy Roman Emperor.

A.D. 850
Polynesians reach New
Zealand and settle there.

This timeline provides an overview of the period from A.D. 400 to 1000. Then a narrative describes this period in greater detail and discusses its significance.

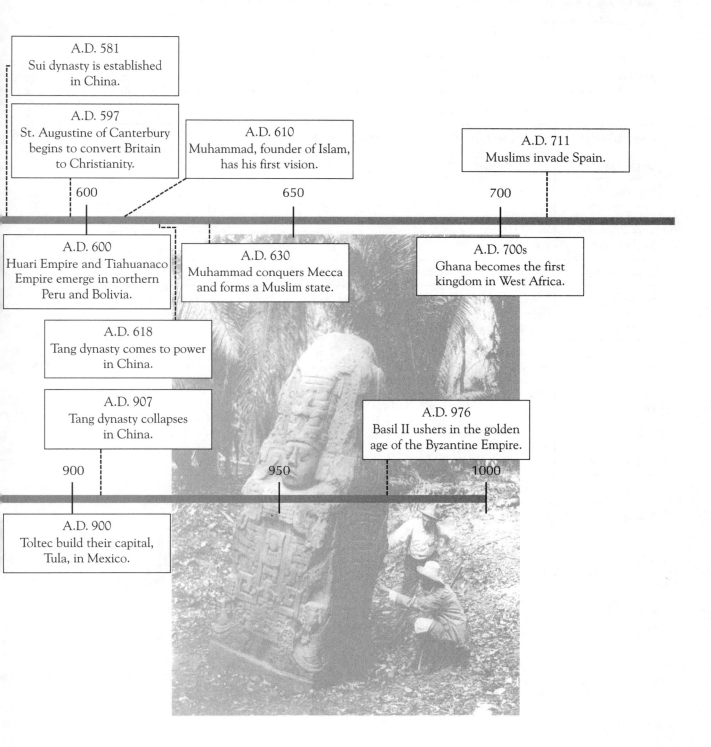

A.D. 581
Sui dynasty is established
in China.

A.D. 597
St. Augustine of Canterbury
begins to convert Britain
to Christianity.

A.D. 610
Muhammad, founder of Islam,
has his first vision.

A.D. 711
Muslims invade Spain.

600

650

700

A.D. 600
Huari Empire and Tiahuanaco
Empire emerge in northern
Peru and Bolivia.

A.D. 630
Muhammad conquers Mecca
and forms a Muslim state.

A.D. 700s
Ghana becomes the first
kingdom in West Africa.

A.D. 618
Tang dynasty comes to power
in China.

A.D. 907
Tang dynasty collapses
in China.

A.D. 976
Basil II ushers in the golden
age of the Byzantine Empire.

900

950

1000

A.D. 900
Toltec build their capital,
Tula, in Mexico.

49

Word Power

The words on the following chart are underscored in the section called "What Your Child Needs to Know." Explain their meanings to your child as needed when they come up in reading or discussion. Keep the list handy for you and your child to use.

Word	Definition
ceramics	objects made out of clay
compulsory	something that must be done by law
deposed	removed from power
hastened	brought on
intolerance	lack of acceptance
laid siege	attacked
missionaries	people who try to spread their faith to others
molest	annoy or injure another person
monasteries	groups of buildings where monks live and work
monks	men who devote their lives to God
mosque	Islamic place of worship
navigable	capable of being sailed on by boat
pagan	one who worships many gods
pillaged	seized goods by force
sacked	stolen from a place conquered in battle
vision	mystical, religious experience

What Your Child Needs to Know

You may choose to use the following text in several different ways, depending on your child's strengths and preferences. You might read the passage aloud; you might read it to yourself and then paraphrase it for your child; or you might ask your child to read the material along with you or on his or her own.

EUROPE

As shown in Chapter 4, by A.D. 400, the old Roman Empire of the West was on the verge of collapse. Soon the period that historians of Europe call the **Middle Ages** would begin. The noun *Middle Ages* and the adjective *medieval* refer to the period between ancient history and modern history.

The Fall of Rome

In A.D. 410, the barbarian **Visigoths** from the north laid siege to Rome. Exhausted and with little food left, Roman citizens opened the city gates and let in the invaders. The Visigoths pillaged much of Rome, but **Alaric** (AL uh rik), who was a Christian convert, commanded his soldiers not to molest women, destroy churches, or steal church valuables.

Soon after, there appeared an enemy that the Romans and their invaders could unite against. In A.D. 433, **Attila** (uh TIH luh) became ruler of the **Huns,** a people from Mongolia in Asia. He conquered much of eastern Europe and helped create a new Hun homeland in Hungary. Then Attila invaded Gaul (France) and Italy. Romans, Goths, and Franks fought Attila and defeated him. The Huns retreated, and Attila died two years later. No strong ruler took his place, and the empire of the Huns quickly fell apart.

What effect, then, did Attila have on the western Roman empire? By displacing other barbarian tribes who were in his way as he moved toward Rome and driving them west, Attila indirectly hastened the final fall of Rome. The Vandals sacked the city in A.D. 455. Then in A.D. 476, the German chief deposed the last western Roman emperor and took over the throne. The western Roman Empire was no more.

Western Christianity Spreads

With Rome gone as a political power, Christianity was the one unifying force left in Europe. The church of Rome sent missionaries to other lands to convert the people to the Christian faith. One of these was the man who would become **St. Patrick.** He converted the population of Ireland beginning in A.D. 432. Irish monasteries became great centers of learning. Scholars went there from all over Europe, and monks there copied important works of religion and literature. In A.D. 597, the man who would become **St. Augustine** (AW guh *steen*) **of Canterbury** traveled from Rome to southern England. There he converted the pagan king to the Christian religion and spread the faith among the people who lived in that part of the world.

Later, in A.D. 751 in Gaul, **Pepin** (PE puhn) **the Short** became king of the Franks, who had earlier invaded Rome. Now Pepin's coronation was blessed by the Roman church. Then Pepin's son, **Charlemagne** (SHAR luh *mayn*), or "Charles the Great," conquered the rest of France, Germany, and Italy. He created the largest empire since that of Rome, the Holy Roman Empire. Charlemagne spread Christianity throughout his empire and built schools and churches.

In Rome, **Pope Leo III** wanted to strengthen the king's ties to the church even more. Therefore, on Christmas Day A.D. 800, he intended to crown Charlemagne the first **Holy Roman Emperor.** According to legend, Charlemagne took the crown from the pope and crowned himself as a signal of his power. The title *Holy Roman Emperor* meant that Charlemagne had legitimate claims on Italy. Charlemagne ruled until his death in A.D. 814.

The Birth of Russia

In the northern European lands of Norway, Denmark, and Sweden, there lived a hardy people called the **Vikings.** In the 700s and 800s, many Vikings left those lands and headed south in vessels called **longships** to find new lands to settle. Each longship could hold fifty or more men; the

Reproduction of a Viking ship

men could sail, row, or haul the sturdily built boat overland when necessary and could even take it on <u>navigable</u> rivers to attack cities far inland.

The Vikings probably had heard of Charlemagne's victories and wanted to avoid capture by that brutal emperor. Some Vikings attacked and sacked coastal European cities. But not all Vikings were destroyers. Some were traders and farmers. Many of them settled in western and southern Europe. Other Vikings settled in Iceland and Greenland, and by the year 1000 even sailed to and explored North America.

Swedish Vikings entered present-day Ukraine and Russia and established the city of **Kiev** (KEE *ef*). These Vikings called themselves *Ros*, which means "oarsmen." This is how Russia got its name. Kiev became a great trading center between the East and the West and the capital of the first Russian state. In A.D. 989, **Vladimir** (VLA duh *mir*) **I,** a Kievan prince, married a Byzantine princess and converted to eastern Christianity (discussed next).

THE BYZANTINE EMPIRE

After the fall of Rome in the 400s, the Byzantine Empire with its capital in Constantinople (formerly Byzantium) became the main Christian power in the world. Christianity in the Byzantine Empire was influenced by Greek culture, so it developed differently from Christianity in the west. Western Christians—who would later call themselves Roman Catholics—regarded the pope as the only leader who could speak for the church. Eastern Christians—who would call themselves Eastern Orthodox Christians—did not see the pope that way.

The Byzantine emperor **Justinian** (*juh* STIH nee uhn) ruled from A.D. 527 to 565. Justinian tried to win back most of the lost western empire in Italy, Spain, and North Africa. He was successful, but after his death most of these lands were lost again—some to the religion Islam (discussed later). Justinian's more lasting legacy was a set of important laws called the **Justinian Code.** This code was based on Roman laws and became a model for European lawmakers for centuries.

By the time **Basil II** became emperor in A.D. 976, the Byzantine Empire (even without the lands it had lost) was experiencing its golden age. Literature and art flourished. The emperor built libraries, schools, and museums. After Basil's death in 1025, the Byzantine Empire began a long decline.

THE RISE OF ISLAM

Arabia is the general name given to the large peninsula in southwest Asia, east of Egypt. Nowadays, we consider Arabia part of what we call the Middle East. In A.D. 610, a forty-year-old Arab trader named **Muhammad** (mu HAH muhd) said he had a <u>vision</u> in which the Archangel Gabriel appeared to him and told him to spread the faith of God—in Arabic, **Allah.** This message and many others form the religious book called the **Koran** (also spelled Qur'an), from the Arabic verb meaning "to read." Muhammad founded a new religion, Islam. In Arabic, *Islam* means "surrender to Allah."

Islam stresses the importance of love, equality, and the unity of all Arab people. Believers in Islam consider Allah the same God worshiped by Christians and Jews and consider Muhammad the prophet of Allah. According to the Koran, Muhammad is the *last* prophet of God and the messages he received from God are more authoritative than those received by Moses and Jesus.

Islam attracted many followers, called **Muslims,** and the rulers of Muhammad's home city, **Mecca** (ME kuh), felt threatened by his power. Muhammad and his followers fled to **Medina** (muh DEE nuh) for their safety in A.D. 622. Their flight was called the **Hegira** (hih JYE ruh) and marks the first year of the Muslim calendar. In A.D. 630, a Muslim army led by Muhammad captured Mecca. By Muhammad's death in A.D. 632, Islam had spread throughout Arabia. Today there are more than a billion Muslims throughout the world.

After Muhammad died, Muslim religious and political leaders called **caliphs** conquered Persian lands and other parts of today's Middle East and central Asia. The Muslim army also marched on Egypt and Libya in North Africa, conquering lands once held by the Byzantine emperor Justinian. In A.D. 711, the Muslims invaded Spain. They might have succeeded in conquering the rest of western Europe, but in A.D. 732 the Franks, led by **Charles Martel** (mar TEL), a great-grandfather of Charlemagne, defeated them at the **Battle of Poitiers** (pwah TYAY) in France. The Muslims retreated from France but remained in control of Spain for almost eight hundred years. By A.D. 751, the Muslim domain stretched from the borders of France to the edge of China.

Although fierce fighters, the Muslims were not cruel conquerors. They did not force conquered peoples to adopt their religion and were tolerant of other religions. They built schools, libraries, and great universities throughout their growing empire.

The Muslims made great advances in mathematics—especially in algebra—and medicine. They also produced fine works of literature such as *The Rubáiyát* (ROO bee *aht*), by the twelfth-century Persian poet **Omar Khayyám** (*oh mar kye YAHM*), and *The Arabian Nights,* a collection of stories that was produced between the 800s and the 1400s.

From the late 700s until the 1200s, the capital of the Muslim world was **Baghdad** (BAG *dad*), in present-day Iraq. Baghdad had a great <u>mosque</u>, the place of worship for Muslims, but it also had an international flavor, with products from India, Africa, Russia, and China. Baghdad even had a paper mill after merchants learned about paper from the Chinese (see next section).

ASIA

China

China broke up into three kingdoms after the fall of the Han dynasty in A.D. 220. A period of political turmoil lasted until A.D. 581, when **Yang Jin,** a general of one kingdom, founded the **Sui** (SWAY)

dynasty. He called himself Emperor Wen. Over the next eight years, he once again unified China and reformed government to better serve the people. He cut taxes, ended <u>compulsory</u> military service, and redistributed land to the people. The last Sui emperor was overthrown and killed in A.D. 618. It seems he had raised taxes too high! Then the **Tang** dynasty came to power.

The Tang era began with a long period of peace and prosperity. China experienced a golden age in the arts and sciences. Movable wood type was invented, and paper books were mass-produced for the first time. Chinese artists created beautiful <u>ceramics</u> and sculptures. Chinese culture spread to **Korea, Tibet,** and **Thailand** (TYE land). Then rebellion shook the empire beginning in A.D. 755 and weakened the state. The Tang dynasty collapsed in A.D. 907. Fifty years of civil war followed.

Japan

Japan's religion at around A.D. 400 was still Shinto (see Chapter 4). Chinese and Korean immigrants to Japan carried with them **Confucianism** and Buddhism. In A.D. 538, Chinese Buddhist monks converted Japanese rulers to Buddhism, and that became the country's official religion. In time, Shinto, Buddhism, and Confucianism blended together in Japan to form a unique way of life.

By A.D. 800, Japanese government and culture were largely based on Chinese standards. Then Japanese culture became more independent of China and produced great art and literature, such as **Lady Murasaki Shikibu's** *Tale of Genji.*

India

In the 400s, the Guptas in India (see Chapter 4) beat off an invasion by the Huns. Then in the early 500s, another attack by the Huns caused India to break up into small kingdoms, and so it remained for much of the next 650 years. During this period in India, Buddhism declined; Hinduism developed new, rich traditions; and, in the tenth century, Islam made inroads.

AFRICA

The Muslims dominated most of northern Africa by the 600s. In the east, Aksum became more prosperous through trade and its conversion to Christianity. Then in the 700s, a new kingdom named **Ghana** (GAH nuh) emerged in West Africa. (This Ghana was farther north than today's country named Ghana.)

Trade and gold formed the basis for Ghana's wealth. Gold mines provided gold dust that Ghana traded for cotton, salt, and copper with other parts of Africa. Ghanaians also had iron that they made into weapons. In addition, officials collected taxes from other traders who had to travel across Ghana. For five hundred years, Ghana remained one of the most powerful kingdoms in West Africa.

POLYNESIA

Polynesia (*pah* luh NEE zhuh) is a region of widely scattered islands in the southern Pacific Ocean. *Polynesia* is a Greek name that means "many islands." Polynesians may have originated farther west, in the Malay Archipelago. At any rate, from about A.D. 400 to A.D. 800, they visited and settled on many other islands in the Pacific—for example, Tahiti, the Marquesas, the Hawaiian Islands, and what is now New Zealand. In New Zealand, they became known as the **Maori** (MOWR ee), who hunted, fished, farmed, and skillfully carved wood. The Maori dominated New Zealand's two large islands until Europeans arrived in the 1700s.

Like the Vikings, the Polynesians were adventurous and skillful navigators. Their ships were large double canoes designed for long voyages and were big enough to carry many people as well as pigs and plants and seeds for crops. The Polynesians navigated by the stars and knew how to use wind currents to the best advantage.

One of the most impressive feats of the Polynesians was their sail of two thousand miles (thirty-two hundred kilometers) from one of their islands to what we now call Easter Island, off the coast of Chile in South America. Historians offer various dates, but this astounding journey probably took place between A.D. 400 and A.D. 500.

THE AMERICAS

The Americas remained untouched by all the developments in Christianity, Islam, Shinto, Buddhism, and Hinduism from A.D. 400 to 1000.

Mexico and Central America

The Maya built the important city of **Chichén Itzá** (chee *chen* eet ZA) in the early sixth century, abandoned it around A.D. 670, and then rebuilt it about three hundred years later. The many structures in the ruins include the Ball Court, used for religious games that called for throwing a ball through a high ring of stone; El Castillo, a large temple; and the Round Tower, probably an astronomical observatory. Archaeologists say that some Chichén Itzá architecture from the second time the Maya inhabited the city shows Toltec influence.

The **Toltec** (TOHL tek) were a warlike people who migrated into central Mexico from the north. They built their capital city, **Tula** (TOO luh), about A.D. 900. Over the next century, the Toltec may have driven the Maya to abandon some of their original cities and move farther north.

South America

The **Huari** (hoo AH ree) Empire appeared in northern Peru about A.D. 600. The Huari were a strong,

Ancient Mayan monument, Quirigua, Guatemala

warlike people. About the same time, the **Tiahuanaco** (*tee* uh wuh NAH koh) people appeared to the southeast near **Lake Titicaca** (*ti* ti KAH kuh), the highest navigable lake in the world. The Tiahuanaco were a peaceful people who devoted themselves to making beautiful pottery and fine jewelry. They also erected enormous stone monuments and carved statues.

For a time, the Huari and Tiahuanaco empires joined together. Huari was probably the political center and Tiahuanaco, the religious center of the empire. Their civilization reached its peak between A.D. 900 and 1000. Then both peoples mysteriously vanished. Some historians believe a severe drought may have driven them from the region.

North America

By about A.D. 700, the **Anasazi** (*ah* nuh SAH zee) began to flourish in today's Four Corners region, where Utah, New Mexico, Arizona, and Colorado meet. The Anasazi are perhaps best known for their apartment-style dwellings, built into the sides of steep cliffs. The outer walls of the dwellings were made from **adobe,** bricks of mud and water baked dry in the sun. Anasazi culture flourished for hundreds of years, but the circumstances of its decline remain a mystery. By 1300, few traces of the people or the culture remained.

 # Implications

To answer the question, "Why does all this matter?" or "What does it mean?," share the following insights with your child.

Religion played a major role in shaping the world that rose from both the successes and the failures of the ancient civilizations. The Muslims built a military empire in the Middle East and Asia. Christianity spread through Europe and became a key ingredient in both the Byzantine and Holy Roman empires. Buddhism spread from China to Japan and other parts of Asia.

These religions united peoples who often had little else in common. They helped preserve civilization and forge the modern nations we live in today.

There was a dark side to these religious empires too. At times, <u>intolerance</u>, prejudice, and corruption motivated religious states to persecute minorities and go to war against each other.

Today, religious wars of various kinds continue to cause destruction and division. When the ideals put forth by Jesus, Muhammad, Buddha, and others are colored by worldly, political motives, the results are all too often devastating to individuals and their families.

Fact Checker

To check that your child knows or can find the basic facts in this chapter, here are questions about its major concepts. Your child should circle his or her answer—*T* for "true" or *F* for "false."

TRUE OR FALSE?

1. T F A caliph was a Muslim religious and political leader.
2. T F Between A.D. 400 and 1000, the Chinese made great advances in the branch of mathematics called algebra.
3. T F Attila the Hun destroyed Rome.
4. T F Some Vikings settled in Russia.
5. T F During the period from A.D. 400 to 1000, the Americas were greatly influenced by Christianity, Islam, Shinto, Buddhism, and Hinduism.
6. T F Charlemagne became the first Holy Roman Emperor.
7. T F The kingdom of Ghana emerged in the Americas.
8. T F The Polynesians who migrated to New Zealand became known as the Maori.
9. T F Chichén Itzá was a principal city of the Maya.
10. T F The Anasazi established towns and villages in what is today the Southeast of the United States.

Answers appear in the back, preceding the index.

 # The Big Questions

The following questions encourage your child to think critically rather than simply recall facts. If necessary, review the specific information from the preceding pages that will help your child make the appropriate inferences to come up with reasonable answers.

1. The invention of movable type allowed people to produce many more books than had been possible when each letter had to be written by hand. Why was the production of more books important?
2. If you could go back to A.D. 1000, which part of the world would you want to visit? Why?

Answers

1. *Production of more books meant more people would be able to read religious books for themselves. In general, information would be able to travel more easily between people.*
2. *Accept any supported answer.*

 # Skills Practice

The following activities give your child practice in applying the skills basic to social studies. For some of the activities, your child may need to review the information in the preceding pages.

A.   CONNECTING HISTORY AND LITERATURE

Many libraries and bookstores shelve *Arabian Nights* in both the adult and the children's sections. Tell your child to select a tale to read and then to answer the following questions.

1. What did you like and not like about the characters in this tale?
2. Were you pleased, surprised, or disappointed in how the tale ended? Why?
3. What did this tale teach you about life in Arabia hundreds of years ago?

Answers

Accept any reasonable answers, especially if your child supports opinions with reasons. For Question 3, your child may talk about a feature of daily life, differences between Arabia then and life in the United States today, or the similarities in emotions across time and place.

Evaluating Your Child's Skills: **In order to succeed with this task, your child needs to select a story and engage with it. If your child has difficulty finding a tale he or she can "get into," suggest "Ali Baba," "Aladdin," or "Sinbad the Sailor."**

B.   READING A BAR GRAPH

This chapter and parts of previous chapters discuss origins of world religions. Explain that organizations such as the United Nations count the world's population in terms of religion as well as many other factors.

A student prepared the following bar graph based on statistics she found in various books published in the late 1990s (she rounded the first five figures to the nearest hundred million). Examine the graph, and then answer the questions that follow.

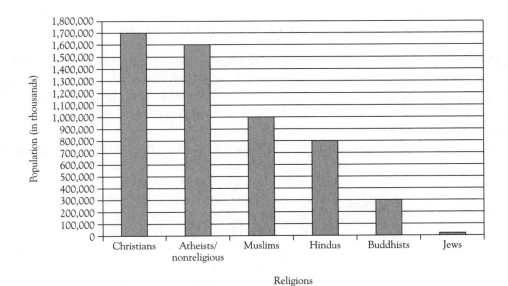

Populations of world religions in the 1990s

1. According to the graph, what is the most popular religion in the world today?
2. Which is the larger group—Christians or atheists/nonreligious?
3. Jews, worldwide, number about 14 million. How many times more Muslims are there than Jews?

Answers

1. *Christianity*
2. *Christians*
3. *Approximately seventy times more Muslims*

> ***Evaluating Your Child's Skills:*** **In order to answer these questions, your child has to feel comfortable using big numbers. Remind him or her that a billion is a thousand million (1,000,000,000). Then, your child needs to understand what each bar stands for. If necessary, tell him or her, "The first bar tells how many Christians live in the world today." Then ask the child to tell you what the other bars mean.**
>
> **For the third question, tell your child that there are approximately 14 million Jews today, and ask him or her how many Muslims there are according to this graph (1 billion or 1,000 million). Then your child must divide 14 into 1,000.**

C.   WORD STUDY

> **Send your child to a dictionary—or to several dictionaries—for the following project. He or she may share the information with his or her class.**

This chapter deals with the Byzantine Empire. Here are some questions about the word *Byzantine*.

1. How did that empire get its name?
2. What are the characteristics of the style of painting and architecture called Byzantine?
3. What does the word *byzantine* (without a capital letter) mean?

Answers

1. *The empire got its name from the capital city, Byzantium (which later changed to Constantinople).*
2. *Byzantine painting has formal design; rich colors, usually gold; religious subject matter. Byzantine architecture is notable for a central dome resting on a cube made of four arches; it uses much marble and decoration out of colored glass mosaics.*
3. *Without a capital letter, byzantine means either "devious" or "highly complicated."*

> ***Evaluating Your Child's Skills:*** **In order to succeed with this task, your child needs to understand that a dictionary often gives more than one definition for a word. Your child must match the meaning to the way the word is being used. If he or she needs help, point out the numerals separating the definitions.**

 # Top of the Class

> **Here is a variety of activities children can do on their own or share in class to show that they have been seriously considering the period from A.D. 400 to 1000.**

CRITIQUING A BOOK

> **The legendary hero King Arthur was based on a sixth-century Celtic warrior, whom you can have your child read about and then talk about in class.**

People have told stories about Arthur for hundreds of years. One of the most famous sets of stories about him was composed by Sir Thomas Malory.

More recently, writers have prepared special versions of the King Arthur stories especially for students in upper elementary grades and middle school. See if you can find a book about King Arthur by Roger Green, Sidney Lanier, Rosemary Sutcliffe, or Jane Yolen. You might even read *two* of those authors to see if they differ in how they present Arthur.

RESEARCHING A RESEARCHER

This project will take your child into science and anthropology, as well as history.

Who was Thor Heyerdahl, and what was *Kon-Tiki*? What was Heyerdahl's theory about Polynesians? What did his experiment involve? What was his conclusion? What do historians and scientists today believe about the origin of Polynesians?

CHAPTER 6
New Social Orders
1000–1350

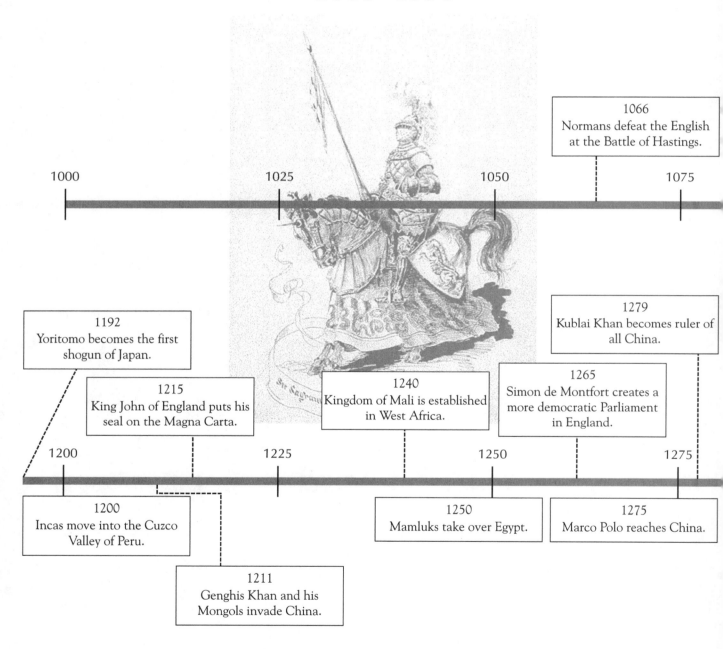

1000   1025   1050   1075

1066
Normans defeat the English at the Battle of Hastings.

1192
Yoritomo becomes the first shogun of Japan.

1215
King John of England puts his seal on the Magna Carta.

1240
Kingdom of Mali is established in West Africa.

1279
Kublai Khan becomes ruler of all China.

1265
Simon de Montfort creates a more democratic Parliament in England.

1200   1225   1250   1275

1200
Incas move into the Cuzco Valley of Peru.

1250
Mamluks take over Egypt.

1275
Marco Polo reaches China.

1211
Genghis Khan and his Mongols invade China.

This timeline provides an overview of the period from 1000 to 1350. Then a narrative describes this period in greater detail and discusses its significance.

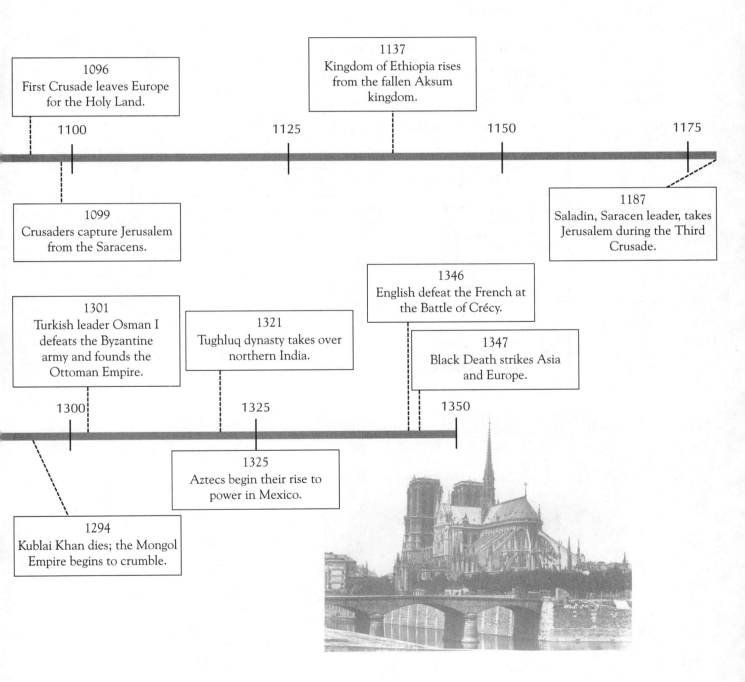

1096
First Crusade leaves Europe for the Holy Land.

1137
Kingdom of Ethiopia rises from the fallen Aksum kingdom.

1100   1125   1150   1175

1099
Crusaders capture Jerusalem from the Saracens.

1187
Saladin, Saracen leader, takes Jerusalem during the Third Crusade.

1346
English defeat the French at the Battle of Crécy.

1301
Turkish leader Osman I defeats the Byzantine army and founds the Ottoman Empire.

1321
Tughluq dynasty takes over northern India.

1347
Black Death strikes Asia and Europe.

1300   1325   1350

1325
Aztecs begin their rise to power in Mexico.

1294
Kublai Khan dies; the Mongol Empire begins to crumble.

Word Power

Word	Definition
causeways	raised roads built across water
charter	document stating people's rights
famine	time of severe shortage of food
hygiene	actions taken to stay healthy and clean
inevitable	sure to happen
moat	deep, wide ditch built around a building
mortar	mixture of lime, sand, water, and cement used for building
pilgrims	people who travel to worship at a holy place
refuge	protection, shelter from danger
seal	stamp to make a document official
sect	religious group that breaks away from a larger church
truce	temporary agreement to stop fighting
tyrant	severe, unfair ruler; dictator

What Your Child Needs to Know

You may choose to use the following text in several different ways, depending on your child's strengths and preferences. You might read the passage aloud; you might read it to yourself and then paraphrase it for your child; or you might ask your child to read the material along with you or on his or her own.

THE CRUSADES

Two great religions—Christianity and Islam—dominated Europe and Asia by the year 1000. It was perhaps <u>inevitable</u> that supporters of these two faiths would clash.

Palestine, where Jesus had lived and where Muhammad was said to have ascended to heaven, came to be called the **Holy Land.** Geographically, the Holy Land is in the Middle East, also referred to as *southwest Asia.*

Muslim Arabs had controlled the Holy Land since 637, but they had allowed Christian <u>pilgrims</u> safe passage to the holy city of Jerusalem. In 950, however, the **Seljuk** (SEL jook) **Turks,** a warlike people from central Asia, began to take over the Middle East. They were Muslim converts who shut off Jerusalem to Christians.

In 1095, the pope called for Christian kings to free the Holy Land from the Seljuk Turks, also called **Saracens** (SAR uh suhns). A year later, a European army of knights (described later), priests, and other pilgrims joined a Byzantine army from Constantinople to fight the Saracens. The Christians took control of Jerusalem in 1099 and held it for almost a hundred years. This was the first of a series of religious wars called the Crusades, which continued for 170 years. They were bloody and destructive fights.

The great Saracen leader **Saladin** (SA *luh* deen) came to power in Egypt in 1171. He led an army against the Christians in 1187 and recaptured Jerusalem. The English king Richard I, known as **Richard the Lionhearted** for his bravery in battle, was a leader of a crusade in 1189. He regained control of parts of Palestine but failed to take Jerusalem. Instead, he and Saladin made a <u>truce</u> in which they agreed to share Palestine for five years.

Crusades continued to 1272. The Christians, on the whole, were unsuccessful. After more than 160 years of fighting, Jerusalem remained in Muslim hands.

But the Crusades had some positive results for the Christians. Warriors returned to Europe with new products from the East. These included spices and silks, which the Europeans liked very much. Trade between the East (Asia) and the West (Europe) developed. Europe, which had been cut off from the rest of the world after Rome fell in the 400s, was beginning to look beyond its borders again.

EUROPE

The same religious passion that drove soldiers to travel hundreds of miles from home to fight a foreign war drove others to become monks, priests, and nuns. As noted in Chapter 5, many of these religious people lived, prayed, and worked in monasteries. From there, the religious community took care of people outside their walls. Monks cared for

Notre Dame

63

the sick, provided jobs for workers, taught the uneducated, and offered a place of <u>refuge</u> in times of trouble.

In addition to monasteries, grand cathedrals began to rise around Europe—for example, Chartres (SHART) and Notre Dame (NOH truh DAHM) in France and Salisbury (SAWLZ buhr ee) in England.

Also on the religious front, this was the period in which Christianity split into two divisions. Western Christians had both kings and popes. The western Christians would eventually call themselves Roman Catholics. Eastern Christians, centered on Constantinople, recognized their emperor as leader of both state and church. They called themselves Eastern Orthodox.

The Norman Conquest

In England, **King Edward the Confessor** promised that on his death the throne would go to the French duke William of Normandy, but when Edward died, the English nobles didn't want William to rule them. They offered the throne to **Harold,** the earl of Wessex. William was furious and crossed the English Channel from France with an army. The **Normans** and the English clashed at the **Battle of Hastings,** one of the most decisive battles in history. William's troops killed Harold and defeated the English. William, now called **William the Conqueror,** soon controlled all of England. The year was 1066.

The Normans brought a new way of life to England—**feudalism.**

The Feudal System

In feudalism, all land and property belonged to the king. He allowed nobles (lords) to own large estates known as **manors.** In return, the nobles, called **vassals,** paid taxes to the king and raised armies to defend him from enemies. The soldiers in these armies were **knights,** and they received land or other benefits for their services. In battle, these knights wore chain-metal or steel armor to protect themselves. The manors were worked by peasants called **serfs,** who were considered nothing more than a lord's property.

Feudal life took place in and around **castles**—elaborate (but drafty) homes for lords and vassals. These constructions also acted as fortresses. Out-

A knight in armor

side the castle walls, towns grew up. In this castle culture, the lords and knights were supposed to act gallantly. Their code of behavior was called **chivalry.**

The Magna Carta

Richard the Lionhearted was a member of a dynasty of English kings named **Plantagenet** (plan TA juh nut). After his death in 1199, his brother **John** came to the throne. John was a mean-tempered <u>tyrant</u>. He placed heavy taxes on his nobles, who then rebelled. They wrote up a document containing sixty-three demands that would limit the power of English kings from that point forward. The document is the **Magna Carta,** or "great <u>charter</u>." On June 15, 1215, in a meadow called **Runnymede,** the nobles forced King John to put his <u>seal</u> on their charter.

The Magna Carta was the first great declaration of human rights in western Europe and the beginning of the **parliamentary system** of government—

a system by which representatives of the people must consent to laws made by the government. The document declared that, while the king was the ruler, he must obey laws just as everyone else did. It said the king could not tax land without the approval of the **Great Council,** made up of important nobles and clergymen. The Magna Carta gave only a few rights to the common people—that is, to people outside nobility. One of these rights stated that the king could not put a free person in prison without a trial.

After John's death, his son **Henry III** became king. The nobles made Henry agree to consult the Great Council on all important issues, not just on taxes. In 1265, representatives of knights and common people were added to the body of nobles, laying the groundwork for a parliament of two bodies—the **House of Lords** and the **House of Commons**—and the beginning of modern European democracy.

The Hundred Years' War

England soon sought to dominate its neighbor, France. In 1337, **Edward III** of England challenged the rule of the new French king, **Philip VI.** Edward invaded France with an army and fought the French at the Battle of Crécy (KRAY see). The French fought with crossbows, while the English used a new weapon, the longbow. The longbow could shoot an arrow farther and faster than any other weapon. It could pierce armor at 200 yards (183 meters). The longbow gave the English a great victory at Crécy.

The war ended with a truce that lasted from 1347 to 1355. But the Hundred Years' War would resume after that.

The Black Death

One reason for the temporary halt to the fighting was the appearance of a terrible plague called the Black Death. This disease was carried by fleas living on rats. When the rats died, the fleas spread the disease to people. The plague began in southern China and quickly spread to central Asia, the Byzantine Empire, and finally western Europe. When it ended in 1351, between one-fourth and one-third of the population of the Middle East and Europe was dead. We know today that the illness was the **bubonic**

plague and that poor <u>hygiene</u> and crowded living quarters helped spread it.

In the devastation left by the Black Death, feudalism died. A new kind of social order would replace it in Europe.

THE BYZANTINES AND THE OTTOMANS

During this period, the Byzantine Empire was under attack from the Seljuk Turks and the Mongols (MAHNG guhlz). Then in 1301, **Osman** (ohs MAHN) **I,** from another Turkish group in central Asia, won a victory over the Byzantines. His followers called themselves Osmanlis ("sons of Osman") or Ottomans. By 1361, the Ottoman Turks had taken over much of the Byzantine Empire. But they did not yet possess Constantinople.

ASIA

The Mongols, Kublai Khan, and Marco Polo

The Sung (or Song) dynasty had taken over in China in 960 and reunited much of the country. The Chinese then went on to a relatively peaceful period, during which they invented paper money and the compass. But in the early 1200s, China and many other parts of Asia were threatened by terrible invaders.

The Mongols were fierce warriors from Mongolia, to the north of China. In 1206, Mongol chiefs gave their tribal leader the title **Genghis Khan** (*jeng* guhs KAHN; *geng* gus KAHN), which means "Emperor of All Men." Genghis Khan set out to live up to his new name. He led his warriors on horseback into China in 1211 and four years later captured the Chinese city of **Beijing** (BAY JING). The Mongols went on to conquer Korea, Afghanistan, Persia, and part of Russia and eastern Europe.

Genghis Khan's grandson Kublai Khan (*koo* bluh KAHN) conquered the Sung dynasty and completed the Mongol domination of China by 1279. Fierce though he and the Mongols were, Kublai Khan was a wise and, in many ways, a good ruler. He encouraged the arts and architecture, gave rights to women, increased trade, and respected the religions of the different peoples of his empire. He provided for the sick and gave surplus food to the hungry in times of <u>famine</u>.

Kublai Khan also opened the overland trade routes between East and West for the first time in many years. One of the first people to travel these routes to China was seventeen-year-old Marco Polo and his merchant father and uncle. They came from Venice.

When they arrived at Kublai Khan's court in 1275, they were probably the first westerners to visit China. The Great Khan liked young Marco and made him one of his closest advisors. He also sent him on many missions across his vast empire.

The Polos returned to Venice after spending seventeen years in China. People were fascinated by Marco Polo's accounts of the Mongol Empire. Later, a book of Polo's would inspire ocean explorers such as **Christopher Columbus.**

When Kublai Khan died in 1294, the Mongol hold on China and on the rest of the Mongol Empire began to fall apart.

Japan

Japan was one of the few Asian kingdoms to escape Mongol conquest. Twice Kublai Khan tried to invade the island, and twice his army and navy were driven off by powerful sea storms.

In 1192, the leader **Yoritomo** seized power and declared himself **shogun,** which means "great general" or "the emperor's general." The shoguns continued to rule Japan as military dictators until 1868. The emperor ruled now in name only. Under the shoguns were a class of nobles supported by strong warriors known as **samurai** (SA muh *rye*). Like the knights of medieval Europe, the samurai swore loyalty to a nobleman, and they lived and fought by a strict code of conduct.

The Khmer Empire

The Khmer (kuh MER) Empire in southeast Asia dates back to A.D. 802. About A.D. 900, the Khmer ruler built a new capital, **Angkor** (ANG kawr) **Thom,** which means "great city." About two hundred years later, during the high point of the empire, a ruler added a great Hindu temple, called **Angkor Wat** ("great temple"), built of red sandstone and surrounded by a <u>moat</u> 590 feet (180 meters) wide. In the 1400s, the Khmer abandoned Angkor Wat, and jungle growth covered the temple. Explorers rediscovered it only in the 1800s. Descendants of the Khmer live in what is now called Cambodia.

AFRICA

The kingdom of Ghana fell in 1203. In 1240, the new kingdom of **Mali** (MAH lee) was established in West Africa along the **Niger** (NYE juhr) **River.** Mali became rich by exporting gold, ivory, and slaves to Muslims in northern Africa and Italy. Its greatest city was **Timbuktu** (*tim buhk* TOO), situated at a crossroads of several trade routes. Timbuktu was also a great center of learning, with a famous university and about one hundred other schools. Around 1325, the people of Mali converted to Islam.

The kingdom of **Ethiopia** (*ee thee OH pee uh*) emerged in eastern Africa about 1137. It grew out of the fallen Aksum kingdom. Ethiopia's founding dynasty may have been Jewish, but most Ethiopians were members of a Christian <u>sect</u> called the **Copts** (KAHPTS). For many centuries, Ethiopia was protected and isolated from the rest of Africa by mountains.

In 1250, slaves who worked as soldiers for the Egyptian Muslims took over rule of Egypt and created their own empire that included Syria and Palestine. In 1260, they defeated an invasion by the land-hungry Mongols.

During the period beginning in 1000, some eastern coastal cities of Africa became linked to Asia by trade. In fact, Arabic words from southwest Asia entered the African Swahili language, and Islam itself surfaced in Swahili cities.

THE AMERICAS

In the 1200s, two new cultures emerged in Mesoamerica and South America. Farther north, the last of the mound-building peoples flourished along the Mississippi River in the central United States.

The Aztec

The Aztec were a nomadic people who settled in the fertile Valley of Mexico in the 1200s. Around 1325, they began to build their capital city of **Tenochtitlán** (tay *nawch* teet LAHN). The name means "place of the prickly pear cactus." The Aztec built the city on an island in Lake Texcoco. They floated huge baskets of soil into the lake's marshes. Then they planted trees to bind the land areas together. Finally they constructed <u>causeways</u> across the lake to their city. Tenochtitlán eventually grew to have a population of over 250,000.

The Aztec quickly became the dominant people in Mexico and Central America. They traded with other peoples and created a large marketplace in Tenochtitlán, where people came from all over Mexico to exchange goods.

The Aztec emperor held complete power over the nobles, priests, and common people. The Aztec were highly religious and warlike. Their chief god was god of the sun and war. They offered him and other gods human sacrifices on the altars of their tall stone temples. The victims were usually prisoners of war and slaves, although sometimes they offered up their own people.

The Inca

The Inca moved into the **Cuzco** (KOOS koh) **Valley** high in the Andes Mountains of Peru by 1200. *Cuzco* means "center of the world." The first Inca rulers, according to legend, were a brother and sister who were called "the children of the Sun." All Inca rulers after that were worshiped as gods.

Like the Aztec, the Inca were great builders. They created magnificent cities such as their capital, Cuzco. They built their temples and other buildings without <u>mortar</u>. The builders placed the stones so tightly together that many Inca structures still stand today. The Inca also developed a method of counting and recording numbers by tying knots in strings. They were one of the first people to freeze-dry food to preserve it for future use. Some potatoes found in Inca ruins were still fresh after five hundred years.

By 1350, the Aztec and Inca were developing what would become the greatest empires in the Americas.

North America

Anasazi culture (see Chapter 5) started fading out, and by 1300 few traces of the people or culture remained. The circumstances of the decline remain a mystery.

Farther east, great towns were appearing around 1200 along the Mississippi River. These **Mississippi peoples** built rectangular, flat-topped mounds that served as the base for large homes and temples.

The largest Mississippi settlement was at the junction of the Missouri and Mississippi rivers in present-day southern Illinois. Of the more than one hundred mounds discovered there, the largest is over ninety-eight feet (thirty meters) high. Little is known of the Mississippi people. They may have lived in houses made of tree branches and twigs plastered together. They may have worshiped their chiefs as gods and buried them in great tombs, some of which have been uncovered. The Mississippians were the ancestors of a number of later Native American peoples.

! Implications

To answer the question, "Why does all this matter?" or "What does it mean?," share the following insights with your child.

Throughout history, people have set out to achieve a goal and have ended up achieving something very different. This phenomenon happened many times in the period from 1000 to 1350. For example, although the Crusaders failed to win back the Holy Land, they returned to Europe with new products and ideas, which would stimulate trade with the East and pave the way for the great age of exploration.

Another example: The English nobles who forced King John to accept the demands of their Magna Carta had no thought of helping the common people of England. Yet the Magna Carta was the blueprint for the democratic rights enjoyed today by millions of people.

Even such a catastrophe as the Black Death had

its positive side. It left towns throughout Europe empty. People from the countryside repopulated these towns and created a new system that replaced feudalism in the 1400s.

Regarding religion in this period, we see that knights, Muslim warriors, and samurai came from different cultures, but all went into battle in the name of their leaders and their beliefs. People in many different societies around the world continued to pray for a better life in heaven or in their next lives. How, if at all, would attitudes about religion change in the coming centuries?

 ## Fact Checker

To check that your child knows or can find the basic facts in this chapter, here are multiple-choice questions. You may want to ask your child the questions as if he or she were competing on a televised game show.

"IS THAT YOUR FINAL ANSWER?"

Choose the correct answer to each of the following questions about this period in world history.

1. Twelfth-century crusaders traveled to
   a. the Sahara Desert
   b. Normandy
   c. the Holy Land
2. William the Conqueror earned his name by conquering
   a. the English at the Battle of Hastings
   b. the Black Death
   c. the kingdom of Ghana
3. Marco Polo was one of the first Europeans to visit
   a. Tenochtitlán
   b. China
   c. Jerusalem
4. The Hundred Years' War was between England and
   a. France
   b. Genghis Khan
   c. Japan
5. Ruins in what is now Peru are remains of buildings by the
   a. Mongols
   b. Romans
   c. Incas

Answers appear in the back, preceding the index.

 ## The Big Questions

The following questions encourage your child to think critically rather than simply recall facts. If necessary, review the specific information from the preceding pages that will help your child make the appropriate inferences to come up with reasonable answers.

1. What role did religion play in the world from the year 1000 to the year 1350?

2. Which parts of the world were aware of one another during this period, and which parts of the world had no idea that there were other continents?

Answers

1. *Answers should acknowledge that the urge to convert people to one's religion or to claim power and glory for one's religion led to warfare—for example, to the Crusades.*

   Religious sites such as monasteries were important to spread learning.

   Faith in a religion may have helped believers during bad times such as the plague years. Alternatively, people may have lost faith during such a period.

   Other answers are also possible.

2. *Asia and Europe were aware of each other, given the Crusades and Marco Polo.*

   Asia and cities on the east coast of Africa had trade relationships.

   Europe and Africa knew about each other, going back at least to A.D. 711, when north Muslims invaded Spain from northern Africa.

   Australia was not aware of other continents. No humans had reached Antarctica yet.

   North and South America may or may not have known about each other; they did not know about other continents, and other continents didn't know about North and South America yet.

Skills Practice

The following activities give your child practice in applying the skills basic to social studies. For some of the activities, your child may need to review the information in the preceding pages.

A. FINISHING A GRAPHIC ORGANIZER

Teachers often ask students to work with graphic organizers. A graphic organizer helps the viewer see the relationships between various pieces of information related to a topic.

The graphic organizer on the right shows some of the people involved in the medieval system called feudalism. What was the title or function of the person in the empty box?

Answer

Accept any of the following answers: knight, soldier, lesser noble.

Evaluating Your Child's Skills: In order to succeed with this task, your child needs to "read" the graphic organizer and to understand that it shows a social structure,

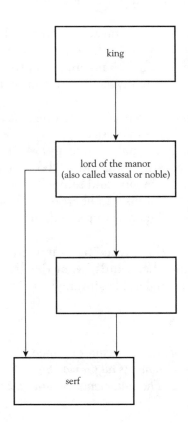

with the most powerful person at the top and the most powerless person at the bottom. If your child has trouble, review the definitions of *king, vassal, knight,* and *serf.*

B. GENERALIZING ABOUT A PRIMARY SOURCE

Ask your child to read the following excerpts (put into modern English) from the Magna Carta and then answer the question. Explain that the entire document contained sixty-three articles.

We have granted to all freemen of our kingdom for us and our heirs forever all the liberties written below.

• No widow shall be forced to marry so long as she wishes to live without a husband.
• A free man shall not be fined for a small offense.
• No sheriff, or anyone else, shall take horses or wagons of anyone without permission.
• No freeman shall be taken, or imprisoned, or banished, or in anyway injured, except by the law of the land.
• To no one will we sell, to no one will we deny or delay, rights or justice.
• All merchants shall be safe and secure in leaving and entering England . . . both by land and by water, for buying and selling.
• All these customs and liberties . . . shall be observed by all men of our kingdom.

What do all the preceding statements have in common? In other words, what did they provide for people in England beginning in 1215?

Answer

Accept any of the following or similarly worded responses: The statements all provide protections or freedoms to people. The statements are laws that everyone

must follow. The document in part refers to freemen. People who were serfs did not have these protections or rights.

Evaluating Your Child's Skills: In order to answer these questions, your child has to think about particulars and come up with a generalization that applies to all of them. If your child has trouble understanding the essence of the document, point out the word *liberty* in the first sentence.

 # Top of the Class

Following is a variety of activities children can do on their own or share in class to show that they have been seriously considering the period from A.D. 1000 to 1350.

VIEWING MEDIEVAL ARTS AND CRAFTS

Take your child on a trip to a real or virtual museum to see European medieval arts and crafts. Local museums may have exhibitions of tapestries, illuminated manuscripts, and knights' shining armor. An alternative is to visit New York City's Metropolitan Museum of Art online at www.metmuseum.org/collections, where your child can click on "Arms and Armor" and "The Cloisters."

What can you learn from a museum about daily life during the Middle Ages in Europe? By looking at books, arms and armor, or tapestries (or all three), tell which were made by hand with simple tools. How would you compare and contrast them with today's books, weapons, and wall decorations?

PLAYING TRAVEL AGENT

Help your child locate articles, brochures, or Web sites for this activity.

Select a building that was constructed between 1000 and 1350 and that still stands. The building can be in the Americas, in Africa, or in Asia. Prepare an advertisement designed to attract tourists to the building. Tell readers what they will see, hear, touch, smell, and taste on a trip to the locale you are advertising.

CHAPTER 7
A World Reborn
1350–1500

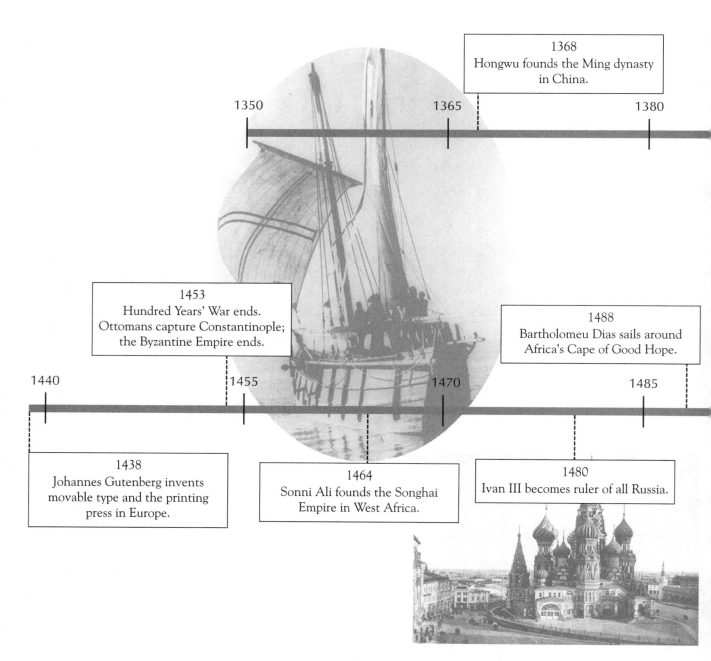

1350   1365   1380

1368
Hongwu founds the Ming dynasty in China.

1440   1455   1470   1485

1453
Hundred Years' War ends.
Ottomans capture Constantinople;
the Byzantine Empire ends.

1488
Bartholomeu Dias sails around
Africa's Cape of Good Hope.

1438
Johannes Gutenberg invents
movable type and the printing
press in Europe.

1464
Sonni Ali founds the Songhai
Empire in West Africa.

1480
Ivan III becomes ruler of all Russia.

This timeline provides an overview of cultural and political developments between approximately 1350 and 1500. On the following pages, a narrative describes this period in greater detail and discusses its significance.

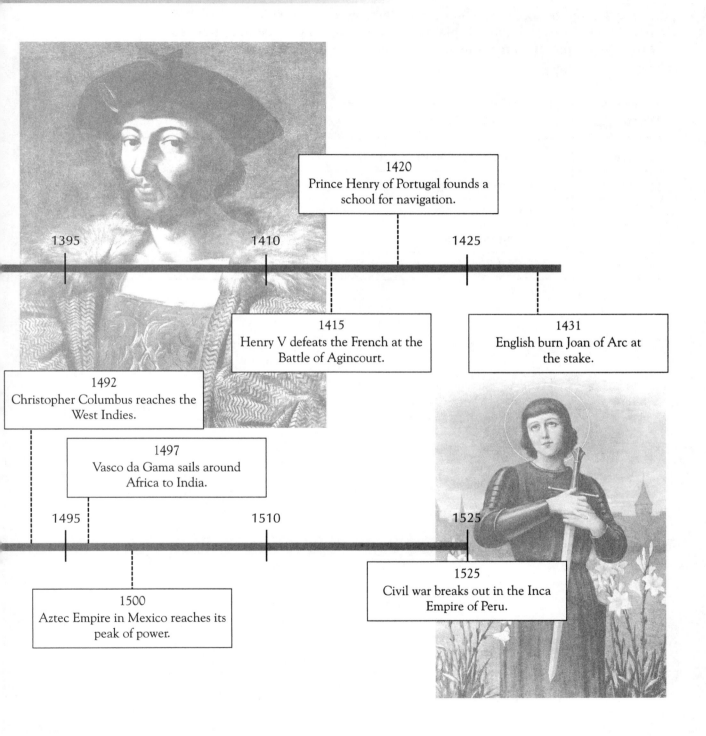

1420
Prince Henry of Portugal founds a school for navigation.

1395

1410

1425

1415
Henry V defeats the French at the Battle of Agincourt.

1431
English burn Joan of Arc at the stake.

1492
Christopher Columbus reaches the West Indies.

1497
Vasco da Gama sails around Africa to India.

1495

1510

1525

1500
Aztec Empire in Mexico reaches its peak of power.

1525
Civil war breaks out in the Inca Empire of Peru.

73

Word Power

The words on the following chart are underscored in the section called "What Your Child Needs to Know." Explain their meanings to your child as needed when they come up in reading or discussion. Keep the list handy for you and your child to use.

Word	Definition
alliances	agreements to work together
grisly	gruesome, horrible
patrons	people who give money and support to artists and writers
stately	grand, majestic
terraces	raised flat land with sloping sides

What Your Child Needs to Know

You may choose to use the following text in several different ways, depending on your child's strengths and preferences. You might read the passage aloud; you might read it to yourself and then paraphrase it for your child; or you might ask your child to read the material along with you or on his or her own.

The title of this chapter refers to a sense of newness, to a sense of change and adventure, that came over parts of the world during this period. As is always the case, some continents felt the changes and participated in them more than others.

EUROPE

End of the Hundred Years' War

The English wanted the French throne and launched a new invasion of France in 1355. A break in the Hundred Years' War came forty years later, when an English king, **Richard II,** married the daughter of the king of France, and the two countries agreed to a truce.

Twenty years later, a new English king, **Henry V,** declared *his* right to the French throne. In the Battle of Agincourt (AH juhn *kohrt*), which followed, Henry, with only thirteen thousand troops, decisively defeated the French force of fifty thousand. As a result, in 1420, the French king once again gave a daughter in marriage to an English king and named the king heir to the French throne. But King Henry died less than two years later, and war soon resumed between the two countries.

Then in France, seventeen-year-old **Joan of Arc,** a simple farmer's daughter, claimed she had had a vision in which the saints directed her to save France. Joan approached the French prince who believed he was heir to the French throne. She persuaded him to let her gather an army to fight the English so that he could win the throne. She and the army marched to the town of **Orléans** (AW lay

Joan of Arc

AHN) in 1428 and defeated the English. But then her luck changed. She lost a battle at Paris and fell into the hands of the English, who called her a witch because she had heard voices. On May 30, 1431, the English burned Joan of Arc at the stake. Almost five hundred years later, the Catholic Church named Joan a saint.

Joan's life and death inspired the French, and they soon began to win back their land from the English. By 1453, the year that the Hundred Years' War finally ended, little of France remained in English hands.

The Early Renaissance

Somehow, out of the Crusades, the misery of the Black Death, and the warfare of the late fourteenth and early fifteenth centuries, there arose in Europe a new enthusiasm for art, literature, and trade. Towns,

Lorenzo de Medici

repopulated after the plague, grew again. Italy's city-states, in particular, prospered.

Florence, in northern Italy, became a great center of the arts. There the wealthy **Medici** (MEH duh *chee*) family served as <u>patrons</u>, paying artists and craftspeople to produce many works. The most famous of the Medici was **Lorenzo the Magnificent.** Historians named this period the **Renaissance** (reh nuh SAHNS), which has come to mean "rebirth of learning and the arts."

What were the characteristics of the Renaissance? For one thing, scholars in Florence, in other parts of Italy, and then across Europe discovered and appreciated the culture of the ancient Greeks, Romans, and Arabs. They began to appreciate ancient writings and ancient statues. They developed a new love of ancient architecture—especially the dome.

These works of art and architecture fed a growing interest in a philosophy known as **humanism.** A second major characteristic of the Renaissance, humanism focused on human life and human tal-

ents in the present day instead of emphasizing life after death, as did the Christian Church. Many people during the Renaissance were still very religious, but they also wanted to create and expand possibilities in this life. Rather than accepting handed-down theories and knowledge, these people questioned everything.

In addition to showing high regard for ancient, classic texts and for humanism, Europeans during the Renaissance turned their attention to sciences. Arabs had preserved scientific knowledge and, during the Renaissance, passed on to Italians and others the urge to look at the world scientifically. For example, Renaissance artists began to observe nature more closely, and, using math and science, they figured out how to portray depth in a painting. Renaissance scientists also observed the world closely and questioned everything they saw. As a result, scientists in Europe during the Renaissance made huge strides in fields such as navigation and astronomy.

Among the outstanding minds and hands working during the period from 1350 to 1500 were the following: **Petrarch** (PEE *trark*), the most famous poet in Europe at the time; the painter **Sandro Botticelli** (*bah* tuh CHEH lee) and the sculptor **Donatello** (*dah* nuh TEH loh), both of whom created realistic works that celebrated human achievements; **Johannes Gutenberg** (GOO tuhn *buhrg*), who perfected printing from movable type around 1450 and so made possible large-scale production of books and newspapers in the West.

These people and others helped Europeans leave the Middle Ages and begin to create our modern world.

Exploration

One of the newest countries in Europe was Portugal, which had won its independence from Spain in 1385. Facing the Atlantic, Portugal made its living largely from the sea in fishing and trade.

As part of the Renaissance spirit of questioning and investigation, Portuguese prince **Henry the Navigator** believed that people could reach the trading centers in Asia by sea. In 1420, Henry founded a school that taught seamen how to make long voyages. Henry encouraged the development of better navigational tools and a new kind of ship, the **caravel.** The caravel was longer and narrower than other ships and easy to maneuver. It also could sail safely in violent storms. Yearly, Henry sent out ships to explore the coast of western Africa. Later, explorers went farther.

The explorer **Bartholomeu Dias** (DEE *ahsh*) became the first person to sail around Africa's southern tip in 1488; the explorer **Vasco da Gama** then sailed not only around the cape, named the Cape of Good Hope by Dias, but also up the east coast of Africa in 1498. Da Gama went on to India and returned to Portugal with a cargo of spices. Spices were valuable in Europe because they disguised the taste of the salt sprinkled on meat to reduce its rotting.

While the Portuguese sailed eastward, the Spanish headed west. (Spain had once again become a Christian country. The Muslims, who had invaded in A.D. 711, were forced out hundreds of years later.) Italian navigator Christopher Columbus persuaded the Spanish king and queen to back an expedition across the Atlantic Ocean. He believed that such an expedition would reach Japan and China. Columbus didn't realize the Americas would block his way. In 1492, he landed in an island group that he named the **Indies** and that eventually became known as the West Indies. He became the first European since the Vikings (see Chapter 5) to "discover" America. On three additional voyages, Columbus reached what we now call Central and South America. The race for the riches of the New World was under way.

Europe and the Mongols

As noted in Chapter 6, warriors from Mongolia, in northern Asia, overran Russia. Soon after they entered Russia in 1238, these Mongols, called **Tartars** (TAHR tuhs), established a kingdom named the **Golden Horde** on the Volga River. The only part of Russia that withstood them was the area eventually known as Moscow. Slowly, Moscow took over surrounding Russian states, and in 1380 Russians from there defeated the Golden Horde.

In 1462, **Ivan III** became Grand Prince of Moscow. Ten years later, Ivan married the niece of the last Byzantine emperor and appointed himself protector of the Eastern Orthodox Church. Ivan enlarged his territory and in 1480 defeated the Tar-

Caravel (sailing ship)

tars in a final decisive battle. He declared himself ruler of all Russia.

Known as **Ivan the Great** for his accomplishments, he rebuilt the **Kremlin,** the fortified center of Moscow, with great churches and other stately buildings. When he died in 1505, Russia was one of the largest and most powerful countries in Europe.

By 1450, another group of Mongol invaders, the Ottoman Turks had taken over much of the Byzantine empire (see Chapter 6) but still had not won the Christian city that had been the capital of the Byzantine Empire for a thousand years. Then in 1451, **Mehmed II** became the new Ottoman **sultan,** or emperor. In 1453, he attacked Constantinople with an army of more than a hundred thousand soldiers. For nearly eight weeks, the Ottoman Turks bombarded the city walls with cannon. The Ottoman Turks finally broke through the walls and entered the city. It was defended by ten thousand Christians, who fought bitterly. Among the defend-

Kremlin

ers was the Byzantine emperor **Constantine XI,** who was killed in the fighting. With his death, the thousand-year-old Byzantine Empire came to its final end.

Mehmed II made Constantinople the new capital of the Ottoman Empire, which remained in power for five hundred years. He changed the city's name to Istanbul. He turned its largest Christian church, **Hagia Sophia** (Church of Holy Wisdom), into a **mosque,** a Muslim place of worship. Today, Istanbul is the largest city of the modern country of Turkey. Geographically, it is partially in Europe and partially in Asia.

ASIA

Many of the countries in Asia were focused on themselves during this period. For example, Korea managed to get out from under Mongol control and then Chinese control, the kingdom of Siam (today's Thailand) established itself, and Japan experienced internal warfare. China, on the other hand, was willing—if only for a while—to go beyond its borders in the spirit of adventure that was sweeping Europe.

China

After Kublai Khan (see Chapter 6), the Mongol emperors of China were weak, and the last one was driven out of China by a former monk and rebel leader. In 1368, this leader became the first emperor of the **Ming dynasty.** He established a strong government that served the people's needs. He abolished slavery in China and repaired the Great Wall, which the Mongols had ruined in places.

In 1402, another emperor took over the Ming dynasty. He put almost a million people to work on building the fabulous **Forbidden City** in Beijing. The Forbidden City (which only the emperor, his family, and servants could use) is a vast complex of palaces and temples that still stands today.

China at this time also extended its influence by sending out seven naval expeditions westward to make friends and to trade with peoples in areas bordering the Indian Ocean region. In the later decades of the century, however, China worried about possible new Mongol invasions from the north. Therefore, rulers concentrated on strengthening the country from within rather than on shipbuilding and exploring beyond its borders. That is, China became isolated once again.

The Ming period is famous to this day for its blue-and-white porcelain dishes and vases.

AFRICA

Here are examples of cultures in different parts of the continent in the years before European dominance. At this time, Christianity, Islam, and old, local religions had followers in Africa.

Western Africa

For centuries, the people of **Songhai** (song GYE) had lived in the shadow of the Mali Empire (Chapter 6). But in 1462, **Sonni Ali,** a strong and ruthless leader, came to power, and, within two years, he gained independence for Songhai and captured the great trading center of Timbuktu. By 1475, the Songhai Empire swallowed up Mali.

Southern Africa

Bantu peoples of West Africa migrated southward by A.D. 500, and around 1100 some of them emerged as the **Zimbabwe** (zim BAH bwee) people. *Zimbabwe* means "great stone enclosure," and for three hundred years workers labored to put up massive stone walls around **Great Zimbabwe,** their capital and a great religious and trading center. Later, in about 1450, the Zimbabwe people were absorbed by another kingdom, which itself would be overtaken shortly by the Portuguese. The modern African nation of Zimbabwe has no connection to the original kingdom, except its name.

East Africa

The people who lived in present-day Tanzania (*tan* zuh NEE uh) did not develop a culture on the level of these other kingdoms. They were mostly farmers who found creative ways to adapt to their hilly land. They built stone platforms to level off the land and placed their communities on top. They created <u>terraces</u> on hillsides to plant their crops. Stone-lined canals carried river water to irrigate fields, and stone walls surrounded their settlements. These people disappeared mysteriously. Some historians think they left the region during a long drought.

Ethiopia, in the meantime, was experiencing its high point. Under Christian leaders, workers expanded churches carved out of solid rock and built monasteries.

Central Africa

Around 1380, the Kongo kingdom took hold in central Africa. A century later, Portuguese explorers in Africa traveled from the Atlantic along the Congo river to this kingdom.

THE AMERICAS

People living in what is now North America had no concept of Europe and no idea that Europeans would soon threaten their ways of life. In the meantime, farther south, the two great cultures of the Aztec and the Inca reached their peaks during this period.

The Aztec Empire

By 1430, the Aztecs had begun to expand their lands. The Aztecs traded as far north as the present-day United States and as far south as Colombia in South America. They brought neighboring peoples into their empire either by peaceful <u>alliances</u> or through conquest in war. By 1500, the Aztec empire stretched across today's Mexico from coast to coast.

War was a way of life for the Aztec. They believed their gods required a steady source of blood and human hearts, the symbol of life. Gods who did not receive these gifts would destroy the world, the Aztec feared. One of the <u>grisly</u> purposes of war was to capture prisoners to sacrifice. As many as twenty thousand people were sacrificed in one day at the great temple at Tenochtitlán.

The Inca Empire

The Inca created an empire in South America as great as the Aztec Empire to the north. In the middle 1400s, they built one of their greatest cities, **Machu Picchu** (*mah* choo PEE choo), on a plain between two mountain peaks in the Andes. It was so remote and well hidden that it remained a secret for nearly four centuries. An American archaeologist finally rediscovered it in 1911.

In 1471, the Inca emperor added new land to his empire, including parts of what today are

Ecuador, Chile, and Bolivia. When the emperor died, his son took power. But when *he* died in 1525 and his two sons replaced him, civil war erupted as the two brothers fought for control of the empire.

OCEANIA

In the late 1400s, while the Americas were being "discovered" by Europeans, another region, Oceania, remained cut off from the rest of the world, as it had been for centuries. But within its own area, Oceania at this time included highly developed cultures in the **Society Islands,** the Hawaiian Islands, **Samoa** (suh MOH uh), and **Tonga** (TAHNG guh).

The Maori in New Zealand were reaching the high point of their civilization. To the west, the **Aborigines** (*ah* buh RI juh neez) of Australia, however, were still living a simple Stone Age existence, as they had for centuries.

 # Implications

To answer the question, "Why does all this matter?" or "What does it mean?," share the following insights with your child.

When the Ottoman Turks captured Constantinople, many Greek scholars who had lived there left and went to cities in Italy. They brought with them vast knowledge of the golden days of ancient Greece and Rome, and they shared this knowledge with Italians and then with the rest of western Europe.

Once Europeans learned about the art, literature, philosophy, and architecture of bygone civilizations, they started thinking more deeply about and questioning everything that touched their lives. Once such questioning started in Europe, Europe itself would become a collection of advanced societies.

As part of their questioning, Europeans—especially the Portuguese and Spaniards—started exploring other parts of the world. This exploration would lead to both good and bad. On the one hand, Europeans would open up trade with Africa and the Americas, but, on the other hand, Europeans would cause disasters for people in Africa and the Americas—disasters called slavery and disease.

Just about the time that Europeans started exploring other lands, the Chinese stopped their ocean voyages and began looking inward. As a result, Europeans of the next few centuries would have more direct effects on the Americas than Asians.

Fact Checker

To check that your child knows or can find the basic facts in this chapter, here is an acrostic for him or her to solve.

ACROSTIC

For each clue, write the answer at the right, one letter to each blank. The first letter of each answer, when read vertically, will spell the name of an important city in Italy in the fifteenth century.

1. Opponent of England in Hundred Years' War   _ _ _ _ _ _
2. First name of an important Medici   _ _ _ _ _ _ _
2. Empire that Istanbul was part of   _ _ _ _ _ _ _
3. Word that means "rebirth of learning"   _ _ _ _ _ _ _ _ _ _ _
4. Where churches were carved out of rock   _ _ _ _ _ _ _ _
5. Nickname of Prince Henry of Portugal   _ _ _ _ _ _ _ _ _
6. Home of Ming dynasty   _ _ _ _ _ _
7. Continent where Renaissance took place   _ _ _ _ _ _

Answers appear in the back, preceding the index.

? The Big Questions

The following questions encourage your child to think critically rather than simply recall facts. If necessary, review the specific information from the preceding pages that will help your child make the appropriate inferences to come up with reasonable answers.

1. How was it that Europeans did not become familiar with the ancient Greek, Roman, and Arab cultures until the Renaissance? Who had preserved the contributions of the ancient cultures?
2. If Gutenberg, who invented the printing press for Europeans, could come back from the dead and see what we read today, what might surprise him?
3. How did it come to pass that Europeans sailed to the Americas before Asians did?

Answers

1. *Europeans had been caught up in their own day-to-day lives ever since the fall of the Roman Empire in the fifth century. War and disease occupied them. People in Constantinople and in Arabia kept alive the work of ancient Greeks, Romans, and Arabs.*
2. *What Gutenberg might be amazed to see: the quantity of books we have and that we publish each year; photographs in books; how we treat books (carelessly compared to treatment in his time). He might also be amazed to see electronic books.*
3. *The Chinese decided to stop exploring and to concentrate on problems at home. Europeans, still looking for a shortcut to Asia, ran into the Americas by accident.*

Skills Practice

The following activities give your child practice in applying the skills basic to social studies. For some of the activities, your child may need to review the information in the preceding pages.

A. DISTINGUISHING FACT FROM OPINION

Review with your child the definitions of the words *fact* and *opinion*. Establish that statements of fact can be checked to find out whether they are true or false, while statements of opinion are neither true nor false; they represent the *judgments* people have made. Then ask your child to identify the following statements as facts or opinions. Encourage your child to explain each identification.

1. Gutenberg printed a Bible, the first large book to be manufactured this way in Europe, in 1455.
2. Prince Henry the Navigator wanted to reach the trading centers in Asia by sea.
3. The Zimbabwe were the most important people in Africa in the year 1100.
4. Henry V of England defeated the French at the Battle of Agincourt even though he had fewer soldiers.
5. Botticelli and Donatello were the best artists of the Renaissance.

Answers

1. fact; 2. fact; 3. opinion; 4. fact; 5. opinion

Evaluating Your Child's Skills: If your child has trouble, point out key words and phrases that are typical in statements of opinion: *most important* and *best*.

B. USING RESEARCH TOOLS

Your child will gain confidence if he or she learns how to find additional information on his or her own.

For each of the following topics and questions, write on the blank the place where you will most likely find the answer. A list of research tools follows the exercise.

1. TOPIC: the painter Botticelli
   QUESTION: Where can I see a painting of his to find out if I like it?
   FIND ANSWER IN: _____
2. TOPIC: Joan of Arc
   QUESTION: What was her life like before she said she had her vision?
   FIND ANSWER IN: _____
3. TOPIC: Florence, Italy
   QUESTION: Today, what other cities are close by?
   FIND ANSWER IN: _____
4. TOPIC: Ivan III of Russia
   QUESTION: Throughout the course of history, how many men named Ivan ruled Russia?
   FIND ANSWER IN: _____
5. TOPIC: Great Zimbabwe
   QUESTION: How tall and how thick are the stone walls?
   FIND ANSWER IN: _____

Research Tools

almanac   biography
atlas   encyclopedia

Answers

1. encyclopedia; 2. biography; 3. atlas; 4. almanac; 5. encyclopedia

Evaluating Your Child's Skills: In order to succeed with this task, your child needs to know what kinds of information each research tool contains. If your child has trouble, tell him or her about the tools or point them out in a library, in a bookstore, or at home.

Top of the Class

Following are a couple of activities children can do on their own or share in class to show that they have been seriously considering the period from 1350 to 1500.

AZTEC INFLUENCE ON MEXICO

This activity will help your child see the connection between historical Mexico of the Aztecs and contemporary Mexico.

Use dictionaries and encyclopedias (you may have to check several) to answer the following questions. Alternatively, you may seek answers from a friend or relative who comes from or has lived in Mexico.

1. The name *Mexico* comes from an Aztec word. What is that word, and what does it mean?
2. According to legend, how did the Aztecs decide where to settle in Mexico? What is the connection between that story and the design of the Mexican flag or Mexican money?

ASIA IN YOUR KITCHEN

Let your kitchen serve as a laboratory in which your child can appreciate the variety and power of spices that originally came from Asia.

European explorers wanted to find a sea route to Asia so that they could more easily and quickly get Asian spices. Here is a list of spices that grew originally in Asia but that today you may find in your kitchen. Design a game in which you blindfold someone and challenge him or her to name a spice by smelling it.

clove	juniper
coriander	mustard (dry)
garlic	nutmeg
ginger	saffron

CHAPTER 8
The Sixteenth Century

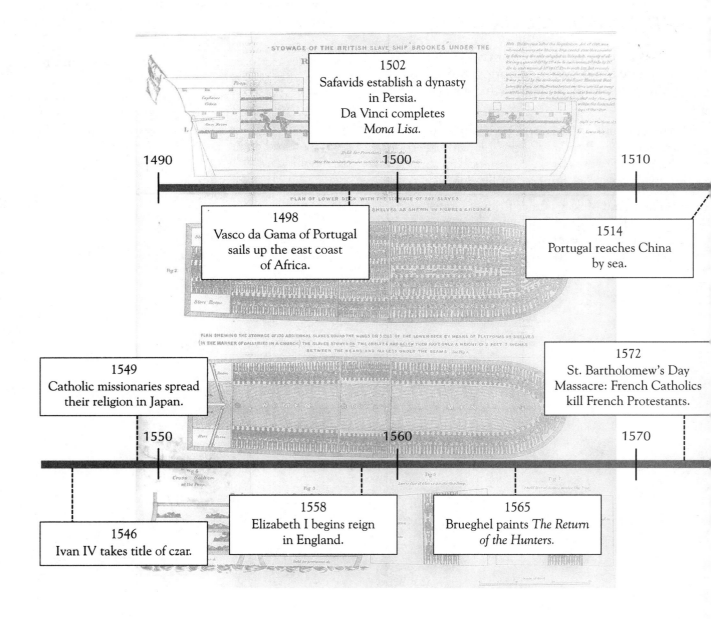

1502
Safavids establish a dynasty in Persia.
Da Vinci completes *Mona Lisa*.

1490

1500

1510

1498
Vasco da Gama of Portugal sails up the east coast of Africa.

1514
Portugal reaches China by sea.

1549
Catholic missionaries spread their religion in Japan.

1572
St. Bartholomew's Day Massacre: French Catholics kill French Protestants.

1550

1560

1570

1546
Ivan IV takes title of czar.

1558
Elizabeth I begins reign in England.

1565
Brueghel paints *The Return of the Hunters*.

This timeline provides an overview of cultural and political developments between, approximately, 1500 and 1600. On the following pages, a narrative describes in greater detail how this period played out on stages in Africa, Asia, the Americas, the Middle East, and Europe—and the significance of those details.

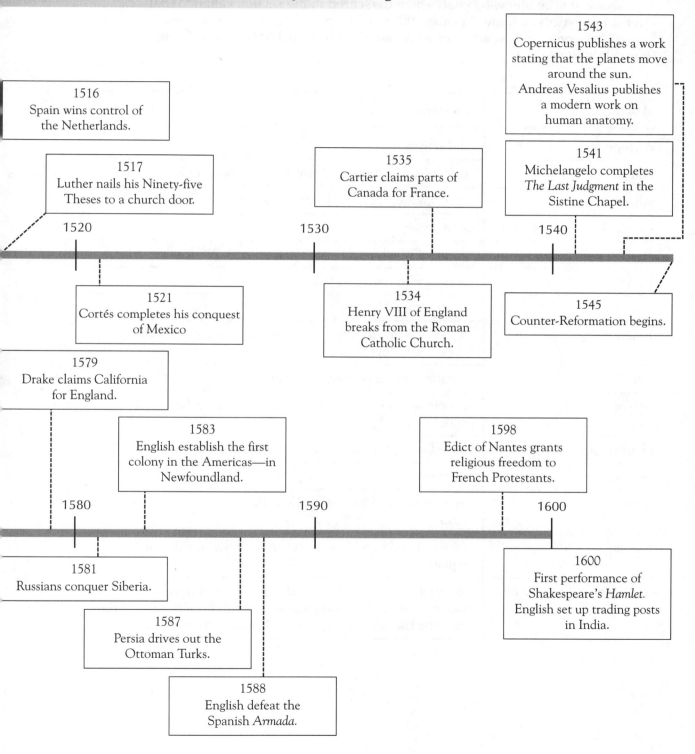

1543
Copernicus publishes a work stating that the planets move around the sun.
Andreas Vesalius publishes a modern work on human anatomy.

1516
Spain wins control of the Netherlands.

1517
Luther nails his Ninety-five Theses to a church door.

1535
Cartier claims parts of Canada for France.

1541
Michelangelo completes *The Last Judgment* in the Sistine Chapel.

1520

1530

1540

1521
Cortés completes his conquest of Mexico

1534
Henry VIII of England breaks from the Roman Catholic Church.

1545
Counter-Reformation begins.

1579
Drake claims California for England.

1583
English establish the first colony in the Americas—in Newfoundland.

1598
Edict of Nantes grants religious freedom to French Protestants.

1580

1590

1600

1581
Russians conquer Siberia.

1587
Persia drives out the Ottoman Turks.

1588
English defeat the Spanish *Armada*.

1600
First performance of Shakespeare's *Hamlet*.
English set up trading posts in India.

Word Power

The words on the following chart are underscored in the section called "What Your Child Needs to Know." Explain their meanings to your child as needed when they come up in reading or discussion. Keep the list handy for you and your child to use.

Word	Definition
corruption	dishonesty
czar	title in Russia meaning "emperor" (sometimes spelled *tsar*)
edict	proclamation or order by an authority
expelled	sent away
fleet	group of warships
heir	person who inherits a title
institution	organization
isolationism	nation's policy to stay out of economic or political relationships with other nations
murals	paintings made directly on a wall
natives	people who were born and lived in an area before other people arrived
plantations	large farms in warm climates; often associated with slave labor
reform	improve
tolerated	permitted, allowed (especially with regard to religious practice)
tropical	very hot and humid, as in the areas of the world near the equator
woodcuts and engravings	art works made by cutting a design onto a surface (usually metal or wood), applying ink or paint to the surface, and then pressing the surface on paper or fabric to print the design

What Your Child Needs to Know

You may choose to use the following text in several different ways, depending on your child's strengths and preferences. You might read the passage aloud; you might read it to yourself and then paraphrase it for your child; or you might ask your child to read the material along with you or on his or her own.

AFRICA

Africa in the sixteenth century saw the flowering of the Songhai Empire, which dominated old Mali (see Chapter 7), and the kingdom of **Benin** (buh NEEN) along the Niger River. Islam, the Muslim religion, was gaining followers in Africa, especially in the north and west, but people over most of the continent continued to practice their traditional religions. European explorers, especially from Portugal, became attracted to Africa.

The Songhai Empire

By the year 1500, the most powerful empire in Africa was the Songhai Empire. The Songhai emperor was **Askia** (AHS kyuh) **Muhammad,** a good ruler. A Muslim himself, he practiced religious freedom, allowing the older African religions to exist alongside Islam. Askia Muhammad had several new ideas that made his empire even more powerful than Mali had been. He divided his empire into provinces and appointed a loyal governor to rule each province. He kept a full-time professional army and a police force. He created a tax system. Askia Muhammad respected education. Among his most important assistants were **griots** (GREE-ohs), or storytellers, who taught people about the past. He supported a library and a large university in Timbuktu.

Many thousands of people lived in the city of Timbuktu, a center of culture and learning, as well as an important marketplace where the Songhai traded gold from their mines with the Arabs and the Portuguese.

In 1528, Askia Muhammad's son took over the empire. He was not as good a ruler as his father, and those who followed him were worse. In 1591, an army from Morocco, in North Africa, invaded the Songhai Empire. The Moroccans had guns, which the Songhai had never seen. They defeated the Songhai, bringing their empire to an end.

Benin

By the middle of the sixteenth century, the powerful kingdom of Benin had grown up in the West African rain forest where Nigeria is now. Benin's great capital city, also called Benin, had wide streets, well-built houses, and a majestic palace. Merchants traded cotton cloth, pepper, and animal skins for copper, clothing, and other goods from North Africa. Benin craftsmen made beautiful sculptures out of brass and bronze.

Unlike the Songhais, the people of Benin kept their old religion and did not accept Muslim ideas. In other ways, Benin and the Songhai Empire were similar. Benin, too, had a strong government, governors who were loyal to the king, a system of laws, and police to enforce them.

Other Parts of Africa

There were other great kingdoms and cities in Africa in the sixteenth century. For example, there was the kingdom of **Kanem-Bornu** (KAHN uhm BOR noo), to the east of Timbuktu, and Zimbabwe, in southeastern Africa. But many people all over the African continent lived in small villages and farmed. Many others wandered, leading their herds of cattle from one grazing place to another. These farmers and herders, even though they did not live in wealthy cities or form powerful empires, achieved much. They governed themselves by complex systems of laws and leadership, they developed advanced farming and herding methods that have been used in other tropical countries, and they devised ways to mine and work with gold.

The Portuguese in Africa

In 1498, the Portuguese explorer Vasco da Gama sailed up the coast of East Africa. His visits were friendly, but less peaceful Portuguese sailors followed him, attacking cities, taking what they wanted, and killing the inhabitants.

Later in the sixteenth century, the Portuguese turned their interest to West Africa. The reason for this interest was the slave trade. Europeans were settling tropical areas of the Americas, growing sugarcane, pineapples, cotton, tobacco, and coffee on huge plantations. Africans knew tropical farming, and, as slaves, they would provide free labor. Slave catchers captured Africans and made them walk miles to the coast to be sold, crammed into ships, and transported to the Americas. Many Africans died crossing the Atlantic, and many more died after they arrived in the "New World." As the slave trade grew, it spread to East Africa, and other European and African nations took part in it.

ASIA

Marco Polo, and perhaps other Europeans, traveled overland to Asia as early as 1271 (see Chapter 6), but only during the 1500s, with better shipbuilding techniques and navigation equipment, did Europeans establish sea trade with Asia. Some Asian leaders eyed nearby lands, continuing the age-old desire to control more and more property.

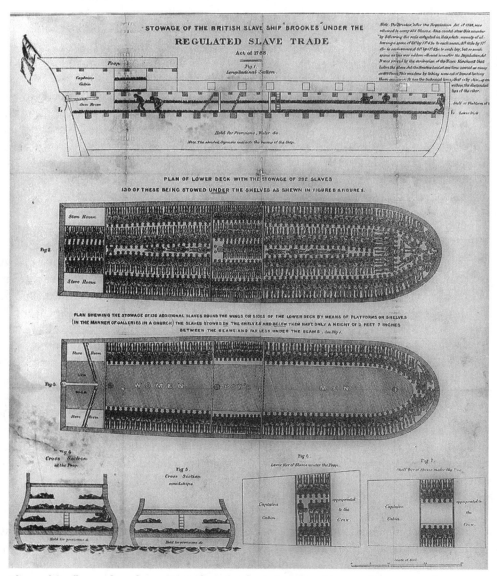

Slave ship floor plan document showing how to crowd in maximum number of slaves

India

In 1500, people in parts of India practiced the Hindu religion, while people in other parts practiced Islam, the Muslim religion. These religious groups clashed. Eventually, a group of Muslims with roots in Turkey, Afghanistan, and Mongolia conquered northern India and established the **Mogul Empire.** Ferocious in battle, the Moguls practiced for war by hunting tigers. (The term *Mogul* comes from the Persian word that means *Mongol*, or person from Mongolia.)

The greatest Mogul leader of this period was **Akbar** (AK buhr), who ruled from 1556 to 1605. Unlike preceding rulers, Akbar tolerated Hindus, did not force them to convert to Islam, stopped the destruction of Hindu temples, and even married a Hindu princess. As a result of Akbar's open-mindedness, Indian culture flourished in the second half of the century.

At the same time, the Portuguese were building up sea trade with India. Then, in 1600, **Queen Elizabeth I** of England allowed English merchants to set up trading posts along the coast of India. This development would mark the beginning of British domination in India for several hundred years.

China

In the 1400s, the Chinese had gone on seafaring missions to trade with India, parts of the Middle East, and Africa. But then around 1500, the Ming emperor of China (see Chapter 7) stopped sending out ships, partly because the Japanese were attacking the coast. Still, foreigners came to China by land and by sea. Portuguese sailors arrived at different ports throughout the century—even though the Chinese expelled Europeans at least once. Then, in midcentury, Moguls from India invaded China, further weakening the country. The late 1500s saw unpopular emperors, as well as famine, heavy taxes, and corruption. All these problems of the sixteenth century would lead to a major change in the ruling class of China in the years ahead.

Japan

Before the 1540s, Japan and Europe knew little of each other. As in preceding centuries, Japan had an emperor, a shogun (military dictator), and samurai (warriors who fought with swords and bows and arrows). Civil wars between great warriors were common, and some purchased firearms from Portuguese traders who arrived by ship in the 1540s. Warriors armed with guns could defeat a much larger force relying on traditional weapons.

In 1585, a general named **Hideyoshi** (*hee* duh YOH shee) came to power. Within a few years, he was ruler of all Japan with plans to rule all of Asia. He failed in that dream, but he succeeded in uniting Japan. Nevertheless, by 1596, the Japanese had come to fear European influence. They ceased to allow Christian missionaries to enter Japan. So began Japan's move toward isolationism once again.

Other Parts of Asia

Just as the Portuguese opened trade with India, China, and Japan, so did they with other parts of Asia—Southeast Asia, the East Indies, the South Pacific, and so on. (All these general names have been given to the area that now includes Myanmar, Thailand, Laos, Cambodia, Vietnam, Malaysia, Indonesia, Singapore, Brunei, and the Philippines.) Spices from this part of the world—cinnamon, cloves, and nutmeg, to name three—would bring the Portuguese great wealth, so they began to establish colonies in order to control as much of the spice trade as possible. Toward the end of the sixteenth century, Spain inherited the Portuguese Empire, including its holdings in Southeast Asia and the Indies.

THE AMERICAS

After Columbus's first voyage to the New World, Europeans set out to search for gold and to colonize the Americas—usually with negative consequences for the natives. First, Spaniards moved in on the **Caribbean** islands. Within twenty years, almost the entire population of Caribbean natives died, either from bad treatment by the Spaniards or from diseases they carried. The Spaniards moved on to cause more damage on the mainland.

Destruction of the Aztec Empire

The Spanish word *conquistador* (kahn kees tah DOR) means "conqueror." A conquistador named

Hernando Cortés (ur NAHN doh kor TEZ) traveled in 1519 from Cuba to the capital of the Aztec Empire, Tenochtitlán in present-day Mexico. There Cortés found magnificent palaces, wide streets, and pyramid temples to many gods. According to legend, the emperor, **Moctezuma** (mok tuh ZOO muh), welcomed Cortés. Later, though, Cortés and his army attacked Moctezuma. Using horses and guns—both unknown to the Aztec—Cortés destroyed the capital, killed Moctezuma and many warriors, and became governor of the region, rich in gold and silver.

Destruction of the Inca Empire

About a dozen years later, farther south, in what is present-day Peru, Spaniards in search of treasure again destroyed an empire. The conquistador was **Francisco Pizarro,** and the target was the Inca, who had built an empire along the Andes Mountains, connecting cities with impressive stone-covered roads. On one of these roads, Pizarro attacked—with horses and with soldiers wearing armor. The Spaniards killed the whole Inca party they came across and then tricked the new emperor into giving up a fortune in gold before they killed him. This raid in the early 1530s was the beginning of the end of the Inca empire.

Spanish Settlers

The Spaniards sent colonists to their territories in the Americas, which they called the Viceroyalty of New Spain and the Viceroyalty of Peru. Under a system called *encomienda,* the Spaniards took land from the Indians and gave it, along with the Indians themselves, to the settlers. The settlers were supposed to care for the Indians in exchange for their work, but the Spaniards usually mistreated the Indians—overworking them as they mined for gold and silver, constructed buildings, farmed, and tended cattle. Disease, murder, and mistreatment of the Indians of Mexico during the sixteenth century reduced the native population from 25 million to 1 million. Spanish missionaries came to the New World in the 1500s to protect the Indians from the colonists, but they destroyed local temples and idols while converting the natives to Catholicism.

In addition to Spain, other European powers that sent expeditions to Mexico and South America in the sixteenth century included Portugal, Florence, and Germany.

North America in the Sixteenth Century

In 1500, there were about 6 million Native Americans in what is now the United States and Canada. They lived differently from region to region. For example, the people of the **Iroquois** (IR uh kwoi) Confederation in what is now the Northeast farmed and used poles and bark to build homes called longhouses, which several families shared; the **Cheyenne** (shye AN) and **Pawnee** had a nomadic, or wandering, lifestyle on the Plains, hunting buffalo, gathering wild foods, and living in tents called tipis; the **Navajo** (NAH vuh hoh) and **Hopi** (HOH pee) lived in villages called pueblos, irrigated the land, grew crops, and raised sheep; in the subarctic region, the **Chippewa** (CHI puh waw) built homes called wigwams by bending branches and covering the structures with bark or skin to keep out the cold.

These and other North American tribes would eventually suffer at the hands of Europeans, who made inroads on the continent in the 1500s. Spaniards, moving north from Central America, came upon California in the 1540s, and by 1598, they had established missions in the Southwest and West. Earlier, in 1535, **Jacques Cartier** (kahr tee AY), under the French flag, explored parts of Canada and claimed the area for the French. In 1572, the navigator **Francis Drake** attacked Spanish ports in North America and by 1579 claimed California for England. In 1583, the English established their first colony in the Americas—in **Newfoundland.**

THE MIDDLE EAST

During much of the 1500s in the Middle East, two great powers—the Ottoman Empire and the Persian Empire—were in conflict. The Ottoman Empire included the lands around the Black Sea that are now Turkey and Iraq, as well as parts of Hungary and Egypt. The Persian Empire bordered the Ottoman Empire on the east. It included Persia (now Iran) and most of Mesopotamia, including parts of present-day Iraq. Both empires were ruled by dictators who, though warlike, supported culture and the arts.

The Ottoman Empire

By the end of the fifteenth century, the Ottoman Empire had become an important power in the Mediterranean. It reached its height under the rule of the sultan **Süleyman I** (SOO lay *mahn*), who reigned from 1520 to 1566. Under Süleyman, the Ottoman Empire became one of the most powerful empires in the world, spreading over parts of three continents—Europe, Asia, and Africa. The empire's capital city was Istanbul in Turkey, which Süleyman turned into a great Muslim city—an international trade center and a great cultural center. By the middle 1500s, the population of Istanbul was almost half a million.

In the Ottoman Empire, the sultan was an absolute dictator. Besides the chief religious leader, all those who worked for the sultan, including soldiers and political advisors, were slaves. When Süleyman died, his son became sultan. He was not as strong a leader as his father had been.

European powers were afraid that the Ottoman Empire would overrun Europe. They fought with the Turks (another name for Ottomans) for control of important trading routes and cities, but the Turks retained control of most of the Mediterranean.

Persia

Persia, now called Iran, had been controlled by the Mongols since the thirteenth century. Then, in 1501, **Shah Ismail,** ruler of the **Safavids** (sah FAH weedz), a group of **Shi'ite** (SHEE *ite*) **Muslims** in northwest Persia, conquered the Persian city of **Tabriz** (tuh BREEZ). By 1508, the Safavids controlled all of Persia and most of Mesopotamia, including parts of Iraq. They made Tabriz their capital and converted the people to their religion, **Shi'ism** (SHEE *i* zuhm).

Both the Ottomans and the Safavids were Muslims, but the Ottomans were **Sunni** (SOO *nee*) **Muslims,** not Shi'ites like the Safavids. Religious wars between the two continued through most of the 1500s. **Shah Abbas the Great,** whose rule began in 1587, finally drove the Turks from Persia. Shah Abbas moved the capital from Tabriz to **Isfahan** (*is* fuh HAHN), which became one of the world's finest cities, with a magnificent palace, a mosque, and a covered marketplace around a main square. Shah Abbas was known for his cruelty, but he succeeded in making peace with the Ottomans.

EUROPE

Russia

When **Ivan IV,** at age seventeen, became the first czar of Russia in 1547, Russia began to come out of isolation by trading with Europe and trying to expand. Ivan conquered territory south of **Moscow** but lost other territory to Poland and Sweden. Finally, just before he died in 1584, Ivan conquered western Siberia.

Ivan IV's nickname, Ivan the Terrible, sums up his ruling style: he terrorized everyone. In a fit of anger in 1581, Ivan killed his son and heir. So after Ivan IV's death, his mentally unstable son took over. His reign led to civil war and then, in 1613, to the beginning of the long-lasting Romanov dynasty.

The High Renaissance

The European nations that sent ships to Asia and the Americas in the 1500s were experiencing major movements in religion, politics, the arts, and sciences at home. Because art and literature reached such heights in Europe, especially in Italy, during the 1500s, this period in European history is known as the High Renaissance. In the High Renaissance, as in the earlier Renaissance (see Chapter 7), Europeans read and studied extensively, kindling an interest in writers, artists, and thinkers from ancient Greece, Rome, and Arabia.

Religion

By 1500, the Roman Catholic Church was the most powerful institution in Europe. The pope claimed authority over all the rulers of Europe and taxed all the people. But people were beginning to speak out against the Church. A German priest named **Martin Luther** did not approve of the wealthy lifestyles of some popes and bishops. Nor did he think it was right for the Church to excuse people from sin in exchange for money. In 1517, Luther nailed a document called the **Ninety-five Theses** to a church door in **Wittenberg.** (Here, *theses* means "complaints," "arguments," or "proposals for change.")

The Catholic Church put Luther on trial, found him guilty of **heresy** (speaking against the Church), and excommunicated, or cut him off, from the Church. Luther set up the **Lutheran Church,** which did not recognize the pope as its leader. Luther translated the Latin Bible into German so that common people could read it for themselves rather than rely on what Catholic priests said the Bible meant. Because Luther set out to <u>reform</u> the Catholic Church, this period in European history is called the **Reformation.**

Very quickly, the news of the Reformation reached people all over Europe, and soon other **Protestant** churches—churches that *protested* practices of the Catholic Church—were established.

Over the course of the century, many people in Germany, Scandinavia, and Switzerland became Protestant. Most, but not all, the people in Spain, Italy, and France remained Catholic. In England, **King Henry VIII** became angry that the pope demanded so much land and money from him. The pope angered Henry further by refusing to let him divorce his wife so that he could take another who might give him a male heir—a son to become king after him. In 1534, Henry broke with the Catholic Church and made himself head of a Protestant church that became known as the **Church of England,** or the **Anglican Church.**

Then the Catholic Church, in an attempt to keep its members and find new ones, started its own movement, the **Counter-Reformation.** The Counter-Reformation sent missionaries to convert people in other countries to Catholicism and made the church service easier to understand by using European languages rather than Latin. In Spain, Roman Catholic leaders went so far as to suppress, or put down, other religions. A court called the **Inquisition** tortured and killed Protestants, Muslims, and Jews for heresy. Today, Roman Catholics condemn the Inquisition as cruel and unjust.

Politics

The Holy Roman Empire was a collection of states in western and central Europe that had been brought together in A.D. 800 under Charlemagne (see Chapter 5). At the beginning of the sixteenth century, **Holy Roman Emperor Charles V** held more land in Europe than anyone else. Charles was from the Austrian **Habsburg** family, which had long controlled the Holy Roman Empire. But Charles realized that his empire was breaking up because of religious and other rivalries.

Indeed, the real power in sixteenth-century Europe was held not by the emperor but by rulers of individual cities, provinces, and countries. The period saw civil wars and endless conflicts between countries. For example, in France, civil war between Catholics and Protestants began in 1562. On one day in 1572—which came to be known as the **St. Bartholomew's Day Massacre**—three thousand French Protestants were killed in Paris, plus more in the rest of France. Only in 1598, when **Henry IV of France** issued the <u>Edict</u> of **Nantes** (NANTS), granting religious freedom to the Protestants, was there peace for a while.

One of the most famous conflicts between European nations occurred in 1588, when **King Philip II of Spain** set out to punish England for attacks on Spanish ships and to force England to be a Catholic country again. However, Queen Elizabeth I of England surprised the Spaniards. With fewer but faster ships, England defeated the Spanish <u>fleet</u>, known as the *Armada.*

Another example of sixteenth-century European rivalry involved Spain and the Dutch—the people of the Netherlands, a Spanish possession. When Philip II became king of Spain, the Dutch started a fight for independence and for the right to be Protestant. Even though Spain and the Netherlands reached a truce in 1609, it would still be many years before Spain recognized Dutch independence.

Additional wars shook Europe between 1557 and 1582, as Russia, Poland, Sweden, and Denmark took up arms.

Niccolò Machiavelli (*mah* kee uh VEH lee) wrote a book called *The Prince,* which described how a state should be governed. Machiavelli stressed that a leader should govern not on fixed rules but as present circumstances and practicality dictated. In other words, according to Machiavelli, it was more important for a ruler to be successful than right. Many see his work as the foundation of modern political thought.

Arts

During the Renaissance, people talked about certain European artists as creative geniuses, inspired by a divine, or godly, spirit. They were referring, for example, to **Leonardo da Vinci,** (*lee* uh NAR *doh* duh VIN chee) who painted the *Mona Lisa* (1503–1505), with its famous, mysterious smile; to **Michelangelo** (*mih* kuh LAN juh *loh*), whose brilliant religious paintings can still be seen on the ceiling of the **Sistine** (SIS teen) **Chapel** (1508–1512) in Rome; and to **Raphael** (RAH fee uhl), whose <u>murals</u> of the early 1500s captured both religious subjects and classical subjects from Greek and Roman myths.

Michelangelo also gained fame for his sculpture and architecture, inspired by classical styles of ancient Greece in the fifth century B.C. Examples are his famous statue of David (1501–1504) from the Bible and his plans for **St. Peter's Basilica** in Rome.

In northern Europe, the German **Albrecht Dürer** (DUR uhr) made detailed <u>woodcuts and engravings</u>, and the paintings of the Dutchman **Pieter Brueghel** (BROO guhl) **the Elder** went beyond religious subjects to show everyday life as in *The Return of the Hunters* (1565).

William Shakespeare was the greatest writer of the High Renaissance, sometimes called in England the **Elizabethan Age** (for the powerful Queen Elizabeth I). His poetry and plays, such as *Romeo and Juliet* and *Hamlet,* draw immense audiences to this day. Many call Shakespeare's writings the greatest in the English language.

Sciences

In the sixteenth century, invention was slowing down in Asia and in the Middle East, but European thinkers produced a long list of new theories and products; for example, they created the first successful watch, wrote the first book on surgery, traced the circulation of blood and accurately described human anatomy, constructed the first microscope, and thought about concepts such as magnetism and electricity. The Polish astronomer **Nicolaus Copernicus** (koh PUHR ni kuhs) introduced the notion that Earth is not the center of the universe but, rather, revolves around the sun.

The scientists of the High Renaissance laid the foundation for the world we live in today.

Perhaps the individual who best represents the Renaissance man was Leonardo da Vinci. In addition to his accomplishments as a painter, da Vinci was a scientist who studied a wide range of subjects—botany, engineering, zoology, anatomy, air flight.

! Implications

> To answer the question, "Why does all this matter?" or "What does it mean?," share the following insights with your child.

Scholars debate the reasons that the study of science and other fields began to decline in Arab countries at about this time. But they agree that Europe became the place where scientists and artists started asking, "How?" and "Why?"

Indeed, the spirit of the High Renaissance celebrated knowledge and exploration. Europeans wanted to discover the world beyond their shores, and advances in technology allowed them to travel by sea to Africa, Asia, and the Americas. Their motives, however, were not always noble.

Europeans explored in order to gain wealth and power. Spanish conquistadores looking for riches conquered and destroyed great civilizations of Latin America. (*Latin America* is an umbrella name for Mexico, Central America, the West Indies, and South America.) Later, Spain and England established colonies in North America, also with devastating effects on the native peoples. The Portuguese were the first to open trade with India, China, Japan, other parts of Asia, and East Africa, but they also established another kind of trade in West Africa—the slave trade, which supplied the new colonies in the Americas with the cheap labor they needed.

The sixteenth century, then, must be viewed as a complex period of history during which hunger for knowledge in part of the world fueled the urge to explore, which in turn brought out less lofty traits—greed and the inhumane disregard for human rights.

Fact Checker

To check that your child knows or can find the basic facts in this chapter, here is a fill-in-the-blanks activity using facts about the 1500s.

1. The center of culture and learning in the Songhai Empire was _____.
2. The capital city of the kingdom of Benin was called _____.
3. The Portuguese explorer who visited the coast of East Africa in 1498 was _____.
4. Akbar was a great leader of the _____ Empire.
5. The country that opened trade with Japan in the sixteenth century was _____.
6. The Aztecs were conquered by the Spanish conquistador _____.
7. The _____ Empire reached its height under Sultan Süleyman I.
8. The movement to change certain practices of the Roman Catholic Church was called the _____.
9. The sixteenth century in Europe is called the High _____.
10. Leonardo _____ is the artist who painted the *Mona Lisa*.

Answers appear in the back, preceding the index.

The Big Questions

The following questions encourage your child to think critically rather than simply recall facts. If necessary, review the specific information from the preceding pages that will help your child make the necessary inferences to come up with reasonable answers.

1. What important historical role did the Portuguese play in the sixteenth century?
2. Identify at least two examples of religious conflict in the sixteenth century, and explain what happened as a result of these conflicts.
3. How would you describe the High Renaissance in Europe in terms of culture, religion, and exploration?

Suggested Answers

1. *The Portuguese opened trade with Africa and Asia and started the slave trade between Africa and the Americas.*

2. *Conflict between Hindus and Muslims in India led to the conquest of northern India and the establishment of the second Mogul Empire. Conflict between the Sunni Muslims of the Ottoman Empire and the Safavids, who were Shi'ite Muslim, led to war between the two. Conflict in Europe between the Roman Catholic Church and Protestants led to the Counter-Reformation; the Catholic Church sent missionaries to convert people in other countries to Catholicism and also established the Inquisition to suppress other religious beliefs.*

3. *Culture: Art and learning were highly valued. Religion: The Roman Catholic Church was in conflict with the new Protestant church; missionaries tried to spread Christianity to other parts of the world. Exploration: The spirit of exploration and the desire for riches and power motivated Europeans to travel to and conquer other parts of the world.*

Skills Practice

The following activities give your child practice in applying the skills basic to social studies. For some of the activities, your child may need to review the information in the preceding pages.

A. PUTTING EVENTS IN SEQUENTIAL ORDER

Ask your child to fill in the correct date for each of the following events and then put the events in the order in which they happened. To do this, he or she will probably have to look back at the timeline at the beginning of this chapter or into the "What Your Child Needs to Know" section. This activity will help your child put the information in this chapter in a global context.

DATE

1. _____ Three thousand French Protestants are killed in Paris in the St. Bartholomew's Day Massacre.
2. _____ Queen Elizabeth I of England allows English merchants to set up trading posts along the coast of India.
3. _____ Martin Luther nails the Ninety-five Theses to a church door in Wittenberg.
4. _____ King Henry VIII breaks with the Catholic Church and establishes the Church of England.
5. _____ English establish their first colony in the Americas.
6. _____ Cortés travels from Cuba to the capital of the Aztec Empire.
7. _____ Portuguese explorer Vasco da Gama sails up the coast of East Africa.
8. _____ Shah Abbas the Great drives the Turks from Persia.
9. _____ Henry IV of France issues the Edict of Nantes, granting religious freedom to Protestants.

Answers

1. <u>1498</u> Portuguese explorer Vasco da Gama sails up the coast of East Africa.
2. <u>1517</u> Martin Luther nails the Ninety-five Theses to a church door in Wittenberg.
3. <u>1519</u> Cortés travels from Cuba to the capital of the Aztec Empire.
4. <u>1534</u> King Henry VIII breaks with the Catholic Church and establishes the Church of England.
5. <u>1572</u> Three thousand French Protestants are killed in Paris in the St. Bartholomew's Day Massacre.
6. <u>1583</u> English establish their first colony in the Americas.
7. <u>1587</u> Shah Abbas the Great drives the Turks from Persia.
8. <u>1598</u> Henry IV of France issues the Edict of Nantes, granting religious freedom to Protestants.
9. <u>1600</u> Queen Elizabeth I of England allows English merchants to set up trading posts along the coast of India.

Evaluating Your Child's Skills: In order to complete this activity successfully, your child needs to use important reading skills that involve skimming text for a specific type of information. If your child has trouble, suggest that he or she visualize key words (for example, *Henry IV* or *Church of England*) to find in the text. Then suggest skimming the text surrounding the key word for a date. You might also suggest that using boldface subheads is a good way to locate information quickly.

B. COMPARING AND CONTRASTING

Make sure your child understands that *comparing* means finding similarities, or likenesses, between two things or ideas and *contrasting* means finding differences. Then have him or her answer the following questions. (Note: You might also explain to your child that the word *compare* in everyday conversation often means "show both similarities and differences.")

1. Compare the Songhai Empire and the kingdom of Benin in three ways.
2. Contrast the Mogul leader Akbar with his predecessors.
3. Compare the conquistadores Pizarro and Cortés in two ways.
4. Compare the Protestant and the Roman Catholic religions.

Answers

1. *They both had great cities; they were both centers for trade; they both had strong governments.*
2. *Akbar allowed the Hindus to have freedom of religion.*
3. *They both came to South America in search of gold; they both destroyed the cultures they found there.*
4. *They are both Christian religions.*

Evaluating Your Child's Skills: **In order to complete this activity successfully, your child needs to understand what he or she has read well enough to find meaning that may not be directly stated in the text. For example, the text does not directly state that Cortés and Pizarro were alike, but it gives similar information about both men. If your child has trouble, suggest that he or she go back to the "What Your Child Needs to Know" section, use the boldface heads and subheads to locate the needed information, and then look for key words that often signal the reader that a comparison or contrast is being made (such as *like, unlike, again, both,* and *but*).**

 # Top of the Class

Children interested in delving more deeply into the topics covered in this chapter can choose one or more of the following activities. They may do the activities for their own satisfaction or report on what they have done to show that they have been seriously considering the events and ideas that developed during the sixteenth century.

A POINT TO PONDER

Suggest to your child that he or she raise the following issue in class.

The sixteenth century was an age of exploration. Europeans ventured across the seas to lands they never knew existed. They opened trade with countries in Africa and Asia. But the urge to explore led to the spread of slavery, one of the world's greatest evils. Our time is an age of exploration, too. In the twentieth and twenty-first centuries, we have ventured across space to investigate places earlier humans never dreamed they could reach. Will explorations of our time have any negative effects on civilization? What might these effects be? What can we do now to prevent them?

BOOKS TO READ AND RECOMMEND IN CLASS

Suggest that your child read one or more of the following books and respond to it by offering an oral or written critique in class.

Halliwell, Sarah, ed. *The Renaissance: Artists and Writers.* Raintree Steck-Vaughn, 1997.

Husain, Sharukh. *What Do We Know about Islam?* Peter Bedrick Books, 1997.

Kendall, Sarita. *The Incas.* Macmillan, 1992.

Libura, Krystyna, et al. *What the Aztecs Told Me.* Douglas & McIntyre, 1997. Based on a sixteenth-century work, this book describes the Aztec people from observation and eyewitness accounts.

Mann, Kenny. *Ghana, Mali, Songhay: The Western Sudan.* Silver Burdett, 1996.

WEB SITES TO EXPLORE

By simply typing in the word *Renaissance,* your child can find a wealth of information about this rich period in European history. Since the amount of material is overwhelming, you may want to work with your child on how to narrow down a Web search to find material that will address his or her specific interests. Your child can view works of Renaissance art by going to the following two Web sites.

For the Uffizi Gallery, the Web address is www.arca.net/uffizi.

For the Louvre Museum, the Web address is mistral.culture.fr/louvre/louvrea.htm.

CHAPTER 9
Trade and Colonization
1600–1750

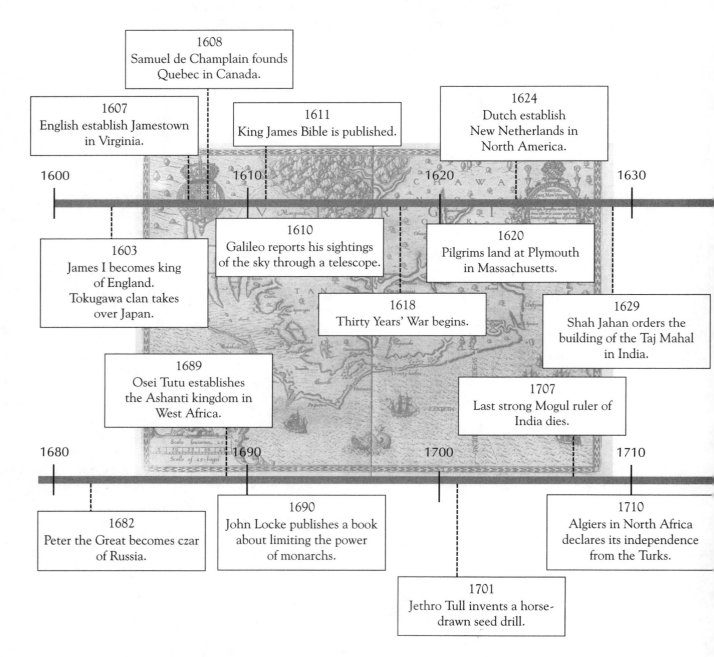

1608
Samuel de Champlain founds Quebec in Canada.

1607
English establish Jamestown in Virginia.

1611
King James Bible is published.

1624
Dutch establish New Netherlands in North America.

1600   1610   1620   1630

1603
James I becomes king of England. Tokugawa clan takes over Japan.

1610
Galileo reports his sightings of the sky through a telescope.

1620
Pilgrims land at Plymouth in Massachusetts.

1618
Thirty Years' War begins.

1629
Shah Jahan orders the building of the Taj Mahal in India.

1689
Osei Tutu establishes the Ashanti kingdom in West Africa.

1707
Last strong Mogul ruler of India dies.

1680   1690   1700   1710

1682
Peter the Great becomes czar of Russia.

1690
John Locke publishes a book about limiting the power of monarchs.

1710
Algiers in North Africa declares its independence from the Turks.

1701
Jethro Tull invents a horse-drawn seed drill.

This timeline provides an overview of the cultural and political developments between approximately 1600 and 1750. Then a narrative describes this period in greater detail and discusses its significance.

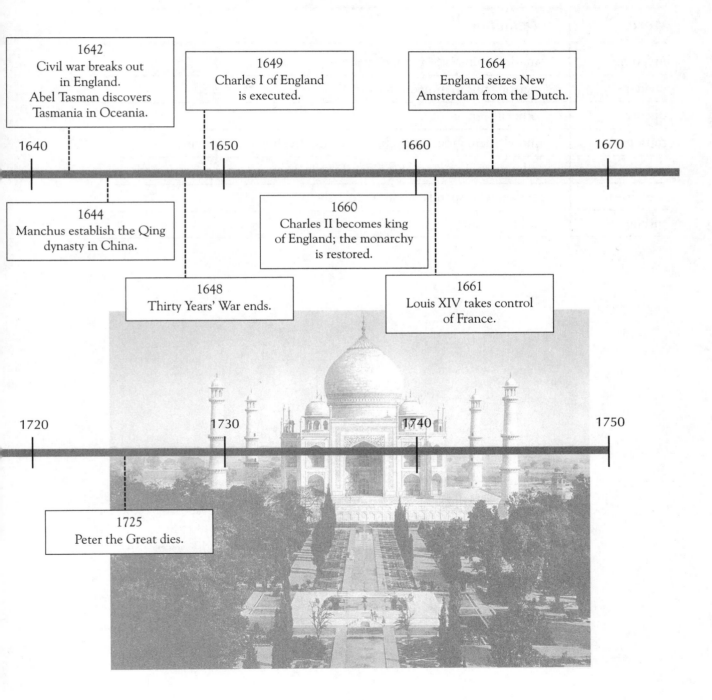

1642
Civil war breaks out in England.
Abel Tasman discovers Tasmania in Oceania.

1649
Charles I of England is executed.

1664
England seizes New Amsterdam from the Dutch.

1640

1650

1660

1670

1644
Manchus establish the Qing dynasty in China.

1660
Charles II becomes king of England; the monarchy is restored.

1648
Thirty Years' War ends.

1661
Louis XIV takes control of France.

1720

1730

1740

1750

1725
Peter the Great dies.

Word Power

The words on the following chart are underscored in the section called "What Your Child Needs to Know." Explain their meanings to your child as needed when they come up in reading or discussion. Keep the list handy for you and your child to use.

Word	Definition
breeding	mating animals to produce young
civilians	persons not in armed forces
dissolved	officially ended
ransom	money demanded in exchange for the freeing of a captive
rotate	take turns doing or using something in a set order that is repeated
spendthrift	person who spends money carelessly
turbulent	wild, violent

What Your Child Needs to Know

You may choose to use the following text in several different ways, depending on your child's strengths and preferences. You might read the passage aloud; you might read it to yourself and then paraphrase it for your child; or you might ask your child to read the material along with you or on his or her own.

EUROPE

The 1600s were a turbulent time in most of Europe. Before European countries would be ready to dominate North America, they would have to fight among themselves and ask themselves the question, How powerful should a king be?

The Thirty Years' War

From 1618 on, the Thirty Years' War in Europe pitted countries and parts of countries against one another, sometimes over religious differences between Catholics and Protestants and sometimes over land. In 1648, the war ended with the **Peace of Westphalia,** which would influence the future of Europe for a very long time. According to the treaty, Catholic lands remained Catholic, and some Protestant states, such as Switzerland and the Netherlands, became independent; the Holy Roman Empire lost much of its power; France emerged as the main power on the continent; and Germany split into three hundred small states. This last result led to economic decline and a general negative and fearful mood.

The Thirty Years' War was different from wars of the past. More deadly firearms and cannon created greater devastation. Many civilians lost their lives. In this sense, it was the world's first modern war.

The Netherlands

With its newly won independence from the Habsburg empire and with profit from trade in the New World, the Netherlands became an exciting place. Scientists worked on problems ranging from light waves to the structure of blood. Artists such as **Rembrandt** and **Vermeer** attracted a lot of attention with their emphasis on indoor scenes of everyday life.

France

France was strong before the Thirty Years' War and even stronger after it. In 1661, at age twenty-two, French king **Louis XIV** took control of the country from his ministers. Louis, referred to as the Sun King, made himself the absolute monarch of France. He built a magnificent palace near Paris called **Versailles** (*vuhr* SYE), which took forty-seven years to complete. French nobles lived at Versailles, where Louis could keep an eye on them, rather than on their own estates.

Louis made France the greatest power in Europe. Late in his reign, however, he got involved in long and costly warfare. When he died in 1715, Louis left France a nation deep in debt.

England

England was not involved in the Thirty Years' War, but it had troubles of its own.

When Queen Elizabeth I died in 1603, she left no heir. She was succeeded by the king of Scotland, James VI. He became England's **James I.** James was not a popular king. The English resented him for being a foreigner, a Catholic, and a spendthrift who taxed his subjects too much. His son, **Charles I,** was not popular either.

When Parliament refused to give Charles I money, he dissolved it for eleven years. In 1642, two years after Parliament became active again, Charles tried to have five parliamentary leaders arrested. Parliament refused to arrest them. The king left London and raised an army for a civil war. The king's supporters were known as **Cavaliers;** those of Parliament, **Roundheads.** The latter, under Parliament leader **Oliver Cromwell,** crushed the king's forces in 1645. Eventually, Parliament captured, tried, and executed the king.

In 1649, Parliament abolished the monarchy. As Lord Protector, Oliver Cromwell ruled as a dictator until his death in 1658. The army ran the country for a time, but the people wanted a king again. Charles I's son, who had been in exile, returned to England and became **Charles II** in 1660. However, Parliament strictly limited Charles's power.

Russia

After Ivan IV (see Chapter 8), Russia existed in isolation from Europe until **Peter I** became czar in 1682 (he would earn the title **Peter the Great**). Peter was an energetic ruler who wanted to make Russia a modern country similar to other countries in western Europe. In 1697, he began a tour of western Europe. He disguised himself as an ordinary person to see how people lived and worked there. He returned to Russia eighteen months later with western European craftspeople and technicians to teach their skills to Russians.

Peter created the first Russian navy, built roads and canals, and founded his new capital, **St. Petersburg,** in western Russia. He called the city his "window on Europe." After Peter died in 1725, his wife and daughter ruled Russia and followed his policies.

The Age of Reason in Europe

During the Renaissance (Chapters 7 and 8), people in Europe found themselves questioning the world around them more than people there had for centuries. By the 1600s, questioning, doubting, and general curiosity were even more widespread.

Beyond the scientific work that was going on during this period in the energetic Netherlands, scientists were hard at work all over Europe. They were enthusiastically observing the world for themselves rather than relying on ideas handed down by tradition.

One of the earliest of these scientists was the Italian named **Galileo** (*gah* luh LEE oh). In 1610, he wrote about his observations of the sky through a telescope. He saw for himself that Copernicus (Chapter 8) had been correct in figuring out that planets move around the sun rather than vice versa.

Toward the end of the century, **Isaac Newton,** an English scientist, proved that the world works according to mathematical laws. He was able to show, for example, that planets follow a precise path and speed. He also observed and wrote about the strength of gravity, or the pull between two objects.

Work such as Galileo's and Newton's was possible because humans at the time had the confidence and the brainpower to figure things out for themselves. They had faith in their ability to reason. Logically enough, then, people in Europe started attaching the label *Age of Reason* to the seventeenth century; the age would go on for quite a while.

On a very practical level, the Age of Reason led to developments that affected day-to-day life. Agriculture, for example, saw advances. In England in 1701, a farmer named **Jethro Tull** created a horse-drawn seed drill that would create straight rows and reduce weeding. Farmers also began to <u>rotate</u> crops. This approach to planting kept the soil productive for many years. Scientific <u>breeding</u> of animals improved livestock. Farmers enclosed farms to increase productivity. All these improvements helped the large-scale farmer but not the small farmer. In fact, many small farmers gave up the land and moved to towns and cities to find new jobs.

New ideas were popping up in other spheres, too. For example, in thinking about politics, the English philosopher **John Locke** suggested that those who governed did *not* have power by **divine right**—that is, by word of God. Rather, he thought, those at the head of a government should hold power only if they have a contract with the people they govern. In spite of (or maybe because of) Louis XIV's actions in France, the political thinking by Locke and others would begin to warm people up to the idea of democracy.

THE MIDDLE EAST

The Ottoman Empire, in the meantime, got bigger before it would get smaller. In the first half of the seventeenth century, under **Murad IV,** the Ottomans captured Baghdad. In the 1660s, the Ottomans beat strong navies and captured land in the Ukraine, Poland, and Crete. Their greatest accomplishment of these years was instilling fear in Europeans.

However, by 1683, the Ottomans suffered a defeat when they tried to conquer the Austrian city of Vienna. From that point on, the Turks would never again be a threat to Europe. Their empire, however, would continue to survive for another 240 years.

THE AMERICAS

The Dutch, English, and French joined the Spanish and Portuguese in the New World. Native Americans began to see the Europeans more as foes than as friends.

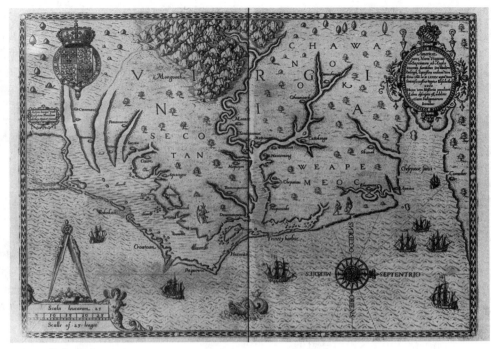

Map of Virginia, 1585

Spanish and Portuguese Colonies

The conquistadors lost their power in New Spain to governors called **viceroys,** who were the king's representatives in New Spain. In 1717, Spain's holdings in the New World expanded to include present-day Panama, Colombia, Ecuador, and Venezuela.

The discovery of gold and diamonds in east central Brazil in the late 1600s and early 1700s brought many more settlers into that Portuguese colony.

The Dutch West India Company

In 1621, the Dutch founded in the Caribbean the trading outfit known as the West India Company. Within two years, eight hundred Dutch ships plied the Caribbean in the sugar, tobacco, and slave trades. Farther north, the company founded the colony of **New Netherlands** along the Hudson River in 1624. From here, the Dutch took back to Europe fur and timber that they traded with Native Americans.

The English Colonies

Jamestown, the first successful English colony in America, was founded in 1607 in present-day Vir-

ginia. Many of the first settlers died from disease, hunger, and conflicts with Native Americans. In 1612, settler **John Rolfe** introduced tobacco as a crop, and Jamestown soon prospered by selling tobacco to England. Slaves from Africa were first brought to Jamestown in 1619 to work the large tobacco plantations. Gradually, Virginia and the Carolinas to the south were settled and dominated by large slave-run plantations of tobacco, rice, cotton, and indigo, a plant with berries used to make dye.

Many of the early southern settlers were well-to-do. The people who settled the New England colonies up north were very different. In 1620, a group of people called **Pilgrims** arrived in New England. They came to America to worship freely. They found life difficult in the wilderness and needed help from friendly Native Americans, who taught them how to grow crops and catch fish.

In 1664, the English seized New Amsterdam, the capital of the Dutch colony of New Netherlands. They accomplished this takeover without firing a shot and renamed the town **New York City.** All told, in New England, the South, and the mid-Atlantic region, the English colonists or their descendants established a total of thirteen colonies.

French Canada

John Cabot, an Italian explorer working for England, first discovered Newfoundland, part of Canada, in 1497. But it wasn't until 1608 that French nobleman **Samuel de Champlain** (duh *sham* PLAYN) founded **Quebec** (kwi BEK) near the St. Lawrence River. By 1663, fur traders, missionaries, and some settlers inhabited New France, and Quebec became its capital.

OCEANIA

For the first time in the 1600s, European explorers reached Oceania. In 1642, Dutch explorer **Abel Tasman** discovered the island later named for him, **Tasmania** (taz MAY nee uh), southeast of the main body of Australia. Tasman also reached the southern island of New Zealand, Tonga, and Fiji. Tasman's voyages were more for trading purposes than for acquiring land. Europe at this point didn't seem interested in establishing colonies so far from home.

In 1644, Tasman visited the northern coast of Australia. The rest of the continent remained untouched. The Aborigines, who had been living in Australia for about 40,000 years, would continue their way of life undisturbed for another 120 years. They related to nature and to their history in ways that would later surprise and impress Europeans, but first the two cultures would clash.

AFRICA

The growing slave trade had a disastrous, crippling effect on African civilization. During the 1700s alone, it is estimated that more than 7 million Africans were sold into slavery and shipped to the Americas to work on Europeans' plantations. Traders also sent slaves to work in North Africa, the Ottoman Empire, and the Arab world.

The Ashanti Empire

In 1689, King **Osei Tutu** (OH say TOO too) founded the Ashanti (uh SHAHN tee) kingdom on the West African coast. The Ashanti traded slaves, gold, and cola nuts with the Europeans for guns. The guns made them the most powerful kingdom in the region.

Ndongo

Not all African leaders supported the slave trade. In 1624, **Queen Nzinga** (en ZHING ah) of Ndongo (en DONG goh) Kingdom in today's Angola refused to sell more slaves to the Portuguese, who needed workers for their sugar plantations in Brazil. The Portuguese drove Nzinga out of Ndongo, but she became queen of neighboring **Matamba.**

Algiers

Algiers (al JIRZ) was a province of the Ottoman Empire on the north coast of Africa. By the late 1600s, Algiers was a haven for pirates who raided European ships and held their passengers for <u>ransom</u>. By 1700, soldiers had largely driven out the pirates and then seized power so that, by 1710, they declared Algiers's independence from the Ottomans and set up their own government.

Cape Town

At the other end of Africa, the **Dutch East India Company** established a trading post called Cape Town in 1652. The post provided supplies to ships passing from Europe to Asia. The Dutch settlers brought slaves from other African lands to work for them and used local people as servants. Relations between the Africans and the Europeans were bad. Soon the white people of Cape Town went farther north to explore more of what someday would be the Republic of South Africa.

ASIA

China and Japan experienced long periods of peace and prosperity during this period, while pursuing policies of isolationism. India experienced its last great period of glory before Europeans began to take control.

China

The last Ming emperor hanged himself during a rebellion in 1644. A chieftain from **Manchuria,** a land north of China, seized Beijing. He made his nephew the first emperor of the **Qing** (TCHING) dynasty. The **Manchus** (MAN chooz) formed an upper class and lived apart from the Chinese but used them to help run their government.

China came to dominate its smaller neighbors, including Burma, Mongolia, Tibet, and Annam (present-day Vietnam). The Emperor **Qianlong** (tchyahn LONG) came to power in 1735 and ruled for sixty years. Qianlong was a great patron of the arts and wrote poetry. Like other Qing emperors, he wanted nothing to do with the "barbarians" of Europe, who were permitted to trade for silk, porcelain, and tea only in one province.

Japan

When the dictator Hideyoshi (see Chapter 8) died, civil war erupted in Japan, with two clans fighting each other for control. When a member of the Tokugawa clan became shogun, establishing the Tokugawa shogunate, he made **Edo** (E doh), then a fishing village, his capital. Today its name is **Tokyo.**

The rulers of Japan feared western influence and further isolated Japan from the rest of the world. They forbade Japanese citizens to travel; did not allow Japanese living outside Japan to return; either expelled or killed foreigners, including Christian missionaries; and even banned the building of large ships for trading.

Most Japanese, however, prospered under the new system of national unity, and there was peace. In 1716, shogun **Yoshimune** (yoh shuh MOO neh) came to power and began to open up Japan to the West. He started economic reforms and allowed new ideas from Europe in science, technology, and medicine to improve Japanese society. Yoshimune retired in 1745.

India

Akbar, the Mogul emperor (see Chapter 8), died in 1605. His grandson **Shah Jahan** (juh HAHN) came to power in 1628 and extended the empire. When his favorite wife died in 1629, he started building a magnificent tomb for her called the **Taj Mahal** (TAHJ muh HAHL). This complex made of white marble took twenty-two years to complete.

Shah's son seized power, imprisoned his father, and reigned until 1707. By that time, the Mogul Empire had weakened. Other countries and tribes began to carve up the empire. Parts of India were invaded and controlled by the Persians, the Afghans, and the French. The British, however, would eventually control nearly all of India.

Implications

To answer the question, "Why does all this matter?" or "What does it mean?," share the following insights with your child.

Taj Mahal

Some of the events in the period from 1600 to 1750, oddly enough, yielded both negative and positive effects. The Thirty Years' War, for example, was horrifically bloody because of new weapons. Still, some good came out of the war. The way it ended led to a more stable Europe with greater religious tolerance.

Another example of an unpleasant event that ultimately led to good is the case of Charles I of England. The civil war he started and his execution were terrible moments in English history, but they did eventually contribute to the development of England as an extremely democratic and stable nation.

The two preceding examples show good coming out of evil. Sometimes the opposite happens. That is, sometimes events that seem to promise positive results wind up bringing unexpected negative consequences. For example, this chapter mentions that better techniques for farming increased the size of farms and helped feed millions of people. Yet when farmers and plantation owners in the Americas applied these techniques, they required a large labor force that was filled by African slaves.

This chapter teaches us that, in studying history and in making our own history, it's not enough to look at the immediate results of an event or action. We must look for long-term developments as well. Only then can we appreciate fully how complicated this world and its inhabitants are.

Fact Checker

To check that your child knows or can find the basic facts in this chapter, here is a matching game for him or her to play.

GEOGRAPHY MATCHING GAME

For each place on the left, find on the right a description that fits it. Use all the descriptions, but do not use any description for more than one place.

Place		Description
1. Netherlands	_____	a. capital established by a tsar
2. Versailles	_____	b. Dutch colony in southern Africa
3. St. Petersburg	_____	c. city captured by Ottomans in the 1600s
4. Baghdad	_____	d. home of painters Rembrandt and Vermeer
5. Jamestown	_____	e. tomb in India
6. Quebec	_____	f. first successful English colony in the Americas
7. Tasmania	_____	g. island off Australia
8. Cape Town	_____	h. Louis XIV's palace near Paris
9. Edo	_____	i. New World city founded by Champlain
10. Taj Mahal	_____	j. village that became Tokyo

Answers appear in the back, preceding the index.

? | *The Big Questions*

The following questions encourage your child to think critically rather than simply recall facts. If necessary, review the specific information from the preceding pages that will help your child make the appropriate inferences to come up with reasonable answers.

1. If you had lived in Europe between 1600 and 1750, would you have wanted to stay there, or would you have tried to get to the Americas? How would you have gone about making your decision?
2. Why did it take 150 years longer for Europeans to find Tasmania, New Zealand, and Australia than for them to "discover" the Americas?
3. This chapter mentions that, in France, the king, Louis XIV, made himself the absolute monarch in the 1660s. At about the same time, what was happening to the power of the king in England?
4. In what way were countries in Africa different from other countries during this period?

5. In China during this period, the emperor referred to Europeans as "barbarians." When else did you hear that term? What generalization can you make about how people use the term?

Answers

1. *Your child may base his or her response on issues such as sense of adventure, economic need, and religious persecution.*
2. *Europeans had been putting their money into looking for a shorter, western route to Asia, a continent that they knew existed. There was no pressing reason for them to think there were lands "down under" and to look for them.*
3. *England was in the process of eliminating the monarchy and then reinstating it with limited powers. Be aware of the difference in attitudes between France and England, but keep in mind that France will undergo a major revolution in the next chapter.*
4. *Many countries were involved in the African slave trade, but only countries in Africa were the source of slaves.*
5. *The term* barbarian *came up in Chapter 4 in a discussion of invaders from the north heading toward the Roman Empire and of invaders bringing trouble to the Han Dynasty in China. People seem to use the term* barbarian *to describe outsiders who hold different values.*

Skills Practice

The following activities give your child practice in applying the skills basic to social studies. For some of the activities, your child may need to review the information in the preceding pages.

A.   COMPARING AND CONTRASTING

This chapter describes the dreams Peter the Great had for Russia. Here is a description of Peter the Great when he was a very young boy in the 1670s. Read the passage to your child, and then ask him or her the question that follows it.

> A doting mother, a proud father and a pleased Matveev [aide to Alexander's father, the emperor] competed to lavish gifts on the child, and Peter's nursery soon overflowed with elaborate models and toys. In one corner stood a carved wooden horse with a leather saddle studded with silver nails and a bridle decorated with emeralds. On a table near the window rested an illuminated picture book, painstakingly made for him by six . . . painters. Music boxes and a small elegant clavichord [musical instrument like a piano] with copper strings were brought from Germany. But Peter's favorite toys and his earliest games were military. He liked to bang on cymbals and drums. Toy soldiers and forts, model pikes [spears], swords, . . . and pistols spread across his tables and chairs and floor. Next to his bed, Peter kept his most precious toy, given to him by Matveev, who had bought it from a foreigner: a model of a boat.
>
> —Robert K. Massie, *Peter the Great: His Life and World* (Knopf, 1980)

QUESTION

Think back to when you were very young. Compare and contrast your childhood toys and games with Alexander's.

POSSIBLE ANSWERS

Similarities and differences may relate to quantity of toys and games, materials that toys and games were made of, who presented the toys, kinds of toys, and favorite toy.

Evaluating Your Child's Skills: **In order to complete this activity successfully, your child needs to understand that** *compare* **means "find similarities or likenesses" between two things or ideas and** *contrast* **means "find differences." (Note: You might also explain to your child that the word** *compare* **in everyday conversation often means "show both similarities and differences.")**

B.   DOING RESEARCH: PLACE NAMES

An important social studies skill is learning where to look to find answers. This activity gives your child a chance to use a few sources of information and to appreciate this country's connection to Europe.

Select three of the following places in the United States, and find out how each got its name: (1) Delaware; (2) Georgia; (3) the Hudson River in New York; (4) Maryland; (5) Plymouth in Massachusetts.

You may find the answers in one or more of the following books (or in a similar electronic source): a regular dictionary, a dictionary of geographical terms, an encyclopedia, a history or geography textbook.

Answers

1. Delaware: *named after Baron De La Warr, the first English colonial governor of Virginia*
2. Georgia: *named after George II, king of England from 1727 to 1760*
3. Hudson River: *named after the Dutch explorer Henry Hudson*
4. Maryland: *named after Queen Henrietta Maria, wife of Charles I, king of England from 1625 to 1649*
5. Plymouth: *named for the seaport in southwest England, from which the* Mayflower *had departed*

Evaluating Your Child's Skills: In order to complete this activity successfully, your child may have to check more than one source. Some, but not all, popular dictionaries and encyclopedias give information about origins of place names. If your child has trouble finding answers, model the role persistence plays in doing research.

 # Top of the Class

Following are a few activities children can do on their own or share in class to show that they have been seriously considering the period from 1600 to 1750.

FASHION AS HISTORY: RESEARCH AND DESCRIPTION

This activity will help your child work with additional research tools and practice verbal skills.

Use books or electronic sources about French history to find examples of clothes worn by Louis XIV, the ladies and gentlemen in his court, and soldiers who fought for him. Then try to describe the fashions you find to someone who cannot look at the visuals that you have found.

BOOKS TO READ AND RECOMMEND IN CLASS

Suggest that your child read an age-appropriate nonfiction book about the African slave trade during this period and respond to it by giving an oral or written critique in class.

Cameron, Ann. *The Kidnapped Prince.* Knopf, 1994. This is a retelling based on a 1789 autobiography by Olaudah Equiano, who was kidnapped at the age of eleven from his home in Benin and forced to work as a slave in England, the United States, and the West Indies. Scenes cover the capture, the conditions on slave ships, the auction, and the forced labor. The introduction is by Henry Louis Gates, Jr.

Haskins, James, and Kathleen Bensen. *Bound for America: The Forced Migration of Africans to the New World.* Lothrop, Lee & Shepard, 1999. This book describes in sharp detail how captives were treated before and during the passage from Africa to the United States. It also deals with slave mutinies (including the *Amistad* revolt).

CHAPTER 10
Industry and Revolution
1750–1850

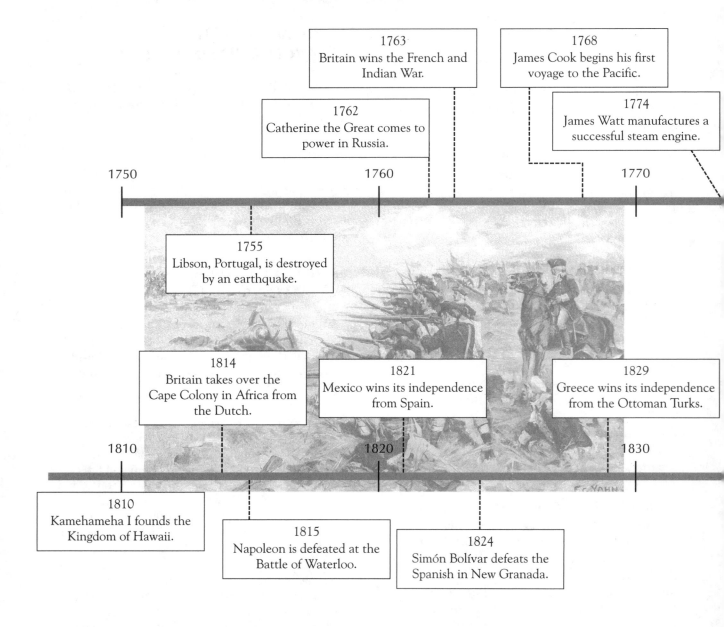

1763
Britain wins the French and Indian War.

1768
James Cook begins his first voyage to the Pacific.

1762
Catherine the Great comes to power in Russia.

1774
James Watt manufactures a successful steam engine.

1750   1760   1770

1755
Libson, Portugal, is destroyed by an earthquake.

1814
Britain takes over the Cape Colony in Africa from the Dutch.

1821
Mexico wins its independence from Spain.

1829
Greece wins its independence from the Ottoman Turks.

1810   1820   1830

1810
Kamehameha I founds the Kingdom of Hawaii.

1815
Napoleon is defeated at the Battle of Waterloo.

1824
Simón Bolívar defeats the Spanish in New Granada.

This timeline provides an overview of the cultural and political developments between, approximately, 1750 and 1850. Then a narrative describes this period in greater detail and discusses its significance.

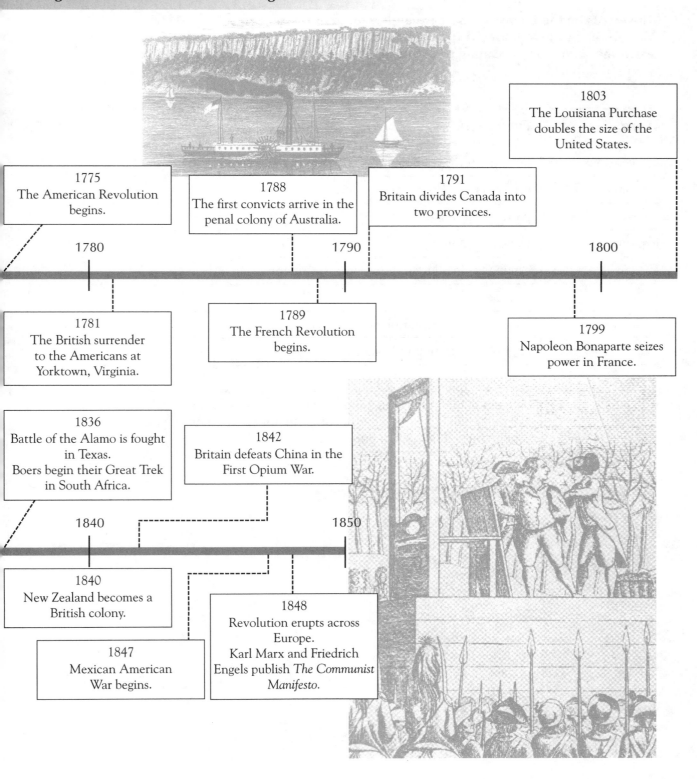

1803
The Louisiana Purchase doubles the size of the United States.

1775
The American Revolution begins.

1788
The first convicts arrive in the penal colony of Australia.

1791
Britain divides Canada into two provinces.

1780

1790

1800

1781
The British surrender to the Americans at Yorktown, Virginia.

1789
The French Revolution begins.

1799
Napoleon Bonaparte seizes power in France.

1836
Battle of the Alamo is fought in Texas.
Boers begin their Great Trek in South Africa.

1842
Britain defeats China in the First Opium War.

1840

1850

1840
New Zealand becomes a British colony.

1848
Revolution erupts across Europe.
Karl Marx and Friedrich Engels publish *The Communist Manifesto*.

1847
Mexican American War begins.

Word Power

The words on the following chart are underscored in the section called "What Your Child Needs to Know." Explain their meanings to your child as needed when they come up in reading or discussion. Keep the list handy for you and your child to use.

Word	*Definition*
convention	large gathering of people for a common purpose
convicts	prisoners found guilty of a crime
course	path of a waterway
exploiting	treating unfairly
faction	group within a larger group or government
fervor	intense feeling
indigenous	native to a particular place
locomotive	engine used to pull railroad cars
penal	used as a place of punishment
woodblock prints	pictures made by carving out a design in a block of wood, applying ink to the carved wood, and pressing the inked wood onto paper or other material to make a print

What Your Child Needs to Know

You may choose to use the following text in several different ways, depending on your child's strengths and preferences. You might read the passage aloud; you might read it to yourself and then paraphrase it for your child; or you might ask your child to read the material along with you or on his or her own.

THE INDUSTRIAL REVOLUTION

Work that produces goods or services on a large scale is called an **industry**. The Industrial Revolution was a revolution based on science, not politics. Even so, the vast changes that the Industrial Revolution brought about led to political and social changes around the world. The middle of the eighteenth century was also a time for great thinkers and the spread of ideas. It was during this time that philosophers such as **Voltaire** (vohl TAIR), John Locke, and **Thomas Paine** were stressing the importance of the individual and were contributing to the spirit of revolution as well. In fact, this period is sometimes referred to as the *Age of Enlightenment.*

New Inventions

Until the 1760s, goods in Europe and elsewhere were made by craftspeople working by hand in their homes. Beginning toward the end of the eighteenth century in Europe, newly invented machines were able to make goods much faster and more cheaply than these craftspeople.

The Industrial Revolution began in Britain for several reasons. British laws protected private property and allowed private enterprise, Britain had avoided the wars that had damaged much of Europe, and Britain had plenty of the coal that was necessary to fuel the new machines.

In 1774, **James Watt** of Scotland manufactured a successful steam engine. Steam power first drove British textile mills and factories. Then the steam engine drove new kinds of transportation. For example, in 1807, the American **Robert Fulton** launched a steamboat on a voyage up the Hudson River in New York. In 1814, **George Stephenson** attached a steam engine to a <u>locomotive</u> and used it to pull wagons along a track. This was the first steam-driven train.

Social Changes

The Industrial Revolution brought about tremendous changes in the way people lived. Cities expanded, as people left villages and farms to work for wages in factories. Traders and merchants grew prosperous from the new industries and formed a

Steamboat

new middle class between the landed, powerful upper class and the working people.

The Industrial Revolution brought new problems, too. Factory workers, including young children, worked long hours, often under terrible conditions. Their families lived in disease-ridden city neighborhoods called **slums.**

Karl Marx and Communism

Some people criticized the industrialization of Europe and sought solutions to the problems it created. Among them was the German philosopher Karl Marx (MARKS). Together with the German writer and revolutionary **Friedrich Engels,** Marx published **The Communist Manifesto** in 1848. This document criticized **capitalism**—an economic system that allows people to own private property and to gain personal wealth from private business. Marx and Engels said that capitalism is bad for society because it allows the owners of businesses and factories to grow wealthy by exploiting the workers. The best system, they said, is one that represents the needs of all the people. Under the form of government they called **communism,** the government, not individuals, would own all businesses. The government would give every person as much as he or she needed to live. As we will see later, in Chapters 12 and 13, communism in practice did not work quite the way Marx and Engels thought it would.

NORTH AMERICA

The Industrial Revolution made colonies in the Americas more important then ever to the nations of Europe because the colonies could supply the raw materials necessary to manufacture goods in European factories and shops. The colonies were also an important market for selling the manufactured goods. Over time, however, the colonists saw their European masters as exploiting them and wanted their independence.

The French and Indian War

By the 1750s, New France extended from Canada to the Great Lakes and along the Mississippi River to the Gulf of Mexico. Britain's thirteen American colonies covered the eastern seaboard of the present-day United States.

In 1754, Britain and France engaged in the last of several wars for dominance in North America. In the French and Indian War, the French and their Native American allies fought against the British. The French won a number of early battles, but in 1759 the British captured Quebec, the capital of New France, and defeated the French. The **Treaty of Paris,** signed in 1763, gave Britain all of Canada and most French possessions east of the Mississippi River. In 1791, Britain proceeded to divide Canada into two provinces: upper Canada became home to English-speaking settlers; lower Canada was home to French-speaking settlers.

The American Revolution

The French and Indian War had been expensive to wage. Britain needed to raise money to pay for the war and the other expenses of running its colonies. The British government decided that the colonies should pay higher taxes to meet these expenses. But many people in America felt that the taxes were unfair because the colonists had no say in them. Furthermore, with the French gone, the colonists felt they no longer needed British soldiers to protect them.

Each new tax imposed by Britain led to American resistance. In April 1775, British soldiers and patriots came to blows in Lexington and Concord, Massachusetts. The American Revolution had begun. Because this revolution was to inspire so many others, the first shot fired at Lexington and Concord is sometimes called "the shot heard round the world."

Only about a third of the colonists were in favor of rebellion, but they included such great leaders as **Benjamin Franklin, Thomas Jefferson,** and **George Washington.** In 1776, Jefferson wrote the **Declaration of Independence,** a document that declared the thirteen colonies "Free and Independent States."

George Washington formed and led the **Continental Army.** Washington's troops were inexperienced compared with the well-trained British soldiers, but the colonists were fighting to defend their homes and families, and they held on. In the end, their determination won out. British troops surrendered to Washington at **Yorktown,** Virginia, in 1781. Two years later, in another **Treaty of Paris,** Great Britain recognized American independence.

Painting of Revolutionary War battle scene

The United States of America

At first, the former colonists governed themselves according to a document called the **Articles of Confederation.** In 1787 a special <u>convention</u> took place in Philadelphia, Pennsylvania, to work out a better plan of government. That plan took the form of the **Constitution of the United States.** The Constitution stated that the new country would have three branches: an **executive** branch (headed by the president); a **legislative,** or law-making, branch (the Senate and the House); and a **judicial,** or court, branch. The Constitution contained a number of **checks and balances** so that no one branch could seize power and turn the new democracy into a dictatorship. In 1791, the **Bill of Rights,** which stated the privileges of individuals, extended the Constitution in the form of ten amendments.

In 1803, France sold its Louisiana Territory to the new nation for $15 million. The Louisiana Territory lay between the Mississippi River and the Rocky Mountains and stretched from the Gulf of Mexico to Canada. The **Louisiana Purchase** more than doubled the size of the United States. When settlers from all over Europe came to the new nation to find a better life, many of them headed to the western territories.

Later, in 1848, gold was discovered in the territory of California. The **California Gold Rush** brought thousands of new settlers and helped make California a state in 1850.

As Americans moved west, they drove out Native Americans who had lived on the land for generations. The **Indian Removal Act** of 1830 forced Native Americans from their lands and moved them to a specially made Indian Territory west of Arkansas. The Indians who resisted removal and fought the settlers died.

FRANCE

Inspired by the example of the American Revolution, the French rebelled against their king. The **French Revolution** ended not in a democratic government but in a military dictatorship. However, out of that eventually came a more just and orderly society.

The French Revolution

By 1750, France had become a nation of extremes. The king and his nobles lived in splendor, while the majority of the French people lived in poverty. When **King Louis XVI** needed money in 1788, he tried to make his subjects pay more taxes. The people refused and formed a new body, the **National Assembly,** to make laws. When the king tried to dismiss the assembly, the people of Paris rose up in rebellion. On July 14, 1789, they stormed the king's prison, the **Bastille** (ba STEEL), freeing the prisoners there, including many popular leaders. The French Revolution had begun.

The king fled Paris, but he was captured, and those who wanted the people to have a say abolished his monarchy. Then in 1793, the people executed Louis XVI and **Queen Marie Antoinette.**

Revolutionary France fell into chaos, as one political <u>faction</u> vied for power against another. Revolutionary leader **Maximilien Robespierre** (rohbz pee EHR) began a **Reign of Terror** in September 1793. Robespierre had anyone who opposed him or the revolution arrested, tried, and executed. During the Reign of Terror, an estimated eighteen thousand people died by the **guillotine** (GIHL uh teen), a machine with a sharp blade that beheaded its victims. The terror finally ended in July 1794, when Robespierre himself was put to death.

Guillotine

Napoleon

In 1795, a group of men called the **Directory** took over the French government. But they were weak rulers, and four years later the brilliant, young general **Napoleon Bonaparte** (BOH nuh PART) seized control of France.

Napoleon was a strong leader who reestablished order in France. Although he made himself a dictator, Napoleon improved the government in many ways. The **Napoleonic Code** consisted of laws that treated all French people equally, whether they were rich or poor. Napoleon also improved the educational system and granted religious freedom. He built up a large army in an effort to conquer Europe and create a French Empire.

Indeed, in 1805, Napoleon defeated the armies of Austria and Russia. He went on to defeat **Prussia,** a powerful German state, in 1806 and 1807 and invaded Spain in 1808. Napoleon placed his relatives on the thrones of the nations he conquered.

Beginning in 1812, however, Napoleon's luck began to change. The British drove the French out of Spain, and then the French army met with disaster when it invaded Russia. In 1814, France itself fell to British forces, and Napoleon had to go into exile on a Mediterranean island. He escaped from exile and returned to France, but in 1815 at **Waterloo** he lost to the British and the Prussians. Once again, Napoleon became an exile, this time on a much more remote island, where he died in 1821.

THE REST OF EUROPE

The French Revolution led to numerous revolutions across Europe. Revolutionary <u>fervor</u>, however, had little effect in Russia, where absolute monarchs continued to hold power.

Greece

After almost four hundred years of rule by the Ottoman Turks, Greece revolted in 1821. When Egypt came to help the Turks suppress the revolt,

Britain, Russia, and France came to Greece's aid. The war ended in Turkish defeat in 1829. It was the start of independence for Greece and the beginning of the end for the Ottoman Turks.

1848: Year of Revolution

The spirit of the French Revolution caught fire across Europe in 1848. The Italian and German states rebelled against the Austrian Empire (which the Habsburg family led after the fall of its Holy Roman Empire). The Hungarians and the Czechs rebelled, too. All these revolts, however, were put down within a year. Still, the spirit of nationalism, once kindled, remained alive. **Nationalism** is pride in and loyalty to one's country and a feeling of unity among people who share a culture. In a short time, the age-old system of kings and nobles would give way to a new democratic Europe.

Russia

After the death of Peter the Great's daughter, Elizabeth, her son **Peter III** came to power. He was deposed and murdered. In 1762, his wife, Catherine, known as **Catherine the Great,** took power.

Catherine was a dynamic ruler and a strong patron of the arts and sciences. Like Peter the Great, she brought new Western ideas to Russia. She established the first schools for girls in Russia and appointed women to important government posts. In a series of wars, Catherine greatly expanded Russia's borders. She divided up Poland and added the Crimea, Siberia, and Turkey to Russia's growing empire. When she died in 1796, Russia was a world power. The Russian people, however, were no better off than they had ever been.

Portugal

While revolution shook most of Europe, Portugal's capital, **Lisbon,** was rocked by an earthquake in 1755. Some fifty thousand people were killed or injured in what was Europe's worst natural disaster of the 1700s. Portugal's prime minister immediately set about rebuilding the city. A great leader, he reorganized Portugal and helped make it into a modern nation.

LATIN AMERICA

Influenced by the American Revolution and the French Revolution, the peoples of Mexico and South America fought for independence from Spain and Portugal.

Mexico

Mexico won its independence from Spain in 1821. In 1824, Mexico declared itself a republic and elected its first president.

Mexico at that time included much of the southwestern United States and California. Mexico's region called Texas had few inhabitants, and the Mexican government welcomed settlers from the United States. In 1835, the people of Texas declared their independence from Mexico. A Mexican army attacked a group of Texan rebels holed up at the **Alamo,** an old mission in San Antonio, in early 1836. All but a few of the two hundred American defenders of the Alamo died, including frontiersman **Davy Crockett.** A few months later, Texans defeated the Mexicans at the Battle of San Jacinto (juh SIN toh) shouting the battle cry, "Remember the Alamo!" Texas remained an independent country for a decade and then joined the United States in 1845.

In 1847, American troops invaded other Mexican land on the Rio Grande. This invasion led to the **Mexican-American War.** American troops captured Mexico City, the capital, and in 1848 the war ended in the **Treaty of Guadalupe-Hidalgo** (GWA duhl *oop* hi DAL *goh*). Under this treaty, the United States gained all of the land north of the Rio Grande, including the present-day states of California, Nevada, Utah, Arizona, and part of New Mexico.

South America

Two great leaders led the fight for independence from Spanish rule in South America. **José de San Martín** (*san* mar TEEN) was an Argentine general who helped win independence for Argentina in 1810 and for Chile in 1824. Farther north, **Simón Bolívar** (see MOHN buh LEE var), a Venezuelan general, led and won the fight for independence for **New Granada** in 1824. Renamed **Gran Colom-**

bia, this territory included Venezuela, Colombia, Ecuador, and Panama. The same year, Bolívar joined forces with San Martín to liberate Peru from the Spanish. Upper Peru was later renamed Bolivia in Bolívar's honor. By 1830, thirteen new nations had established themselves in Latin America.

The revolution in Brazil, in contrast, was mostly bloodless. The son of the king of Portugal was named ruler of Brazil in 1821. He sided with the Brazilians in their rebellion and declared Brazil independent in 1822.

AFRICA

The slave trade slowed down in Africa, and Europeans began to explore the continent's vast interior. The British led the way in exploration and colonization, but one African people remained strong and dominant in South Africa.

Exploration

European exploration was conducted for both scientific and commercial purposes. One goal was to find rivers that would provide trade routes with the interior. In 1796, **Mungo Park** of Scotland reached the Niger River near Mali. He led another expedition to follow the <u>course</u> of the Niger and drowned in present-day Nigeria while trying to escape an African attack.

South Africa

Cape Colony was a Dutch colony at the southern tip of Africa. In 1814, the British took over Cape Colony and freed the slaves there. Earlier, in 1787, the British had established Sierra Leone as a refuge for freed African slaves. By the early 1800s, nearly all European nations but Portugal had ended their slave trade.

The Dutch settlers, called **Boers** (BOHRZ), meaning "farmers," opposed British rule. Some six thousand of them headed north into the interior in 1836. They took lands from Bantu-speaking peoples and established the states of the **Natal** (nuh TAHL), the **Transvaal** (trans VAL), and the **Orange Free State.** The British took over the Natal in 1843, but granted independence to the Transvaal and the Orange Free State.

The Zulu Nation

One African people that remained independent in the face of European conquest were the Zulu (ZOO loo) of South Africa. The Zulu were farmers and cattle herders who lived in villages. In the early 1800s, a great military leader came to power. He created a strong, well-disciplined army that fought with long spears and carried large shields for self-defense. The Zulus clashed with the Boers in the Transvaal in 1837 and 1838. Although the Boers drove them farther north, the Zulu nation remained the most powerful native state in South Africa for forty years.

ASIA

In this period of growing colonialism, India came almost completely under British control. China struggled to keep out Western influence but lost in a war with Britain. Only Japan managed to keep foreigners completely out, as it continued its policy of isolationism.

India

The British and French East India Companies vied for control of India after 1750. British general **Robert Clive** defeated the French in battle in 1752 and seized the rich region of **Bengal** (ben GAHL) in 1757. By 1819, Britain controlled India as far north as the Indus River. That same year, Britain established **Singapore,** in Southeast Asia, as a free port and a stopover for their boats trading with China.

China

Trade with China was extremely limited for the British and other European nations. Frustrated by China's refusal to open more ports to trade, the British smuggled in opium. This powerful drug came from Burma and India. The British traded it for Chinese silver, silks, and tea. Many Chinese workers became addicted to opium and lost all interest in work. The Qing government tried to stop the opium trade and in 1839 seized and burned twenty thousand opium chests in a British warehouse. The result of this action was the **First Opium War.** It ended in British victory in 1842.

The Chinese signed the **Treaty of Nanking,** which gave the British the island of Hong Kong and access to five Chinese trading ports. This only further weakened the corrupt and inefficient Qing dynasty.

Japan

After the reforms of Yoshimune, Japan returned to its policy of strict isolationism. During this time, Japanese culture and arts flourished. **Kabuki** (kuh BOO kee) **theater,** consisting of musical drama performed by actors in colorful costumes, developed. Beautiful woodblock prints celebrated ordinary life. But for many Japanese, isolationism brought hardship. Heavy taxes and severe laws led to uprisings in some regions. The rise in population caused famines. The Tokugawa shogunate was unable to solve these problems.

OCEANIA

This remote part of the world was finally explored. One of the most important island groups was united for the first time. The first European settlers arrived in Australia and New Zealand, causing problems for the indigenous peoples.

James Cook's Expeditions

British navigator and explorer **James Cook** was sent on a scientific expedition to the Pacific islands in 1768. On his first voyage, Cook went around New Zealand and landed at **Botany Bay** on the east coast of Australia. On his second voyage (1772–1775), Cook visited many Pacific islands and explored the continent of Antarctica—the frozen continent that surrounds the South Pole. Cook encouraged scientific study on his voyages and kept detailed journals of his explorations. Cook's third voyage ended in his death in 1779, when he was killed in the Hawaiian Islands during a confrontation with the native people there.

Hawaiian Islands

The Hawaiian Islands in Cook's time were governed separately. In 1810, **Kamehameha I** (kah MAY hah MAY hah) united all the islands and founded the Kingdom of Hawaii. Kamehameha was a wise ruler who developed local industry, kept old customs and religion alive, and encouraged foreign trade.

Australia and New Zealand

The British government used Australia as a penal colony. The first convicts arrived there in 1788. Free settlers first arrived in 1793. Many convicts who served out their sentences stayed on to become landowners and farmers.

The Aborigines resisted giving over their lands to the settlers. By 1821, half of the Aborigine population had been killed in fighting.

Britain declared New Zealand a British colony in 1840 and established **Wellington** as its capital. Driven from their lands, the Maoris in New Zealand rose up in rebellion in 1845 and 1847.

! Implications

To answer the question, "Why does all this matter?" or "What does it mean?," share the following insights with your child.

The idea of government serving the needs of its citizens rather than the other way around was truly revolutionary. It was the idea that inspired the leaders of the American and the French revolutions and all the attempts at revolution that spread across Europe in the year 1848.

Unfortunately, in their thirst for revenge, the ordinary French people were guilty of some of the same injustices as the monarchy that they overthrew. This pattern would repeat itself in later revolutions, especially in the one that would shake Russia nearly seventy years down the road. At times, the chaos of revolution created a desperate desire for order that would bring a strong leader like Napoleon Bonaparte to power.

Yet despite all the backsliding and all the problems with starting democracies, John Locke's idea that governments govern by the consent of the governed has helped people in many countries to form better societies—societies in which individual liberties and responsible leadership can work together.

Fact Checker

To check that your child knows or can find the basic facts in this chapter, here is a puzzle for him or her to solve.

HIDDEN WORD

For each clue, write the answer at the right, one letter to each blank. The letters that fall on the boldface blanks will answer the question that follows the puzzle.

1. She was a great leader of Russia.   _ _ _ _ _ **_** _ _ _

2. His last name was Bonaparte   _ _ _ _ _ **_** _

3. The British surrendered in Yorktown, ____.   **_** _ _ _ _ _ _

4. He explored islands in the Pacific.   _ _ **_** _

5. The British sent prisoners here.   _ _ _ _ _ _ _ **_** _

6. He invented a steamboat.   _ **_** _ _ _ _

7. He perfected the steam engine.   _ _ _ **_**

8. He led fights for independence from Spain.   _ _ _ **_** _ _ _

9. Answer 2 lost a battle here.   _ _ _ _ _ _ **_** _

10. He wrote *The Communist Manifesto*.   _ **_** _ _ _ _

Question: What is this chapter about?

Answer: _ _ _ _ _ _ _ _ _ _

Answers appear in the back, preceding the index.

? The Big Questions

The following questions encourage your child to think critically rather than simply recall facts. If necessary, review the specific information from the preceding pages that will help your child make the necessary inferences to come up with reasonable answers.

1. When the Industrial Revolution took place, many people wanted to own machine-produced goods—for example, clothes and dishes—rather than goods that they or other people had made by hand. Now many people prefer products made by hand over products made by machine. What does this switch tell you about people?

2. This chapter tells about colonies and countries fighting 150 and 200 years ago to become free and independent nations. Why are events that took place so long ago still important to learn about?

3. The chapter says that only about a third of the colonists in the 1700s thought Americans should fight for independence from Britain. How do you explain that most Americans wanted to remain colonies of Britain?

Possible Answers

1. People clamor for the "new thing." Whatever is new and different gets attention. People like to feel they have something different—and better—than their neighbors.
2. If we remember how hard it was to get the kind of government we have, maybe we'll appreciate it more. Learning about these battles of 150 to 200 years ago helps us understand why people in other parts of the world fight today for new governments and more say over their own lives.
3. Change is hard for many people to accept. Many colonists actually felt British and wanted to continue feeling British.

 # Skills Practice

The following activities give your child practice in applying the skills basic to social studies. For some of the activities, your child may need to review the information in the preceding pages.

A.   TAKING A POLL

Sometimes it's easier for a child to think about other countries of the world by contrasting them with his or her own country. Here's an opportunity to contrast forms of government.

This chapter tells about countries that made a break with royal families, but even today some countries (for example, Great Britain, Denmark, the Netherlands) have royal families who perform functions. What opinions do your friends and relatives hold about kings and queens in today's world?

Here are some questions you can ask people who live in the United States. Rewrite the questions on a piece of paper, and leave space to write in people's answers. (You may photocopy the questionnaire so that you have one for each person you poll.) Add other questions if you wish. When you have finished noting the answers of at least ten people, explain the results you came up with.

1. Would you prefer the United States to have a king or queen as the head of government rather than a president?
   ____ YES ____ NO ____ UNDECIDED
2. Why did you give that answer to Question 1?
   _____
   _____
   _____

3. Should Great Britain, Denmark, and the Netherlands eliminate the role of a king or queen?
   ____ YES ____ NO ____ UNDECIDED
4. Why did you give that answer to Question 3?
   _____
   _____
   _____

Evaluating Your Child's Skills: In order to complete this activity successfully, your child must practice social skills, keep good records, and make inferences from the data he or she collects. If your child needs help, model how you would call or visit someone to ask questions for a survey.

B.   CONNECTING CAUSES AND EFFECTS

This activity gives your child a chance to work with a chain of causes and effects.

Item A is the first event in a chain of causes and effects. Item F is the final effect. For the four events in between A and F, figure out which is B, which is C, which is D, and which is E.

A. Loggers clear forests to provide wood for people to use for many purposes, including heating their homes.

_____ Horses carry the coal or pull barges that carry the coal, but horses and barges are slow.

_____ Steam engines help coal miners to work faster, but someone still has to figure out how to get the coal from the mine to people's homes.

_____ People realize they can use coal as an alternative to wood, but mining is hard work.

_____ Wood becomes hard to find and very expensive.

F. Steam locomotives carry the coal more efficiently.

Answers

The four intermediary events as listed should be marked D, E, C, and B.

> ***Evaluating Your Child's Skills:*** In order to complete this activity successfully, your child must see that the effect of a cause can become the cause of another effect. If your child needs help, write the six items on index cards, which your child can then move around easily.

C.   WORKING WITH ANALOGIES

> An important skill in social studies and other subjects involves seeing how the two words in a pair relate to each other and finding a second pair like the first pair.

Fill in the blanks in the following sentence with the names of two leaders mentioned in this chapter.

Sentence

George Washington is to the United States of America as _____ is to Argentina and as _____ is to Colombia.

> ***Evaluating Your Child's Skills:*** In order to complete this activity successfully, your child must understand that the sentence is about the relationship of a person to the

country he helped gain independence. If your child has trouble, ask, "What did George Washington do for the United States?" or a similar question. Then ask, "Who did the same thing for Argentina? for Colombia?"

Answers

1. *José de San Martín*
2. *Simón Bolívar*

 # Top of the Class

> Children interested in delving more deeply into the topics covered in this chapter can choose one or more of the following activities. They may do the activities for their own satisfaction or report on what they have done to show that they have been seriously considering the American Revolution.

A POINT TO PONDER

> Encourage your child to think about a more recent revolution in history—the electronic revolution. Questions and ideas may come up in discussion that your child may want to raise in class.

The Industrial Revolution caused life to change in major ways. In more recent years, we have experienced another historical revolution. It could be called the Electronic Revolution.

Not so long ago, computers were huge objects that took up whole rooms. No one had a computer at home. Now many homes have at least one computer, and everyone in the family—even very young children—knows how to use computers. Have computers changed life for people in the world? In what ways?

BOOKS TO READ AND CRITIQUE

> Make one of the following novels available to your child. The stories are told in the first

person by fictional teenage American boys who lived before or during the Revolutionary War. After your child has finished the book, he or she may want to share thoughts about it with his or her teacher or class.

Forbes, Esther. *Johnny Tremain.* Houghton, 1943. This book won the prestigious Newbery Award in 1944.

Characters in the novel include Paul Revere and Sam Adams.

Collier, Christopher, and James Lincoln Collier. *My Brother Sam Is Dead.* Simon & Schuster, 1974. This title was a Newbery Honor Book. Tim feels caught between his brother's and his father's differing views of the war.

CHAPTER 11
The Triumph of Nationalism
1850–1907

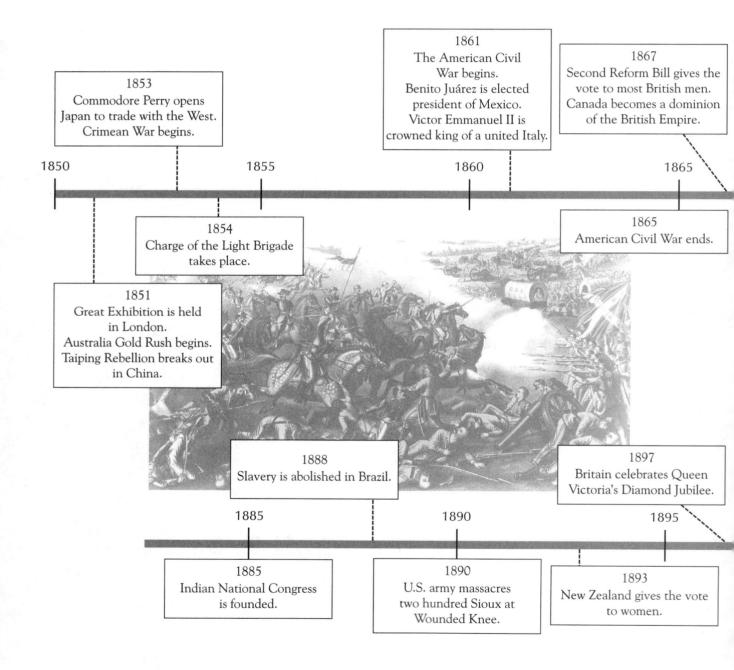

1861
The American Civil War begins.
Benito Juárez is elected president of Mexico.
Victor Emmanuel II is crowned king of a united Italy.

1867
Second Reform Bill gives the vote to most British men.
Canada becomes a dominion of the British Empire.

1853
Commodore Perry opens Japan to trade with the West.
Crimean War begins.

1850

1855

1860

1865

1865
American Civil War ends.

1854
Charge of the Light Brigade takes place.

1851
Great Exhibition is held in London.
Australia Gold Rush begins.
Taiping Rebellion breaks out in China.

1888
Slavery is abolished in Brazil.

1897
Britain celebrates Queen Victoria's Diamond Jubilee.

1885

1890

1895

1885
Indian National Congress is founded.

1890
U.S. army massacres two hundred Sioux at Wounded Knee.

1893
New Zealand gives the vote to women.

This timeline provides an overview of the cultural and political developments between 1850 and 1907. Then a narrative describes this period in greater detail and discusses its significance.

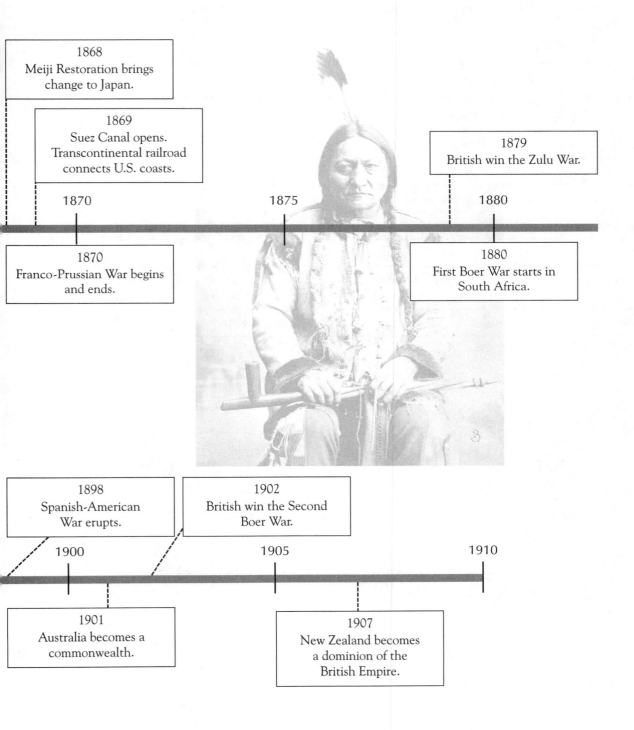

1868
Meiji Restoration brings change to Japan.

1869
Suez Canal opens.
Transcontinental railroad connects U.S. coasts.

1879
British win the Zulu War.

1870

1875

1880

1870
Franco-Prussian War begins and ends.

1880
First Boer War starts in South Africa.

1898
Spanish-American War erupts.

1902
British win the Second Boer War.

1900

1905

1910

1901
Australia becomes a commonwealth.

1907
New Zealand becomes a dominion of the British Empire.

Word Power

The words on the following chart are underscored in the section called "What Your Child Needs to Know." Explain their meanings to your child as needed when they come up in reading or discussion. Keep the list handy for you and your child to use.

Word	Definition
abdicate	give up power
abolished	ended officially
goaded	pushed someone into doing something
incompetent	not qualified, ineffective
infamous	notorious, having a bad reputation
mutiny	revolt against someone in charge
resources	things that a place has and can use to its advantage (for example, the natural resources coal and oil)
strategist	person who creates a clever plan for winning a battle

What Your Child Needs to Know

You may choose to use the following text in several different ways, depending on your child's strengths and preferences. You might read the passage aloud; you might read it to yourself and then paraphrase it for your child; or you might ask your child to read the material along with you or on his or her own.

EUROPE

Nowhere did nationalism triumph more dramatically than in Europe. In the second half of the nineteenth century, many individual states came together to form a unified Germany, and Prussia became the strongest part of the new Germany. Independent Italian states also united during this time. Britain became ruler of the world's largest colonial empire. Russia, however, suffered a serious setback in a disastrous war. Here are more details about each nation.

Germany

Following the failed revolution of 1848, the forty states in the German Confederation remained separate and disunited—in spite of the umbrella name. The states of Austria and Prussia fought over control of the confederation. Then in 1866, Prussian Prime Minister **Otto von Bismarck** (BIZ *mark*) dissolved the confederation; Austria responded to this act by declaring war on Prussia. Bismarck was a brilliant military strategist, and he defeated the Austrians at the Battle of Sadowa in July 1866. He then organized the many individual German states into the North German Conference under Prussian leadership.

When **Napoleon III,** the leader of France, demanded German territory, Bismarck goaded France into the **Franco-Prussian War** of 1870. Prussia won the war and took from France the regions of Alsace (al SAYS) and Lorraine (luh RAYN). In addition, the king of Prussia became the emperor of Germany, **Wilhelm I.**

Italy

Italy, like Germany, was a weak confederation of small states before 1850. In 1852, **Count Camillo Cavour** (kuh VOOR) was named chief minister under **Victor Emmanuel II,** who was king of Piedmont-Sardinia (consisting of Piedmont in northern Italy and the island of Sardinia off the coast of Italy). With French help, Cavour drove the Austrians out of northern Italy, and most of the rest of northern Italy united with the Kingdom of Piedmont-Sardinia.

Then in southern Italy, **Giuseppe Garibaldi** (*gar* uh BAWL dee) led a revolution. He took over the Kingdom of the Two Sicilies. Garibaldi's rebels, called **red shirts** after their clothes, conquered all parts of Sicily in three months and then seized Naples. Cavour met with Garibaldi, and they agreed that the Northern Kingdom would take over Naples, Sicily, and the Papal States (states ruled by the pope). As a result of this agreement, Victor Emmanuel II was king not only of northern Italy but of *all* of Italy—with the exception of Venice and Rome. An Italian parliament began to function as well. Italy gained Venice in the 1860s. Finally, in 1870, the Italian army conquered Rome from France and made it the capital of a new, fully united Italy.

Russia

Russia went to war against Turkey in 1853. Russia wanted control of Turkish territory in order to get to the Black Sea. As Russia began to win this war, called the **Crimean** (krye MEE uhn) **War,** Britain, France, and Sardinia went to Turkey's aid. They feared Russia would take over much of the Ottoman Empire and upset the balance of power in Europe. On October 25, 1854, at the Battle of Balaklava, (*bah* luh KLAH vuh) British horsemen engaged in the infamous **Charge of the Light Brigade.** Incompetent commanders sent the soldiers into a heavily fortified Russian stronghold. Nearly one-third of the British soldiers were killed or wounded.

Many more soldiers during the Crimean War died from disease and infection than in battle. To help the injured, British nurse **Florence Nightingale** established the first modern wartime nursing organization.

The Russian-held city of **Sebastopol** (suh BAS tuh POHL) finally fell to the allies in September 1855, and the war ended the following March. The loser was Russia, but reports about the Charge of the Light Brigade caused the downfall of the British government then in power.

Great Britain

Britain's colonial empire continued to grow during this period. Britain claimed territory all over the world. The period opened with the **Great Exhibition** held in London in 1851. It was the world's first international exhibit and celebrated British industry and technology. The era ended in 1897 with the celebration of **Queen Victoria**'s Diamond Jubilee, which marked sixty years of rule. At the time of her death, several years later, Victoria had been the longest-reigning monarch in British history.

British rights at home were expanding. For example, in 1832, the government granted the right to vote to most middle-class males. The Second Reform Bill in 1867 gave voting rights to many more men. But women in Britain continued to have no vote, and the non-British people—that is, the natives—living in British colonies usually had few rights.

AFRICA

A huge canal in northern Africa gave Britain a dominant role in the trade between Africa and Asia. At the other end of the continent, the discovery of gold twice led to war. Throughout the continent, European powers scrambled to stake their claims. Some more specifics follow.

Egypt

The year 1869 marked the completion of the 107-mile **Suez** (soo EZ) **Canal,** which linked the Mediterranean and Red seas in northern Egypt. British ships no longer had to travel around Africa to transport goods to and from India, its most valuable colony. Britain bought out Egypt's share in the canal in 1875, and by 1882 Britain controlled all of Egypt.

South Africa

A three-way battle was under way for South Africa by the British, the Boers (see Chapter 10), and the Zulu tribe. The **Zulu War** erupted in 1879. Zulu warriors defeated the British in several early battles. But the spears of the Zulus were finally no match for the guns of the British. The British soldiers beat the Zulu warriors at the battles of Rorke's Drift and Kambula, and the Zulu Nation lost what power it had left.

In 1880, the British tried to seize the Transvaal from the Boers. This move led to the **First Boer War.** The Boers won and kept the Transvaal. The discovery of gold there in 1886, however, brought the British back. A secret plan to seize the region failed, and the **Second Boer War** broke out in 1899. This time, the British were the victors. In 1902, the Boer republics became self-governing members of the British Empire.

The Rest of Africa

In 1884, a number of European nations met in Berlin. Their purpose was to divide what remained of Africa among themselves. By the late 1800s, only two African nations remained independent—Liberia and Ethiopia.

The colonial powers established order and stable government in their African colonies but provided few, if any, liberties to Africans. The colonial powers shipped African raw materials to Europe; they left the colonies poor and weak. The colonial powers also ignored African tribal borders, so entire groups of people lost their cultural identity. By the century's end, Africa was basically a European colony.

THE AMERICAS

Unlike in Africa, nations in the Americas got stronger, as the following passages show.

The United States

By the 1850s, the Northern states and the Southern states opposed each other on the issue of slavery. The industrial North had abolished slavery by the early 1800s, but the agricultural South continued to rely on slave labor for its farms and plantations. The Southern states resented the North's pressuring them to end slavery. They felt that policy about slavery should be up to the state involved and that other states and the federal, or national, government should not interfere.

When **Abraham Lincoln,** a member of the antislavery **Republican Party,** was elected president in 1860, the South feared he would attempt to abolish slavery all over the country. One by one, the Southern states **seceded,** or broke away, from the United States. They formed their own government and called themselves the **Confederate States of America** in 1861. On April 12, Southern soldiers fired on federally held **Fort Sumter** in Charleston, South Carolina. This set off the **American Civil War,** or War between the States.

The North had greater <u>resources</u> and a larger army than the South. However, the Confederacy had better generals and the advantage of fighting mostly on their home ground. When Confederate general **Robert E. Lee** attempted to bring the war north in the summer of 1863, he met the enemy at the Battle of **Gettysburg** in Pennsylvania. This three-day battle was horrible for both sides, but the winner was the North.

In 1864, **Ulysses S. Grant,** the Northern general, captured Richmond, Virginia, the capital of the Confederacy. This was another blow for the South. Lee finally surrendered to Grant on April 9, 1865, at **Appomattox** (*ah* puh MAH tuhks), Virginia. Five days later, a Southern sympathizer assassinated Lincoln.

The American Civil War took the lives of about 620,000 soldiers. However, the war had a few important results: it made the United States stronger than ever before. No state would ever again attempt to secede. The war also ended the unjust system of slavery in the South.

After the war, more and more people, including many freed African Americans, headed west looking for land and opportunity. The Homestead Act of 1862 granted every family 160 acres of land in the West on the condition that they cultivate it and not sell it for five years. In 1869, railroads linked the United States from coast to coast. People could more easily travel west, and towns and cities grew quickly.

Western expansion, however, meant the end of a way of life for the Native Americans there. Western tribes resisted giving up their land to settlers and went to war against them, starting in 1866.

Painting of Civil War battle scene

Sitting Bull (1834?–1890)

The **Battle of the Little Bighorn** in 1876 was a temporary victory for the Native Americans, who were led by **Sitting Bull** and **Crazy Horse**. Within fifteen years, however, the U.S. Army had defeated Native Americans and forced many of them to live on Indian **reservations,** small areas of land set apart for them. One of the last confrontations took place at **Wounded Knee,** South Dakota, in 1890. Soldiers massacred two hundred Sioux men, women, and children.

The new settlers changed much of the West into farmland and grazing land for sheep and cattle. Between 1850 and 1900, no fewer than thirteen new states joined the country. These included Colorado, Utah, Nevada, Washington, and Oregon.

In 1898, U.S. troops went to the aid of Cuba, which was fighting for its independence from Spain. The United States won the war and gained the former Spanish territories of Puerto Rico, Guam, and the Philippines. These countries became part of what people now saw as a growing "American empire."

Canada

Like the American colonies, the two provinces of Canada had revolted against Britain in 1837. The rebellion failed, but Britain avoided another revolution by giving Canadians their independence.

The British North American Act of 1867 made Canada a **dominion,** a self-governing land within the British Empire. As such, Canada elects its own political leader, a prime minister, and members of the legislature. Canada also has a governor-general appointed by Britain to represent the monarch, but the governor-general has no political power.

In 1885, a railroad, completed to link the entire country, began to speed up western expansion.

Mexico

The **Mexican Civil War** of 1858 was fought between conservative landowners and middle-class liberals who chose to represent the majority of poor Mexicans. **Benito Juárez** (HWAHR ez), a liberal Indian lawyer, helped his side win the war and was elected president in 1861. But then France invaded Mexico, and Prince **Maximilian** of Austria was installed as emperor.

Juárez led the fight against France. With help from the United States, the French were driven out and Maximilian was executed. Juárez led Mexico again and reformed the land system and education system. He died in 1872. Four years later, **Porfirio Díaz** (pawr FEE ree oh DEE *ahs*) became president and, later, dictator of Mexico. He brought foreign trade and other improvements to the country. However, the poor remained poor, and the rich grew richer. Mexico was ready for another revolution (see Chapter 12).

Brazil

Pedro II had been crowned emperor of Brazil in 1841. He increased the country's output in industry and agriculture. Pedro opened up the Amazon River to trade in 1867. From 1879 to 1888, he passed a number of acts that abolished slavery in

Brazil. The landowners were opposed to ending slavery and forced Pedro to <u>abdicate</u> in 1889. The monarchy was abolished, and Brazil became a republic.

OCEANIA

Oceania's two largest countries became modern, independent nations in this period.

New Zealand

As New Zealand's white population grew, relations with the Maoris worsened. In 1860, war broke out, and the Maoris were driven into the mountains. Peace between the two peoples was established in 1871.

In 1889, the New Zealand government gave the vote to all males over age twenty-one. Based on this new voting block, a liberal government took power in 1890. Three years later, New Zealand became the first country in the world to give the vote to women. Australia followed a year later, in 1894. New Zealand became a dominion of the British Empire in 1907.

Australia

Gold was discovered in the two Australian colonies of Victoria and New South Wales in 1851. The gold rush that followed more than doubled Australia's population. **Melbourne** (MEL buhrn), Victoria's capital, became a major city. Britain granted Australia dominion status by 1890, and the six former colonies formed a new nation, the Commonwealth of Australia in 1901. **Canberra** (KAN buh ruh)—between Melbourne and Sydney—became Australia's national capital.

ASIA

Europeans had influence for good and for ill in Asia during this period.

China

In 1856, the British and Chinese fought the **Second Opium War,** which ended in British victory.

According to the treaty at the end of the war, the Chinese had to open more of their ports to European trade.

Tz'u-hsi (TSOO SHEE), also known as the **Empress Dowager,** came to power in 1861. One of the most powerful women in modern Asian history, she ruled for nearly fifty years. Although harsh with her own people, Tz'u-hsi could not prevent Europeans from taking over more and more of China. The **Taiping** (tye PING) **Rebellion,** led by ordinary Chinese people protesting the ruling Qing dynasty, broke out in 1851 and lasted thirteen years. Millions of Chinese died in what became the bloodiest civil war in history. Britain and other European powers helped to end the rebellion because it was in their best interests to keep the corrupt and weak Qing dynasty in power.

India

In 1857, Indian colonial troops staged a <u>mutiny</u> against their British rulers. The Indians captured the capital, Delhi, but the British quickly put down the rebellion. Then the British government dissolved the East India Company and took direct control of India. In 1876, Queen Victoria was pronounced empress of India, and she named a **viceroy,** an official who represented her interests.

British officials and landowners went on to enjoy lives of wealth and leisure, while most Indians lived in poverty and could not reach positions of power in the government or the army.

Some middle-class Hindus founded the **Indian National Congress** in 1885. Their first goal was to force the British to give better jobs to Indians. Nationalism was on the rise in India.

Japan

In 1853, U.S. president **Millard Fillmore** sent Commodore **Matthew Perry** and four warships to Japan. Using the threat of force, Perry soon persuaded the Japanese to end their isolationism and open two ports to U.S. trade. Within a short time, the Japanese signed similar trade treaties with Russia, Britain, and the Netherlands.

Western influence in Japan further weakened the Tokugawa shogunate, and in 1867 a group of Japanese nobles overthrew the shogunate. This act led to naming fifteen-year-old **Prince Mutsuhito** (moo tsoo HEE toh) to the position of emperor. He took the name **Meiji** (MAY jee), which means, "enlightened rule." The **Meiji Restoration** of the emperor's rule was *not* a throwback to life under Japanese emperors in medieval times. Rather, the Meijis sought to develop Japan into a modern nation based on Western ideas and technology. They imported Western machines for new factories, adapted Western dress and music, and modernized the educational system. In 1890, Japan elected its first national parliament.

This fifty-year period is an interesting study in contrasts. On the one hand, nationalism reached a peak. In Europe, the disorganized states of Germany united, as did those of Italy. In other parts of the world, countries as different as Japan and Brazil started to modernize and grow stronger. The United States endured a terrible civil war but survived as a nation.

On the other hand, as nations grew strong and confident, some felt the need to extend their power and influence. As a result, Africa's many nations, with two exceptions, became European colonies; India became subject to British rule; and China was an economic colony of Europe in everything but name. In other words, in some significant cases, the triumph of nationalism led to empire building. One country's need to make itself more prosperous and powerful was often at the expense of another country's independence. This need to dominate would have disastrous, worldwide consequences in the century to come.

Implications

To answer the question, "Why does all this matter?" or "What does it mean?," share the following insights with your child.

Fact Checker

To check that your child knows or can find the basic facts in this chapter, here is a game based on the names of leaders and nations.

NATION MATCHING GAME

For each leader on the left, find on the right his or her nation. Write the letter of the nation on the blank after the leader's name. Use all the nations, but do not use any nation for more than one answer.

Leader   **Nation**

1. Benito Juárez _____   a. Britain
2. Victor Emmanuel II _____   b. Mexico
3. Queen Victoria _____   c. Italy
4. Otto von Bismarck _____   d. United States of America
5. Pedro II _____   e. Prussia
6. U.S. Grant _____   f. Japan
7. Mutsuhito _____   g. Brazil

Answers appear in the back, preceding the index.

The Big Questions

The following questions encourage your child to think critically rather than simply recall facts. If necessary, review the specific information from the preceding pages that will help your child make the necessary inferences to come up with reasonable answers.

1. During the Civil War in the United States, some brothers took up arms against each other. How did such awful situations come about?
2. Chapter 10 shows that between 1750 and 1850 the British colonies in North America and the Spanish colonies in Latin America became independent countries. Chapter 11 tells us that between 1850 and 1900 India and most of Africa became European colonies. What's your reaction to hearing that some colonies got their freedom but that, shortly afterward, other countries were colonized?

3. A popular statement during this period in history was "The sun never sets on the British Empire." Explain in your own words what that statement meant.

Possible Answers

1. *Brothers who were born and grew up together in one state could become separated as one or another moved to a different state. In the Civil War, one set of states fought another set of states. It's possible that one brother lived in a Union state and one in a Confederate state and would have to take up arms against each other.*
2. *In Chapter 10, it seems like the world is moving forward and following the ideals of the United States of America. But in Chapter 11, it seems like stronger countries want to increase their power and wealth by controlling weaker countries.*
3. *An empire consists of a mother country and colonies. The quotation means, "When it is night in one British colony, it is still morning or afternoon in another British colony." That is, the sun is always shining on some parts of the world, and since Britain had colonies all over the world, some of them must have always been in the sunlight.*

Skills Practice

The following activities give your child practice in applying the skills basic to social studies. To do the activities, your child may need to review the information in the preceding pages.

A. SUPPORTING GENERALIZATIONS

Give your child the following generalizations that can grow out of this chapter. Have him or her support each generalization with specifics from the chapter.

1. Many leaders unified parts of a country or built empires from 1850 to 1900.
2. As in so many other periods in history, between 1850 and 1900, wars raged in parts of the world.

3. From 1850 to 1900, voting for national leaders was catching on as an alternative to rule by dictators or monarchs.

Answers

1. *Specifics may include information about roles played by Bismarck, Cavour, Garibaldi, Queen Victoria, General Grant, the Empress Dowager, Prince Mutsuhito, Benito Juárez, and Pedro II.*
2. *Specifics may include information about the Franco-Prussian War, the Crimean War, the Zulu War, the First Boer War, the Second Boer War, the American Civil War, the Spanish-American War,*

the Mexican Civil War, the Second Opium War, and the Taiping Rebellion.

3. *Specifics include voting practices in Britain, New Zealand, and Australia. Your child may also know that in the United States, (a) African American males gained the right to vote (if not a support system for voting) during this period, and (b) women demanded the right (and would finally get the right in 1920).*

> ***Evaluating Your Child's Skills:*** **In order to complete this activity successfully, your child must understand the meanings of *generalization* (a statement about the overall character of separate details) and *specifics* (particular instances or examples). If he or she has trouble, provide one specific for each question, and then ask for others.**

B. CONNECTING LITERATURE AND HISTORY

> **This activity will illustrate for your child that history moves artists to create.**

The nineteenth-century British poet Lord Tennyson, wrote a poem to honor his countrymen who died or suffered injuries in a battle against the Russians during the Crimean War. First, read the poem to yourself a few times; second, read it aloud. Then answer the questions that follow the poem.

The Charge of the Light Brigade

Half a league, half a league,
Half a league, onward,
All in the valley of Death
   Rode the six hundred.
"Forward, the Light Brigade!
Charge for the guns!" he said.
Into the valley of Death
   Rode the six hundred.

"Forward, the Light Brigade!"
Was there a man dismayed?
Not though the soldier knew
   Someone had blundered.

Theirs not to make reply,
Theirs not to reason why,
Theirs but to do and die.
Into the valley of Death
   Rode the six hundred.

Cannon to right of them,
Cannon to left of them.
Cannon in front of them
   Volleyed and thundered;
Stormed at with shot and shell,
Boldly they rode and well,
Into the jaws of Death,
Into the mouth of hell
   Rode the six hundred.

Flashed all their sabers bare,
Flashed as they turned in air
Sabering the gunners there,
Charging an army, while
   All the world wondered.
Plunged in the battery smoke
Right through the line they broke;
Cossack and Russian
Reeled from the saber stroke
   Shattered and sundered.
Then they rode back, but not,
   Not the six hundred.

Cannon to right of them,
Cannon to left of them,
Cannon behind them
   Volleyed and thundered;
Stormed at with shot and shell
While horse and hero fell,
They that had fought so well
Came through the jaws of Death,
Back from the mouth of hell,
All that was left of them,
   Left of six hundred.

When can their glory fade?
O the wild charge they made!
   All the world wondered.
Honor the charge they made!
Honor the Light Brigade,
   Noble six hundred.

Questions

1. According to the second stanza, why do the British soldiers go forward when they know the order to fight was a mistake?
2. What does the rhythm of the poem remind you of?
3. Many people over the years have memorized this poem, even though they may not know much about the Crimean War. How do you explain that fact?

Answers

1. *The soldiers are trained to follow their commander's orders.*
2. *To some listeners, the rhythm sounds like the beat of horses' hooves.*
3. *The story line and the sounds grab a reader or listener more than a history book might.*

Evaluating Your Child's Skills: In order to complete this activity successfully, your child may need help with vocabulary and figurative language. Explain that "half a league" is a distance of about 1½ miles; "valley of Death" and "jaws of Death" are the poet's way of saying that the British soldiers were facing destruction; sabers are swords.

Top of the Class

Children interested in delving more deeply into the topics covered in this chapter can choose the following activity. They may do the activity for their own satisfaction or report on what they have done to show that they have been seriously considering the period from 1850 to 1900.

QUICK RESEARCH

With your child, use an encyclopedia, the Internet, or a library to find facts about one or more of the following topics.

Find at least two facts about any of the following topics. All the topics come from this chapter.

Commodore Perry
Cossacks
Florence Nightingale
Queen Victoria
Suez Canal

CHAPTER 12
The World at War
1900–1950

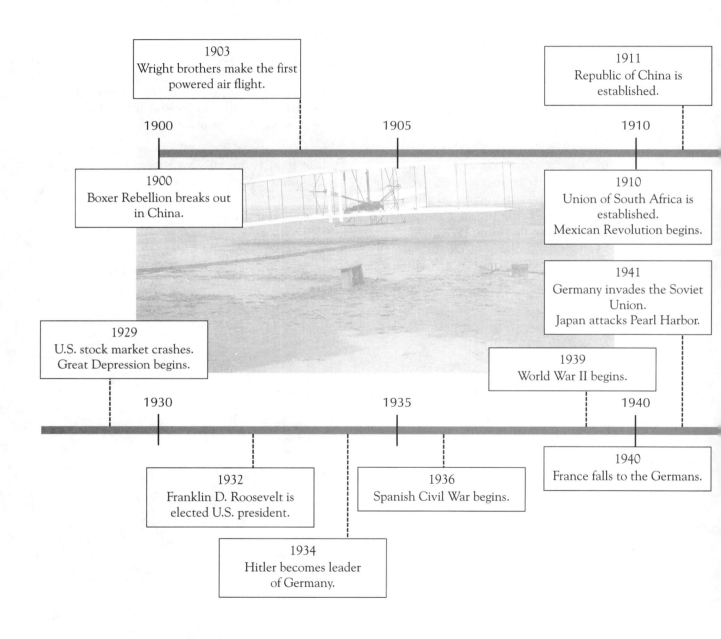

1903
Wright brothers make the first powered air flight.

1911
Republic of China is established.

1900

1905

1910

1900
Boxer Rebellion breaks out in China.

1910
Union of South Africa is established.
Mexican Revolution begins.

1941
Germany invades the Soviet Union.
Japan attacks Pearl Harbor.

1929
U.S. stock market crashes.
Great Depression begins.

1939
World War II begins.

1930

1935

1940

1932
Franklin D. Roosevelt is elected U.S. president.

1936
Spanish Civil War begins.

1940
France falls to the Germans.

1934
Hitler becomes leader of Germany.

This timeline provides an overview of the cultural and political developments between, approximately, 1900 and 1950. On the following pages, a narrative describes this period in greater detail and discusses its significance.

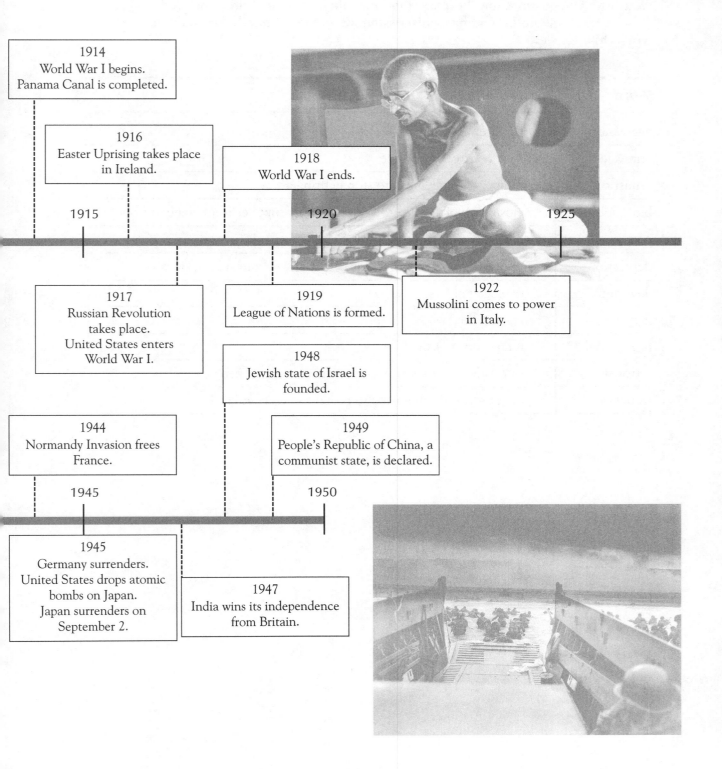

1914
World War I begins.
Panama Canal is completed.

1916
Easter Uprising takes place in Ireland.

1918
World War I ends.

1915

1920

1925

1917
Russian Revolution takes place.
United States enters World War I.

1919
League of Nations is formed.

1922
Mussolini comes to power in Italy.

1948
Jewish state of Israel is founded.

1944
Normandy Invasion frees France.

1949
People's Republic of China, a communist state, is declared.

1945

1950

1945
Germany surrenders.
United States drops atomic bombs on Japan.
Japan surrenders on September 2.

1947
India wins its independence from Britain.

Word Power

The words on the following chart are underscored in the section called "What Your Child Needs to Know." Explain their meanings to your child as needed when they come up in reading or discussion. Keep the list handy for you and your child to use.

Word	Definition
aggression	threatening behavior
annexed	took control of by force
armistice	temporary agreement to stop fighting a war
blockade	closing off of an area to keep people or supplies from going in or out
consumed	used up or destroyed
depression	time when the economy fails and many people are out of work
devastated	damaged or destroyed
illegal	against the law
provisional	temporary, not final
terrorist	someone who uses violence or threats against people
trenches	long narrow ditches used to protect soldiers in battle

What Your Child Needs to Know

You may choose to use the following text in several different ways, depending on your child's strengths and preferences. You might read the passage aloud; you might read it to yourself and then paraphrase it for your child; or you might ask your child to read the material along with you or on his or her own.

PRE–WORLD WAR I

The decade and a half before World War I was a time of peace and growth in most of Europe and the United States. But elsewhere—for example, in China, Mexico, Japan, and southeast Europe—conflicts arose.

Asia

In 1900, resentment against Europeans in China exploded in the **Boxer Rebellion.** The Boxers were members of a secret society supported by the Qing dynasty. During the rebellion, they killed many Europeans and Chinese Christians. An international force that included the United States quickly crushed the rebellion.

In 1911, the **Chinese Nationalist Party** under its leader **Sun Yat-sen** (SOON YAHT SEN) overthrew the Qing dynasty, ending their 267 years of rule. Sun Yat-sen was named <u>provisional</u> president of a new Chinese republic.

Steadily building its military power as the century started, Japan took control of Korea and of Manchuria, the northern province of China. Since Russia also wanted to dominate this Asian region, it went to war with Japan in 1905. Japan totally destroyed the Russian naval fleet in the **Russo-Japanese War.** In doing so, Japan became the first Asian nation to defeat a European country.

The Americas

The United States grew larger and more powerful in the early 1900s. New technology helped its growth. In 1903, the **Wright brothers** made their first flight in a powered aircraft. **Henry Ford** developed his popular **Model T** automobile in 1908.

A million immigrants a year were coming to the United States by 1904. Most of them were from eastern and southern Europe. They came looking for a new life in the "land of opportunity."

Wright brothers' plane at Kitty Hawk

In Mexico, the people overthrew dictator Porfirio Díaz in 1911. The **Mexican Revolution** pitted landowners against the poor and landless. In the north, rebel leader **Pancho Villa** (PAHN choh VEE yuh) organized the revolt against the landowners. In the south, Indian peasant **Emiliano Zapata** (EH mee LYAH noh suh PAH tuh) led the fight. Both men died in the fighting, but their efforts helped to produce a new, more just constitution in 1917.

In Central America, the United States completed the **Panama Canal** in 1914. The canal linked the Atlantic and Pacific oceans and greatly shortened voyages between the western and eastern coasts of the Americas.

Europe

The **Balkan states** in southeast Europe—including Serbia, Montenegro, and Bulgaria—had gained independence from the Ottoman Empire back in 1878. In 1912, these nations and Greece attacked Turkey to gain territory. The **First Balkan War** ended a year later with the defeat of the Turks. The victors carved up much of the remaining Ottoman territory. A dispute over this territory led to the **Second Balkan War.** As Serbia grew larger, neighboring **Austria-Hungary** (a pairing that went back to 1867) grew concerned. The neighbors became bitter enemies.

WORLD WAR I

World War I started with a tiny spark but quickly spread into a roaring fire that consumed Europe. For four long years, the world was at war. While the war was in progress, Russia and Ireland experienced bloody revolutions.

Europe

On June 28, 1914, a Serbian terrorist assassinated **Archduke Franz Ferdinand,** heir to the **Austro-Hungarian Empire.** A month later, Austria-Hungary declared war on Serbia.

What turned a small war into World War I? The answer is in the alliances formed by the nations of Europe. Austria-Hungary was in an alliance with Germany, the strongest military nation in Europe. Serbia was under the protection of Russia, which belonged to an alliance with France and Britain. The purpose of this alliance was to halt German aggression.

Germany came to Austria's aid and declared war on Russia and France. When Germany invaded Belgium a few days later, Britain declared war on Germany. Russia, Britain, and France became known as the **Allied Powers.** Germany and Austria-Hungary became known as the **Central Powers.** The remaining Ottoman Turks later joined the Central Powers.

The Germans advanced on France by September 1914, but the Allies counterattacked and forced them back at the Marne River. In a few months, the Germans and the Allies had dug lines of trenches across a four-hundred-mile imaginary line called the **western front.** Between the two lines of trenches were a few hundred yards of territory called "no-man's-land." In four years of fighting, neither side made much progress along the western front.

The **eastern front** ran from the Baltic Sea to the Black Sea. Along this front, the Russians fought to hold back another advancing line of Germans.

World War I introduced a range of new destructive weapons—including aircraft, German submarines called U-boats, tanks, machine guns, and poison gas.

The Russian Revolution

The way **Czar Nicholas II** handled Russia during the war angered the Russian people. By 1917, food shortages and war deaths led to riots in St. Petersburg. Russian soldiers joined the rioting, and the **Russian Revolution** began. In 1917, the communist **Bolsheviks** (BOHL shuh viks), led by **Vladimir Lenin** (VLAD uh meer LEN in), seized control of the government.

The Bolshevik government made peace with Germany and took no further role in World War I. However, in 1918 a civil war broke out between the Bolsheviks and the anticommunists. The Bolsheviks won after two years of bloody fighting that claimed 15 million lives. In 1920, the Bolsheviks renamed the old Russian empire; they called it the **Union of Soviet Socialist Republics (U.S.S.R.),** or the **Soviet Union.**

Ireland

Ireland had long been struggling for independence from Britain. Things came to a head in 1916. The

Easter Uprising occurred on Easter Monday in Dublin, the Irish capital. Five hundred people died in the rebellion before it ended. But the Irish did not give up their fight. In 1922, the country gained dominion status and became the self-governing **Irish Free State.**

The United States

The United States did not want to get involved in World War I. But, in 1917, after German U-boats sank many U.S. ships, the United States declared war on Germany.

The United States sent a very large number of troops to Britain and France. Finally, the Allies drove the Germans back from the western front, and a sea blockade against Germany drove the German people to near starvation. As a result, Germany signed an armistice, and the war ended on November 11, 1918.

The End of the War

The **Treaty of Versailles** punished the Central Powers severely. The treaty reduced the size of Germany, made Germany give up colonies, and dissolved Austria-Hungary and the remains of the Ottoman Empire.

World War I was the bloodiest war up to that time. The toll was more than 8 million soldiers dead and more than 20 million wounded.

POST–WORLD WAR I

As the following paragraphs show, Europe was left devastated by World War I. The United States emerged as a superpower and enjoyed a decade of prosperity.

Europe

The Paris Peace Conference in 1919 established the **League of Nations.** Its purposes were to keep world peace and to settle disputes between nations. The United States, however, refused to join the League of Nations. As a result, the league was too weak to prevent a number of small wars.

Germany and other European countries experienced economic collapse in the 1920s. In Italy, **Benito Mussolini** (*moo* suh LEE nee) came to power in 1922. Mussolini was a fascist. *Fascism* comes from the Latin word *fasces*, meaning "a bundle of rods with an ax," which was a symbol of power in ancient Rome. **Fascism** is a form of government in which a dictator and the dictator's political party exercise complete power over a country; they do not allow any debate about their policies. Mussolini looked to create an Italian empire as mighty as the Roman Empire. To begin, in 1935, he invaded Ethiopia in Africa and annexed it.

Asia

In 1921, the **Chinese Communist Party** was founded. **Mao Zedong** (MAOO zeh *doong*) emerged as one of its leaders. After the death of Sun Yat-sen in 1925, **Chiang Kai-shek** (jee AHNG KYE SHEK) became leader of the Nationalist Party. Soon, the Communists and the Nationalists faced each other in a civil war. In 1933, Chiang ordered a large attack on the Communist stronghold in southern China. Under Mao's leadership, the Communists moved north in 1934 on the **Long March.** Of the one hundred thousand Communists who started the more than six-thousand-mile march, only twenty thousand reached their destination.

After the fall of the Ottoman Empire, England and France controlled most of western Asia—the area also known as the Middle East. During this period, some nations gained their independence. For example, in Turkey, the last Ottoman sultan fled the capital in 1923. **Mustafa Kemal** (kuh MAL) was elected first president of a new Turkish republic. Kemal took the name *Atatürk* (A tuh *tuhrk*), which means "father of the Turks." He helped to transform Turkey into a modern, Westernized nation before his death in 1938. Similarly, in 1932, after a period of British rule, Iraq gained independence.

The United States

The United States experienced an economic boom in the 1920s. Public pressure against alcohol led to **Prohibition,** a national law banning the making and selling of alcoholic beverages. People ignored the law, however, and gangsters grew powerful making and selling illegal alcohol. The **Roaring Twenties** was a time of carefree behavior, jazz music, and lawlessness in many American cities. The U.S. government ignored events in Europe and pursued a policy of isolationism.

PRE–WORLD WAR II

In the 1930s, a worldwide <u>depression</u> changed life in many countries.

The Americas

The U.S. economic boom ended in 1929, when the stock market crashed. The **Great Depression** saw thousands of businesses close and millions of Americans lose their jobs. Democrat **Franklin D. Roosevelt** was elected president in 1932 and launched his **New Deal** programs, which set out to create new jobs, help banks stay open, and protect people's savings.

In Mexico, **Lázaro Cárdenas** (KAHR duhn ahs) was elected president in 1934. Like Roosevelt, Cárdenas was a great social reformer. He gave land to the people and built schools for the rural poor.

Europe

Economic depression in Germany led to the rise of **Adolf Hitler,** leader of the **Nazi** (or Nationalist Socialist) **Party.** Hitler, like Mussolini, was a fascist. He promised the German people a return to national glory. By 1934, Hitler was *führer,* or "leader," of Germany. He blamed Jews for many of Germany's problems and persecuted them. In 1936, he formed an alliance with Italy and Japan.

In Spain, democratic leaders took control in 1931 and overthrew the monarchy with the goal of setting up a republic. These leaders, called Republicans, believed in **socialism,** a system in which the government, not individuals, control the country's major industries. The Republicans reduced the power of the Army and the Catholic Church. Then in 1936, a group of Spanish army generals rebelled against the Republicans. Led by the fascist general **Francisco Franco,** these rebels called themselves Nationalists. People around the world saw the **Spanish Civil War** as a battle between the forces of socialism and fascism. By 1939, the Nationalists (fascists) had won, and Franco became dictator of Spain for the next thirty-five years.

Asia

In 1937, Japan launched a massive invasion of China. The Chinese Nationalists and the Communists stopped fighting each other and together fought the

Mohandas Gandhi (1869–1948)

Japanese. But by 1938, the Japanese controlled most of eastern China.

The Indian National Congress found a bold leader in **Mohandas Gandhi** (moh HUHN dahs GAHN dee). Gandhi began a movement of peaceful resistance (sometimes called **civil disobedience**) to drive out the British, who had ruled India for many years.

Africa

The **Union of South Africa** was founded in 1910 and consisted of the British Cape Colony and three Dutch colonies. In 1936, the white-run Union took the vote away from nearly all Africans. It left them powerless in their own country.

WORLD WAR II

World War II pitted the **Axis Powers** of Germany, Italy, and Japan against the **Allied Powers** of Britain, France, the United States, and the Soviet Union.

Europe

Germany's Hitler wanted to create a world empire. In 1939, Hitler invaded Poland. Britain and France immediately declared war on Germany. The Soviet Union, meanwhile, had entered a secret pact with Germany.

In early 1940, Germany invaded Denmark, Norway, Belgium, the Netherlands, and, finally, France. When France fell, Hitler began an attack of Britain by air, sometimes referred to as the **blitz.** The British fought back in what became the **Battle of Britain,** which prevented Germany from launching a land invasion. Hitler broke his pact with the Soviet Union and invaded that country in June 1941.

The United States

The United States stayed out of the war for more than two years. Then on December 7, 1941, the Japanese launched a surprise attack on the U.S. naval fleet at Pearl Harbor, Hawaii. The United States declared war on Japan the next day. The United States, however, was ill prepared for this conflict, and it took many months to gear up for the war effort. Eventually, American troops poured into the Pacific area to fight the Japanese and into Europe to fight the Germans.

Asia and Oceania

Southeast Asia, the Philippines, and many Pacific islands quickly fell to the Japanese. In 1942, the Japanese advanced on Midway Island, which was a strategic point in the war. The Americans drove back the Japanese in the **Battle of Midway,** which became a crucial battle in the early point of the war. Then U.S. troops began to take back Japanese-held islands. By early 1945, the United States was closing in and, in fierce fighting, took the Japanese islands of **Okinawa** (*oh* kuh NAH wuh) and **Iwo Jima** (EE woh JEE muh).

Africa

The Italians attacked Egypt in 1940, but the British drove them out. The Germans came to the Italians' aid. German commander General **Erwin Rommel** reclaimed North Africa and pushed the British back into Egypt. But by November 1942, the British were able to reverse their fortunes, and they defeated the Italians and Germans in Egypt. The Axis Powers were trapped in Africa by British and U.S. troops, and they surrendered in May 1943.

The End of the War

The harsh Soviet winter climate played an important role in weakening the invading Germans. A Soviet counterattack at Stalingrad forced the Germans to retreat. In 1943, American and British

Allied troops landing at Normandy, D-Day, 1944

planes began bombing German cities, and Allied forces invaded Italy in September. Mussolini was killed by his own people, and the Italians surrendered to the Allies.

On June 6, 1944, known as **D-Day,** Allied forces invaded Normandy on the northern coast of France. Soon after, the Allies drove the Germans out of France. As the Soviets moved eastward toward the German capital of Berlin, Hitler disappeared, apparently having taken his own life in the underground bunker where he spent his last days. On May 8, 1945, Germany surrendered to the Allies.

As Allied troops moved through German-occupied land, they discovered people in **concentration camps,** where prisoners were forced to work as slave laborers, and millions were executed. An exact count will probably never be determined, but estimates run between 10 and 20 million, including 6 million Jews. This terrible event is called the **Holocaust.**

The war in Europe was over, but the Japanese continued to fight. The Americans developed a new weapon, the atomic bomb. To end the war quickly, the United States dropped atomic bombs on the Japanese cities of **Hiroshima** (*hir* uh SHEE muh) and **Nagasaki** (*nah* guh SAH kee). The bombings devastated both cities and led to the Japanese surrender on September 2, 1945. World War II ended.

The war had caused 50 million deaths, and $1 trillion was spent waging it.

POST–WORLD WAR II

After the war, the United States and the Soviet Union emerged as the world's two superpowers. Developments in those countries and also in China, India, and the Middle East made the biggest headlines around the world right through the end of the twentieth century and into the twenty-first.

The United States

The United States set up the **Marshall Plan** to help the nations of Europe get back on their feet. In 1945, the United States and other nations formed a new peacekeeping organization, the **United Nations (UN)**. The UN's **Security Council** had the power to send arms and peacekeeping troops to problem spots around the world.

Europe

The Allies divided Germany and its capital, Berlin, into four zones; one Allied power controlled each zone. The Soviet Union turned its zone, East Germany, into a communist state. It also established communist governments under its control in Bulgaria, Poland, Czechoslovakia, Hungary, Romania, and Yugoslavia.

Asia

Britain granted independence to India in 1947. Indian Muslims, however, did not want to be ruled by the Hindu majority and demanded a new homeland. Northeast and northwest India became the independent country of **Pakistan.** The new republic of India had **Jawaharlal Nehru** (juh WAH huhr *lahl* NAY roo) as its first prime minister.

In China, civil war between Communists and Nationalists resumed. The Communists had wider support and drove the Nationalists to the island of Taiwan (TYE WAHN) in 1949. Here, Chiang Kai-shek established the Republic of China. Mao Zedong declared the mainland the **People's Republic of China,** a Communist state.

The Middle East

Hebrews had been exiled from Palestine as long ago as 586 B.C. (see Chapter 2). Nevertheless, some Hebrews and their descendants had continued to live there since ancient times. In addition, over the course of hundreds and hundreds of years, some Jews (descendants of Hebrews) who had been born elsewhere moved, or "returned," to Palestine. After World War II, larger numbers of European Jews decided to move there. Then the United Nations agreed to divide Palestine; they planned to establish separate and distinct areas for Arabs and Jews. In May 1948, the Jewish nation of **Israel** was born.

The Arabs in the surrounding nations of Syria, Iraq, Egypt, and Jordan, among others, felt threatened by Israel. They attacked the new nation but were defeated. As many as 750,000 or a million Palestinians who had already been living in the land that became Israel then fled, leaving about 600,000 Palestinians in Israel. The intense Israeli-Palestinian conflict of these days would continue for decades.

 # Implications

> **To answer the question, "Why does all this matter?" or "What does it mean?," share the following insights with your child.**

The first half of the twentieth century saw more destruction than the world had ever seen before. Never before in history had war enveloped the entire world. The colonial empires built by Europe in the preceding decades and the defensive alliances these countries formed to protect their empires almost certainly led to World War I. Most historians agree this war was unnecessary. Few people would say the same about World War II, which was seen as a struggle between fascism and democracy. Yet without World War I, World War II may never have happened.

The punishment and humiliation heaped on Germany at the end of World War I paved the way for Adolf Hitler's rise to power. Both Hitler and Mussolini promised a better tomorrow in troubling times and gained their nations' full support.

The United States, to its credit, was far more generous in victory at the end of World War II. Both Japan and West Germany received economic aid and developed into stable democracies.

Fact Checker

To check that your child knows or can find the basic facts in this chapter, here is a puzzle based on proper and common nouns in the chapter.

1900–1950 PUZZLE

Across

2. Date of invasion of Normandy during World War II
4. Name of Mussolini's political movement
7. Leader who practiced nonviolent protests
8. German leader during World War II
9. Peacekeeping organization

Down

1. Connector of Atlantic and Pacific (two words)
3. Holiday at the time of Irish Uprising in 1916
5. Communist leader in Russia
6. Destruction by Nazis of Jews and others during World War II

Answers appear in the back, preceding the index.

[?] The Big Questions

The following questions encourage your child to think critically rather than simply recall facts. If necessary, review the specific information from the preceding pages that will help your child make the necessary inferences to come up with reasonable answers.

1. In this chapter, the United States is referred to as "the land of opportunity." What kinds of opportunities do you suppose the United States provided to people from eastern and southern Europe at the beginning of the twentieth century?
2. Why do countries make alliances?
3. What was the same about America's entry into World War II and its entry into World War I?
4. Americans still debate the use of atomic bombs on Japan in 1945. Do you think their use was justified? Why or why not?

Possible Answers

1. *The United States offered immigrants opportunities to earn a living, to get an education, to practice their religion freely, and to settle in cities or in rural areas.*
2. *Countries form alliances to protect one another, to share resources, and to scare off other countries from attacking them.*
3. *In both instances, U.S. property was attacked first, and, in response to the attacks, the United States declared war on the attackers.*
4. *Some people believe that no war justifies the use of nuclear weapons. Others believe that shortening a conflict and reducing deaths justify the use of nuclear weapons.*

Skills Practice

The following activities give your child practice in applying the skills basic to social studies. To do the activities, your child may need to review the information in the preceding pages.

A. CONNECTING CAUSES AND EFFECTS

Make sure your child understands that the *effect* of an event is something that happened *on account of* the event. Then have your child fill in the missing words for each numbered item.

In the following activity, each arrow (→) stands for the words *led to*. Finish each sentence by telling what belongs after the arrow.

1. Resentment against Europeans in China → a rebellion by the group called _____.
2. The overthrow of the Qing dynasty in China → the position of president for _____.
3. Russia's desire to dominate Asia → the _____ War.
4. Food shortages in Russia and the people's anger at Czar Nicholas → the _____.
5. The sea blockade of Germany by the Allies → _____.
6. The decision by the United States not to join the League of Nations → _____.
7. Germany's invasion of Poland in 1939 → _____ by Britain and France.
8. Knowledge that the Allies were approaching Germany → _____ by Hitler.
9. The bombing of Pearl Harbor by Japan → _____ by the United States.
10. Dropping atom bombs on Hiroshima and Nagasaki → _____ by Japan.

Answers

1. *the Boxers*
2. *Sun Yat-sen*
3. *Russo-Japanese*
4. *Russian Revolution*

5. *starvation of Germans and their surrender (accept also "armistice")*
6. *failure by the League of Nations (accept also "ineffective League of Nations")*
7. *declaration of war by Britain and France on Germany*
8. *suicide*
9. *declaration of war*
10. *surrender*

Evaluating Your Child's Skills: **In order to complete this activity successfully, your child must think about more than chronology, or time sequence. He or she must see causal relationships, which is what history is all about. If your child has trouble, consider giving him or her two choices (one right, one wrong) for each item. For item 1, you can offer *Boxers* and *czars*, for example.**

B. WORKING WITH GRAPHIC ORGANIZERS

Using graphic organizers such as lists, charts, and diagrams makes facts easier to organize and remember.

Fill in the blanks in each of the following graphic organizers.

Graphic Organizer 1: Sides in World War I

Allied Powers	Central Powers
Russia	_____
France	_____
Britain	_____
Australia	
New Zealand	
United States	

Graphic Organizer 2:
Sides in World War II

Allies	Axis
Britain	_____
France	_____
United States	_____

Answers

Graphic Organizer 1: *In World War I, the Central Powers were Austria-Hungary, Italy, and Germany. (Later, the Ottoman Turks joined these countries.)* Graphic Organizer 2: *In World War II, the Axis Powers were Japan, Italy, and Germany.*

Evaluating Your Child's Skills: **If your child needs help, provide a list of *all* the countries in World War I, and ask him or her to separate them into two categories— Allied Powers and Central Powers. Repeat this process with all the countries in World War II, to be separated into two categories—Allies and Axis.**

Top of the Class

Children interested in delving more deeply into the topics covered in this chapter can choose one or both of the following activities. They may do the activities for their own satisfaction or report on what they have done to show that they have been seriously considering the period from 1900 to 1950.

INTERVIEW

By interviewing a World War II veteran or anyone who lived through the war years, your child can get firsthand information about what it was like to be overseas or at home during World War II.

Consult with your family about people you know who were involved in World War II, either abroad or here in the United States. If possible, arrange to interview one of these people. With this person's permission, you might tape the interview and present it in class.

Be sure to prepare your questions in advance. What you've learned about World War II from this chapter will help you think of questions. Don't ask any embarrassing questions or questions that are too personal. And always be considerate of your interviewee's feelings.

BOOKS TO READ

The titles recommended here focus on the period covered in this chapter. Your child might wish to share one of these books with classmates by preparing an oral report or by bringing up relevant details from the book in class discussion.

Choi, Sook Nyul. *Year of the Impossible Goodbyes.* Houghton, 1991. Historical fiction, this book focuses on Sookan, a Korean girl of ten. She survives harsh treatment by the Japanese and manages to escape from Russian authorities, who take over late in World War II.

Coerr, Eleanor. *Mieko and the Fifth Treasure.* Putnam, 1993. This is the story of a Japanese girl who is injured during the atomic bomb attack on Nagasaki.

Greene, Bette. *Summer of My German Soldier.* Dial, 1973. Taking place in Arkansas during World War II, this story concerns a Jewish girl who offers safety to an escaped German prisoner-of-war.

Rinaldi, Ann. *Keep Smiling Through.* Harcourt, 1996. This book looks at life in the United States during World War II through the eyes of a lonely ten-year-old girl.

Watkins, Yoko Kawashima. Lothrop, *So Far from the Bamboo Grove.* 1986. In this memoir, a family who had been part of the Japanese ruling class in Korea must make its way back to Japan after Japan's defeat in World War II.

CHAPTER 13

The Shrinking World
1950–Present

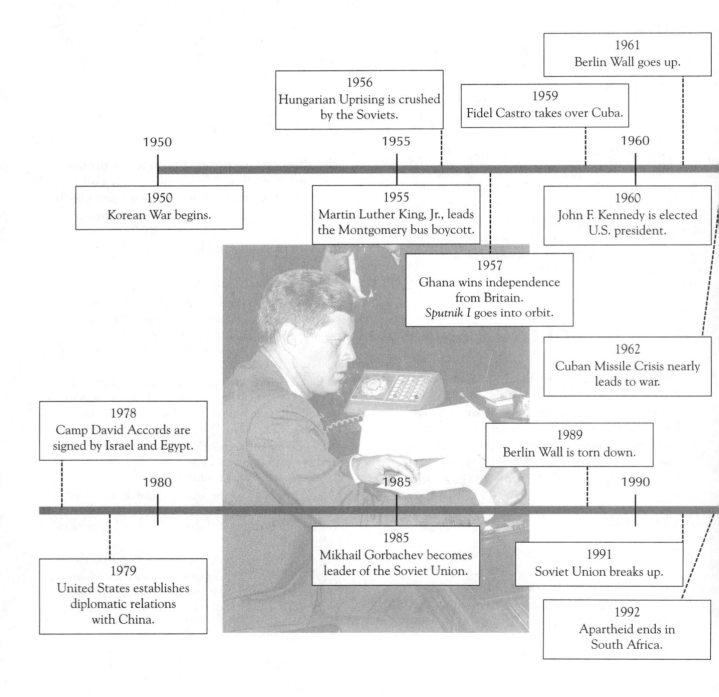

1961
Berlin Wall goes up.

1956
Hungarian Uprising is crushed by the Soviets.

1959
Fidel Castro takes over Cuba.

1950

1955

1960

1950
Korean War begins.

1955
Martin Luther King, Jr., leads the Montgomery bus boycott.

1960
John F. Kennedy is elected U.S. president.

1957
Ghana wins independence from Britain.
Sputnik I goes into orbit.

1962
Cuban Missile Crisis nearly leads to war.

1978
Camp David Accords are signed by Israel and Egypt.

1989
Berlin Wall is torn down.

1980

1985

1990

1979
United States establishes diplomatic relations with China.

1985
Mikhail Gorbachev becomes leader of the Soviet Union.

1991
Soviet Union breaks up.

1992
Apartheid ends in South Africa.

This timeline provides an overview of the cultural and political developments between, approximately, 1950 and the opening years of the twenty-first century. Then a narrative describes this period in greater detail and discusses its significance.

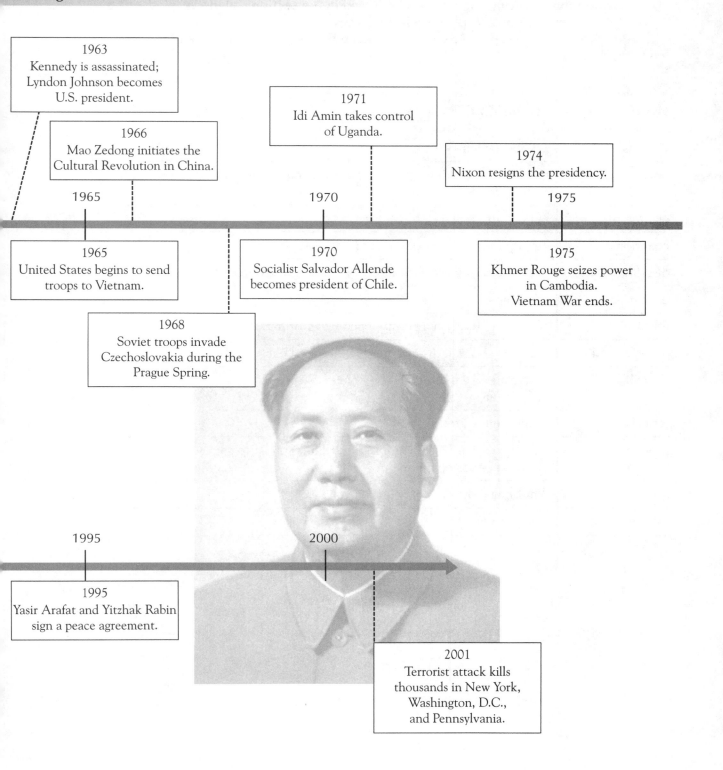

1963
Kennedy is assassinated; Lyndon Johnson becomes U.S. president.

1966
Mao Zedong initiates the Cultural Revolution in China.

1971
Idi Amin takes control of Uganda.

1974
Nixon resigns the presidency.

1965

1970

1975

1965
United States begins to send troops to Vietnam.

1970
Socialist Salvador Allende becomes president of Chile.

1975
Khmer Rouge seizes power in Cambodia.
Vietnam War ends.

1968
Soviet troops invade Czechoslovakia during the Prague Spring.

1995

2000

1995
Yasir Arafat and Yitzhak Rabin sign a peace agreement.

2001
Terrorist attack kills thousands in New York, Washington, D.C., and Pennsylvania.

Word Power

The words on the following chart are underscored in the section called "What Your Child Needs to Know." Explain their meanings to your child as needed when they come up in reading or discussion. Keep the list handy for you and your child to use.

Word	Definition
accords	peace agreements
boycott	as a way of making a protest, refusal to buy something or to use a service
clamored	cried out
coalition	group formed to work for a common purpose
discrimination	act of treating people unfairly based on the group they belong to
dismantled	took apart
ethnic	having to do with a group of people who share the same culture
fundamentalists	people who strictly and literally follow a belief or principle
guerrilla	referring to a fighter who launches a surprise attack against an official army
junta	small ruling group
propaganda	incomplete or biased information that is spread to gain supporters or hurt an opposing group
quadrupled	multiplied by four
radical	extreme

What Your Child Needs to Know

You may choose to use the following text in several different ways, depending on your child's strengths and preferences. You might read the passage aloud; you might read it to yourself and then paraphrase it for your child; or you might ask your child to read the material along with you or on his or her own.

As noted in Chapter 12, the United States and the Soviet Union emerged from World War II as superpowers. The United States practiced democracy and **free enterprise** (an economy based on private ownership); the Soviet Union had a communist government and an economy controlled by the government.

Tension developed between the superpowers and started the **Cold War.** This was a war of words and propaganda, not guns. Nevertheless, part of the Cold War involved *threats* by each superpower to use weapons of mass destruction. After the United States dropped atomic bombs on Japan to end World War II, the Soviet Union created similar weapons. Then both superpowers moved on to develop more deadly hydrogen bombs. This competition in weapons that use nuclear energy became known as the **nuclear arms race.** Here are glimpses of other world developments.

THE 1950s

Asia

After World War II, Korea was freed from Japanese control and divided into the communist North and the democratic South. In June 1950, North Korea invaded South Korea. The United States, as part of a United Nations force, sent troops to counter the North Koreans. China sent troops to help the North Koreans and to keep UN troops from crossing into North Korea. These acts set the stage for the **Korean War,** which lasted for three years, until a cease-fire was declared. The two Koreas remained divided.

In Southeast Asia, the French had been fighting the **Indochina War** since 1946 to maintain control of their colonies. The war ended in 1954, and the French gave up their colonies. Laos and Cambodia became independent countries. Vietnam, like Korea, was divided into a communist North and a democratic South. The United States supported the South.

Africa

African colonies also clamored for independence. For example, led by **Gamal Abdel Nasser** (guh MAHL AHB duhl NAH suhr), Egypt overthrew its British-backed royal government and became a republic in 1953. By 1956, Egypt even achieved sole ownership of the Suez Canal. Ghana (GAH nuh), formerly called the Gold Coast, became, in 1957, the first sub-Sahara country to win independence from Britain. Freedom, however, brought new problems. Many new nations faced civil war, famine, and corruption in government.

Europe

In 1953, **Nikita Khrushchev** (KROOSH chef) became the Soviet leader. In 1955, eastern European communist countries formed the **Warsaw Pact,** a military alliance. In 1956, when Hungary, a member of the alliance, rebelled against communist rule, the U.S.S.R. itself quickly crushed the uprising.

Astounding the United States and the rest of the world, the Soviets sent *Sputnik I* into orbit around Earth in 1957. This first artificial satellite represented a major technical feat and marked the start of the **space race** between the Soviet Union and the United States. The two countries went on to spend millions of dollars on space programs.

The United States

Racial **segregation**—that is, separation of the races—still existed in the United States, especially in the South, in the 1950s. In 1955, African American minister **Martin Luther King, Jr.,** led a boycott of segregated buses in Montgomery, Alabama. This action marked the beginning of the modern **civil rights movement.**

Latin America

In 1959, on the island nation of Cuba, only ninety miles from Florida, rebels led by **Fidel Castro** overthrew the dictatorship government that ruled the country. Castro later declared himself a communist, and hundreds of thousands of Cubans who were anticommunist fled to the United States.

THE 1960s

The United States

President **John F. Kennedy** faced a major challenge in 1962, when the Soviets in Cuba began to build launch sites for missiles with nuclear warheads. In response, Kennedy ordered a naval blockade of the island. The United States and the Soviet Union appeared on the edge of war during the **Cuban Missile Crisis.** After a tense standoff that riveted the world's attention for many days, the Soviets backed down and <u>dismantled</u> the missile sites.

John F. Kennedy (1917–1963)

In November 1963, President Kennedy was assassinated in Dallas, Texas. **Lyndon Johnson** became president. Pressure from the civil rights movement led Johnson and Congress to pass a series of civil rights bills to make racial <u>discrimination</u> illegal in voting, employment, schools, and housing.

Johnson also sent American troops to Vietnam in 1965 to keep the North Vietnamese from taking over South Vietnam. By 1969, the United States had five hundred thousand troops in Vietnam. The **Vietnam War** became one of the most unpopular wars in American history. Many young people across the nation demonstrated against the war, a conflict that eventually claimed the lives of more than fifty thousand Americans.

At about the same time, more <u>radical</u> black leaders started the **black power movement**—usually defined as a more extreme call for civil rights. The assassination of Martin Luther King, Jr., in 1968 led to riots in cities across the country.

Spurred on by the Soviet achievements in space, America took pride in the greatest success of the U.S. space program in 1969: American astronauts **Neil Armstrong** and **Edwin "Buzz" Aldrin, Jr.** became the first humans to land and walk on the moon.

Europe

From 1949 to 1958, 3 million East Germans fled to the West to escape communism. In 1961, the Soviets built the **Berlin Wall** around the city to prevent people from escaping into West Germany.

Khrushchev was removed from power in 1964, and **Leonid Brezhnev** (BREZH *nef*) became the new Soviet leader. Brezhnev pursued a hard communist line. When communist leader **Alexander Dubček** (DOOB tchek) of Czechoslovakia began in 1968 to reform his government and encourage intellectual freedom, Brezhnev sent in Soviet troops. The **Prague Spring,** named for the Czech capital, ended abruptly.

Asia

Famine and other problems weakened Mao Zedong's power in China. In 1966, he started the **Cultural Revolution.** The revolution called for destroying old Chinese religious and cultural be-

Mao Zedong (1893–1976)

liefs, as well as anything American. While Mao developed the country's industry and improved education during the revolution, poor harvests and chaos in the countryside led to the death of millions of Chinese. The communist dream was not working out in China.

The Middle East

Tensions between Israel and its Arab neighbors grew greater in the 1960s. Egypt closed the Gulf of Aqaba (AH kuh buh) to Israel in 1967. Israel responded militarily. What followed came to be known as the **Six-Day War,** during which Israel occupied Egypt's Sinai Peninsula, the West Bank, and other territory formerly held by Arabs.

Africa

In South Africa, the white government had been pursuing a policy of **apartheid** (uh PAHR *tayt*) the separation of people according to their color or race. In 1960, the government went even further by making black political parties illegal.

THE 1970s

The United States

The trip by President **Richard Nixon** to China in 1972 was perhaps the high point of his presidency. But the same year, members of Nixon's staff hired burglars to break into Democratic headquarters in a Washington building called the Watergate. Their capture and the cover-up that followed became known as the **Watergate scandal.** It eventually caused Nixon in 1974 to become the first president to resign from office.

The long Vietnam War finally drew to a close in 1975, when the South surrendered to the North and the United States withdrew its troops.

The Middle East

The Arab nations attacked Israel in the **Yom Kippur War** of 1973. Both sides suffered significant losses before they reached a truce. In a follow-up move, Middle Eastern countries that controlled vast amounts of oil deposits <u>quadrupled</u> the price of oil. This action led to a worldwide energy crisis.

Then in 1978, at Camp David, Maryland, President **Jimmy Carter** helped Egyptian leader **Anwar Sadat** (suh DAHT) and Israeli prime minister **Menachem Begin** (muh NAH kuhm BAY gin) to reach a peace agreement. In the **Camp David <u>Accords</u>,** Egypt became the first Arab nation to recognize Israel's right to exist in exchange for the return of the Sinai Peninsula, an area that the Israelis had taken over in the 1967 war.

However, other hot spots developed in the region. In 1979, **Saddam Hussein** (hoo SAYN) became president and dictator of Iraq, and Islamic <u>fundamentalists</u>, who had earlier overthrown the **Shah of Iran,** held fifty-three U.S. citizens hostage from late 1979 to early 1981.

Europe

Acts of terrorism were also on the rise in Europe. In 1972, members of the **Palestinian Liberation Organization (PLO)** kidnapped and murdered Israeli athletes at the Olympic Games in Munich, West Germany. The **Irish Republican Army (IRA)** carried out shootings and bombings to protest British control of Northern Ireland. Terrorists were also active in Italy and Spain.

Latin America

A military junta (HOON tuh) seized power in Argentina in 1976. This government arrested thousands of people, who were held without trial and never seen again. They became known as *los desaparecidos,* or "the disappeared ones."

Asia

The **Khmer Rouge** (kuh MER ROOZH), a communist guerrilla army, took control of Cambodia in 1975. They killed or starved to death almost 2 million Cambodians—anyone who resisted them. The Khmer Rouge's reign of terror ended in 1979, when they were forced out by Vietnamese troops.

Chinese leader Mao Zedong died in 1976. The new ruler, **Deng Xiaoping** (DENG shyow PING), helped to modernize China and improved relations with the West.

Japan, which had made itself into a strong and vibrant democracy since World War II, developed one of the most successful economies in the world during this period.

Africa

Of the numerous dictators who came to power in Africa during this decade, one of the harshest was **Idi Amin** (EE dee ah MEEN), who took control of Uganda in 1971. During his eight years in power, Amin was responsible for at least 250,000 deaths. He was driven into exile in 1979.

THE 1980s

The United States

In 1980, **Ronald Reagan** became the oldest man to be elected president. Despite his age, Reagan communicated ideas that appealed to many Americans. One reason for Reagan's popularity was a long economic boom during his time in office. But while the rich grew richer, many of the poor grew poorer under **Reaganomics,** a policy that relied heavily on tax and budget cuts.

Another milestone of the 1980s was the release by IBM of the first personal computer, which would significantly change how humans work and play.

Europe

Europe experienced an environmental disaster when a reactor exploded at the nuclear power plant at **Chernobyl** (chuhr NOH buhl) in the Soviet republic of Ukraine in 1986. The radioactivity from the explosion spread as far west as Sweden, Finland, Poland, and West Germany. It killed plants and animals and made some land unlivable.

Mikhail Gorbachev (*gawr* buh CHAWF) became the new Soviet leader in 1985. Gorbachev introduced policies of *perestroika,* or "restructuring," of Soviet society and *glasnost,* or "openness," in Soviet affairs. In 1989, Gorbachev gave eastern European nations permission to elect democratic governments. The same year, authorities tore down the Berlin Wall in East Germany. Communism in Europe was collapsing.

Asia

In China, however, communism was very much alive. Some one hundred thousand students and workers demonstrated in the capital's **Tiananmen** (TYAHN ahn muhn) **Square** in 1989. They were calling for greater freedom. Government troops who broke up the protests killed and wounded thousands.

The Middle East

A war between Iran and Iraq ended in 1988, after eight years, with more than a million people dead. Iraq was the victor. The same year, PLO leader **Yasir Arafat** (ahr uh FAT) recognized Israel's right to exist. This was a major step toward peace in the Middle East.

Africa

New nations of Africa faced serious problems. A civil war in Mozambique (*moh* zuhm BEEK) took close to a million lives; Ethiopia suffered a terrible famine after a civil war. However, things were looking better in South Africa. **F. W. de Klerk** was elected president in 1989 and surprised many whites by beginning to dismantle apartheid.

Latin America

In Nicaragua, the **Contras,** or counter revolutionaries, struggled against the ruling revolutionary **Sandinistas** (*san* dee NEES tahs). U.S. aid to the Contras became the focus of the **Iran-Contra Hearings** in the U.S. Congress in 1987. The hearings revealed that the Reagan White House had sold guns to the Iranians and then had given the money to the anticommunist Contras. Meanwhile, in Argentina, **Raúl Alfonsín** (rah OOL ahl fohn SEEN) became the first freely elected president in forty years. Brazil and Uruguay also saw democracies restored.

THE 1990s ONWARD

Europe

Communist governments fell in East Germany, Hungary, Bulgaria, and Romania. The two Germanys reunited into one nation. The Soviet Union was no more as of January 1, 1991: the fifteen republics of the Soviet Union became independent countries. Russia was the largest, and reformer **Boris Yeltsin** tried to convert Russia to a democratic country with a free-market system. Yeltsin was ultimately unable to solve his country's many problems and stepped down in 1999. At any rate, the Cold War was over, and the world now had only one superpower—the United States.

Ethnic divisions caused problems in the Balkan states. Serious fighting took place between Muslims, Croats, and Serbs, for example. Eventually, the **North Atlantic Treaty Organization (NATO)**, the western military alliance, became involved. By the decade's end, it appeared that parts of eastern Europe were on the road to democracy.

Countries in the **European Union** worked throughout the 1990s and beyond to create a solid organization. A common currency, the **euro,** was in place by 2002.

Africa

In 1990, President de Klerk of South Africa lifted the ban on black political parties and released black leader **Nelson Mandela** (man DE luh), who had been in prison since 1964. Apartheid officially ended in 1992, and Mandela became South Africa's first elected black president.

The Middle East

In 1990, Iraq invaded oil-rich Kuwait. This action led to the **Persian Gulf War,** in which a coalition led by the United States attacked Iraq. The war ended in Iraqi defeat in less than a year, but Saddam Hussein remained in power and continued as a threat.

Meanwhile, hope for peace rose between Israel and its Arab neighbors. In 1995, PLO chief Yasir Arafat signed an accord with Israeli leader **Yitzhak**

Rabin (YIHTS hahk rah BEEN). But peace did not arrive. Through the late 1990s and into the twenty-first century, both peace efforts and fighting continued.

Asia

An economic crisis and then the seizure of Kabul, Afghanistan, by the fundamentalist Taliban were among Asia's—and, by extension, the world's—biggest problems.

The United States

The United States was a key player in the rise of the computer age. Computers and the Internet—especially electronic mail—became essential for conducting everyday activities throughout society.

In September 2001, terrorists hijacked four commercial airliners and crashed two of them into New York City's World Trade Center and one into the Pentagon, headquarters for the U.S. Defense Department in Washington, D.C. A fourth plane crashed into the ground in Pennsylvania. Approximately three thousand people died in what was at that time the worst terrorist attack on U.S. soil.

The terrorists who carried out this act left no messages about their purpose or identity. However, the massive worldwide investigation that was immediately launched quickly revealed the terrorists' ties to the Middle East.

The United States moved forward to forge alliances with countries around the world to battle terrorism. The battle promised to be long and costly, but President **George W. Bush** vowed to wipe out terrorism. As this book goes to press, the world waits to see how the events of September 11, 2001, will affect everyone's future.

! Implications

To answer the question, "Why does all this matter?" or "What does it mean?," share the following insights with your child.

In the second half of the twentieth century, the world shrank to a global village—but a global village with many voices, many opinions. The very issue of **globalization**—decision making by international groups rather than by individual nations—found both supporters and critics.

Within this global village, communications technology from television to the Internet brought the world's peoples closer together than ever before. One of the reasons so many Americans protested the Vietnam War was that they watched its horrors daily on TV news reports.

People are coming to recognize the downside of lightning-quick technology: an Internet virus can shut down worldwide communications. By the same token, a deadly medical virus or bacterium can quickly spread across the globe via jets and giant ships—accidentally or on purpose.

Obviously, political, economic, and social problems abound, as they have throughout the history of the world. We solve some problems, and others come along. On the hopeful side, diplomacy continues where possible, and significant parts of the world still want democracies to endure. Yet all of us must answer for ourselves the question of how we should look at the world's future.

 # Fact Checker

To check that your child knows or can find the basic facts in this chapter, here is a scramble puzzle.

RECENT HISTORY PUZZLE

Each scrambled clue word is a person, place, thing, or idea associated with the second half of the twentieth century. Unscramble each of the clue words in the list. Copy the letters in the numbered boxes to the boxes at the bottom of the list. The word at the bottom tells what changed between the end of the twentieth century and the beginning of the twenty-first.

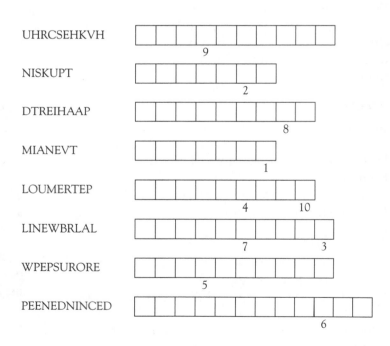

UHRCSEHKVH

NISKUPT

DTREIHAAP

MIANEVT

LOUMERTEP

LINEWBRLAL

WPEPSURORE

PEENEDNINCED

Answers appear in the back, preceding the index.

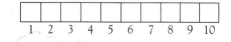

The Big Questions

The following questions encourage your child to think critically rather than simply recall facts. If necessary, review the specific information from the preceding pages that will help your child make the necessary inferences to come up with reasonable answers.

1. The last fifty years have seen a movement toward independence for countries in Africa, the Caribbean, and the former Soviet Union. What may have caused this trend?

2. What do you think of the way the world has responded to the 2001 terrorist attack on New York City and Washington, D.C.?

Possible Answers

1. *Increased worldwide communication—for example, television and the Internet—may account for the trend toward independence.*

2. *Your child may comment on responses by individuals and responses by states or organizations—the Taliban, the United States and its allies, countries that are not usually allies of the United States, religious groups, and so on.*

Skills Practice

The following activities give your child practice in applying the skills basic to social studies. To do the activities, your child may need to review the information in the preceding pages.

A. INTERVIEW

By interviewing someone who served (in or out of the armed forces) in Vietnam during the U.S. engagement there, your child can get firsthand information about the war.

Consult with your family about people you know who were involved in the Vietnam War. If possible, arrange to interview one of these people. With this person's permission, you might tape the interview and present it in class.

Be sure to prepare your questions in advance. What you've learned about Vietnam from this chapter will help you think of questions. Don't ask any embarrassing questions or questions that are too personal. And always be considerate of your interviewee's feelings.

Evaluating Your Child's Skills: **In order to get the most out of this activity, your child needs to think of questions that only** the interviewee can answer—not questions that your child can find answered in a book or article. He or she could ask about the interviewee's thoughts at the time and the interviewee's reflections between that time and today.

B. VISUAL LITERACY: READING POLITICAL CARTOONS

After discussing a current issue covered in the news media, share with your child a relatively easy-to-understand political cartoon about that issue. You may locate such a cartoon in a newspaper or news magazine or even on the Internet. The following questions can guide a conversation with your child.

1. What is the topic of the cartoon?
2. If the cartoon has a caption or text, what is its point?

3. What, if any, symbols appear in the cartoon? (The Eiffel Tower, for example, is a symbol of France; Uncle Sam is a symbol of the United States.)

4. Based on the picture and the text, what is the cartoonist's opinion about the topic?

> ***Evaluating Your Child's Skills:*** In order to complete this activity successfully, your child needs to notice details. He or she must realize that political cartoons—like editorials—are not neutral; they announce an opinion.

 # Top of the Class

> Children interested in delving more deeply into the topics covered in this chapter can choose one or both of the following activities. They may do the activities for their own satisfaction or report on what they have done to show that they have been seriously considering the world they live in.

CHILDREN AROUND THE WORLD

> Your child can learn about his or her peers around the world by exploring a variety of media. Here are examples of materials you can make available to your child.

Books

Zlata's Diary by Zlata Filipovic (Penguin, 1994) is a first-person account by a girl who lived through trauma in Sarajevo in the early 1990s. Janet Bode specialized in books of interviews with young people. *The Colors of Freedom: Immigrant Stories* (Franklin Watts, 1999) focuses on teenagers who moved to America from around the world and had to adjust to life here.

Recordings

The musical *Sarafina* illustrates life under apartheid in the South African township of Soweto, and its cast album is available. The show focuses on high school students.

Internet Sites

The United Nations Children's Fund maintains an up-to-date site about children around the world: www.unicefusa.org.

Answers to "Fact Checkers"

Chapter 1

wheel: Sumerians

system of laws: Babylonians

paper: Egyptians

silk: Shang

glass: Sumerians

written language: Sumerians

potter's wheel: Sumerians

Chapter 2

Across

2. Chavin
3. India
6. Rome
7. Babylon
10. Etruscans
12. Hebrews
13. Kush

Down

1. Phoenicians
4. Assyrians
5. Greece
8. Olmec
9. Persians
11. Nok

Chapter 3

1. Pericles
2. Plato
3. Alexander
4. Hannibal
5. Octavian *or* Augustus
6. Confucius, Lao-tzu
7. Qin
8. Adena

Chapter 4

1. Diocletian
2. Christianity
3. Vandals
4. caravans
5. emperor
6. Hinduism
7. glyphs
8. Mexico
9. Arizona
10. ivory

Chapter 5

1. T
2. F
3. F
4. T
5. F
6. T
7. F
8. T
9. T
10. F

Chapter 6

1. c
2. a
3. b
4. a
5. c

Chapter 7

1. France
2. Lorenzo
3. Ottoman
4. Renaissance
5. Ethiopia
6. Navigator
7. China
8. Europe

Chapter 8

1. Timbuktu
2. Benin
3. Vasco de Gama
4. Mogul
5. Portugal
6. Cortés
7. Ottoman
8. Reformation
9. Renaissance
10. da Vinci

Chapter 9

1. d
2. h
3. a
4. c
5. f
6. i
7. g
8. b
9. j
10. e

Chapter 10

1. Catherine
2. Napoleon
3. Virginia
4. Cook
5. Australia
6. Fulton
7. Watt
8. Bolívar
9. Waterloo
10. Engels

Question: What's this chapter about?

Answer: Revolution

Chapter 11

1. b
2. c
3. a
4. e
5. g
6. d
7. f

Chapter 12

Across

2. D-Day
4. Fascism
7. Gandhi
8. Hitler
9. UN

Down

1. Panama Canal
3. Easter
5. Lenin
6. Holocaust

Chapter 13

Khrushchev

Sputnik

apartheid

Vietnam

petroleum

Berlin Wall

superpower

independence

Question: What changed . . . ?

Answer: millennium

INDEX

Singapore, 89
Sistine Chapel, 93
Sitting Bull, 130
Six-Day War, 153
Skara Brae, 12
slavery:
    in China, 78
    in the United States, 128
slaves, 22, 66, 67, 88, 91, 103,
    106
slums, 114
socialism, 142
Society Islands, 80
Socrates, 31
Solomon, 19
Solon, 21
Songhai, 79, 87
Sonni Ali, 79
Sophocles, 31
South Africa, 128
South America:
    A.D. 400–1000, 54–55
    1750–1850, 117–118
Soviet Union (*see* Union of Soviet
    Socialist Republics)
space race, 151
Spain, 142
Spanish Civil War, 151
Sparta, 21, 31
Sputnik I, 151
steamboat, 113
steam engine, 113
Stephenson, George, 113
Stonehenge, 12
Suez Canal, 128, 151
Sui dynasty, 53
Süleyman I, 91
sultan, 77, 91
Sumer, 7–8
Sumter, Fort, 129
Sung (Song) dynasty, 65
Sunni Muslims, 91
Sun Yat-sen, 139

Tabriz, 91
Taiping Rebellion, 131
Taj Mahal, 104
Tang dynasty, 53
Taoism, 34
Tartars, 77
Tasman, Abel, 104

Tasmania, 104
taxes, 9, 53, 89
technology, 43
Tenochtitlán, 67, 79
Thebes, 9
Thirty Years' War, 101
Thucydides, 31
Tiahuanaco, 55
Tiananmen Square, 154
Tiber River, 22
Tibet, 53
Tigris River, 7
Tikal, 34, 44
Timbuktu, 66, 79, 87
Titicaca, Lake, 55
Tokugawa shogunate, 104, 131
Tokyo, 105
Toltec, 54
Tonga, 80, 104
Tower of Babel, 19
trade, 7, 10, 42, 43, 54, 63, 66, 78
Transvaal, 118
tribunes, 33
Trojan War, 11, 21
Tula, 34
Tull, Jethro, 102
Tutankhamen (king of Egypt), 9
Tutu, Osei, 102
Tz'u-hsi, 131

Ukraine, 51
Union of South Africa, 142
Union of Soviet Socialist Republics,
    140, 144, 151
United Nations, 144
United States:
    founding of, 115
    in years 1850–1907, 128–130
    Civil War in, 129
    1900–1950, 141
    in World War I, 141, 143
    in World War II, 143
    in 1950s, 151
    in 1960s, 152
    in 1970s, 153
    in 1980s, 154
    in 1990s onward, 155

Vandals, 42
vassals, 64

Vedas, 20
Vermeer, 101
Versailles, 101
Versailles, Treaty of, 141
viceroys, 103
Victor Emmanuel II (king of Piedmont-
    Sardinia), 127
Victoria (queen of England), 128, 131
Vietnam War, 152
Vikings, 51–52
Villa, Pancho, 140
Visigoths, 51
Vladimir I (king of Kiev), 52
Voltaire, 113

war, 19, 21, 67, 79, 80, 89, 92
    (*See also specific wars*)
Warring States Period, 34
Warsaw Pact, 151
Washington, George, 114
Watergate scandal, 153
Waterloo, 116
Watt, James, 113
Wellington (New Zealand), 119
western front, 140
Westphalia, Peace of, 101
Wilhelm I (emperor of Germany),
    127
William the Conqueror, 64
Wittenberg, 91
World War I, 139
World War II, 142–144
Wounded Knee, 130
Wright brothers, 139

Yamato dynasty, 43
Yeltsin, Boris, 155
Yom Kippur War, 153
Yoritomo (shogun of Japan), 65
Yorktown, Virginia, 114
Yoshimune (shogun of Japan), 105

Zapata, Emiliano, 140
Zeus, 21
Zhou, 20–21
ziggurat, 8, 19
Zimbabwe, 79, 87
Zulu, 118, 128
Zulu War, 128